DRIVING EUREKA!

Doug Hall

FOUNDER OF EUREKA! RANCH,
INNOVATION ENGINEERING INSTITUTE,
AND BRAIN BREW CUSTOM WHISK(E)Y

Other Books by Doug Hall

Jump Start Your Brain
A Proven Method for Increasing Creativity up to 500%
with David Wecker

Maverick Mindset
Finding the Courage to Journey from Fear to Freedom
with David Wecker
(Paperback Title: *Making the Courage Connection*)

Jump Start Your Business Brain
The Scientific Way to Make More Money

Meaningful Marketing
100 Data-Proven Truths and 402 Practical Ideas
For Selling MORE with LESS Effort
(Paperback Title: *Jump Start Your Marketing Brain*)

North Pole Tenderfoot
A Rookie's Adventures and Misadventures
Walking in Admiral Peary's Footsteps

Jump Start Your Brain 2.0
How Everyone at Every Age
Can Be Smarter & More Creative

DRIVING EUREKA!

Problem-Solving with Data-Driven Methods & the Innovation Engineering System

Doug Hall

FOUNDER OF EUREKA! RANCH,
INNOVATION ENGINEERING INSTITUTE,
AND BRAIN BREW CUSTOM WHISK(E)Y

CLERISY PRESS

Driving Eureka!

Copyright © 2018 by Eureka! Institute, Inc.
All rights reserved
Published by Clerisy Press
Printed in the United States of America
Distributed by Publishers Group West
First edition, first printing

Library of Congress Cataloging-in-Publication Data
Names: Hall, Doug, 1959- author.
Title: Driving Eureka! : problem-solving with data-driven methods &
    the innovation engineering system / Doug Hall.
Description: Birmingham, AL : Clerisy Press, [2018]
Identifiers: LCCN 2017022462 | ISBN 9781578605811 (hardback) |
    ISBN 9781578605828 (eISBN)
Subjects: LCSH: Creative ability in business. | Systems engineering—
    Technological innovations. | Creative thinking. | Problem solving. |
    Industrial productivity—Measurement. | Eureka! Ranch (Firm)
Classification: LCC HD53 .H349 2018 | DDC 658.4/063—dc23
LC record available at https://lccn.loc.gov/2017022462

Cover design: Travis Bryant
Book design: Annie Long
Illustrations: Steve Jones
Indexer: Meghan Brawley

CLERISY PRESS
An imprint of AdventureKEEN
306 Greenup St., Covington, KY 41011
800-678-7006; clerisypress.com

THIS BOOK IS DEDICATED TO
THE INNOVATION ENGINEERING PIONEERS.

Acknowledgments

This book covers my life's work and learnings. However, I am not the sole author. To paraphrase Sir Isaac Newton, if there is anything on these pages or in our college courses and tools that is valuable, it's because I have stood on the shoulders of giants. The following people helped create the Innovation Engineering movement and this book—some in small ways, many in big ways. **They are the heart, brains, and soul of Innovation Engineering.** It is a challenging thing to make a list like this. I am sure that this list of more than 350 is wrong, but it is a useful start. I am sure that I have missed some important people. I apologize for my mistakes. I will correct this list in a future edition. Thank you to those mentioned and those whom I have missed.

Tom Ackerman, David Ahlert, Louise Aitcheson, Todd Allison, Laurie Allison-Jones, Ash Andrews, Maribel Asensio, Peter Athanas, Tripp Babbitt, Anne Badanes, Jen Bailey, Jarrod Ball, Tyson Bauer, Chip Baumgardner, Danielle Beaupre, James Beaupre, Steve Bebko, Jesse Bechtold, April Bertram, Nancy Bettcher, Art Bierschbach, Gerald Biser, Beth Bittenbender, Ken Bloemer, Paul Bolesta, Mark Bond, Jarnell Bonds, Fred Botterbusch, Bob Bowen, Wade Bowles, Lani Boyer, Jim Brennon, Scott Broughton, Carla Brown, Scott Brown, Iain Bruce, Barry Bruns, Shelby Buell, Amy Burmeister, Deanna Burwell, Nick Busch, Kevin Cahill, Eric Canter, David Carrick, Lydia Carson, David Cassady, Connie Casteel, Todd Centers, Scott Chadwick, Mark Chalfant, Chris Chapman, George Chapman, Sandie Chapman, Walter and Lillian Chapman, Wendy Chapman, Andrew Clist, Beth Colbert, Chris Coleman, Jane Coleman, Bryan Colpo, Greg Conder, Gary Conley, Bill Conway, Greg Cozzolino, Blake Craig, Jason Craig, Pat Crane, Graeme Crombie, Selene Crosby, Will Culp, Lenny Cumberledge, Dan Curtis, Todd Daniels, Andy Davis, Fernando de Vicente, Keith Decker, Keith Deibert, Misty DePriest, Schelli Dittmann, Aimee Dobrzeniecki, Darrell Donahue, Liz Downing, Rory Drennan, Jesse Dunbar, Corinne Dupuy, Kirbie Earley, Eric and Anne Eifrig, Kit Eisel, Randy Elkins, Mike and Margaret England, Ralph

Eschenwecker, Bill Fararr, Stephanie Ferking, Lily Ferrante, John Ferris, Wendy Ferris, Florin Flortis, Bruce Forsee, Andy Francis, Steve and Mary Friedberg, Kate Galbraith, Shawn Gants, Victor Garcia, Julian Gardner, Scott Gardner, Mark Geary, Joe Genet, Tod Gentille, Paige Gianetti, Patricia Giavara, Joe Girgash, David Goebel, Gary Gottenbusch, Dan Gowin, Kevin Grayson, Virginia Green, Ken Grier, Don Groom, Dane Gross, Colin Guthrie, Jennifer Hagan-Dier, Brad Hall, Bruce Hall, Buzz Hall, Debbie Hall, Jean Hall, Kristyn Hall, Linda Leibert Hall, Lois Hall, Rebecca Hall, Victoria Hall, Mitch Hamm, Elaine Hanna, Colleen Harris, Mark Hartwell, Kimberly Haywood, Brad Helfman, Keith Helfrich, Lisa Henderson, Rick Henry, Margaret Henson, Laura Herrin, Stephen Hinton, Patty Hogan, Tim and Sue Hogan, Rhonda Honke, Dave and Debbie Horn, Brianna Hughes, Richard Hunt, Hutch Hutchison, Petar Ilchovski, Joe Jacobs, Erick James, Lance and Robin Jensen, Adam Johnson, Alex Jones, Michele Jones, Stephan Junion, Lynn Kahle, Joe Kanfer, John Karp, Mike Kelleher, Renee Kelly, Emily Kennedy, Robert Kennedy, Darren Kidd, Dave Kilbury, Roger Kilmer, James Kim, Jessa Kippel, James Kirby, Nikos Kiritsis, Matt Kirk, Kip Knight, Mike Kosinski, Robert Kosobucki, Ea Ksander, Aaron Kurchev, Phillip Kurtz, Craig Kurz, David Lafkas, Jack Lamon, Jeremy Lancaster, Cassie Larson, Jeff Lawrence, Russ Lawrence, Toby Lay, Casey Leaman, Mike Legary, Greg Leman, Kristen LeMastus, Greg Lemmon, Mike Levy, Gary Lewandowski, John Lingenfelter, Nicholas Loyd, Margo Lukens, Angela Marcolini, Annette Marksberry, Clare and Bob Mason, Jaime Matayas, Helen Mayer, Scott McAuley, Stephen McClanahan, Angela McCue, Jeff McCurrach, Kelly McDonald, Eddie McGlamery, Pat McKay, Whitney McKuhen, Kari and Kevin McNamara, Carol Meagly, Matt Melinkovich, Michele Menegotto, Molly Merkle, Tom Merrill, Chad Meyer, Rich Meyer, Wade Milek, Brad Miller, David Mixson, Bruce Montgomery, Will Moody, Perry and Liz Moore, Patricio Morales, Jesse Moriarity, Michael Moriarity, John Muldoon, Jim Mundy, Earl Murphy, William Murray, Shawn Nason, Ann Herrmann Nehdi, Maggie Nichols, Bob Oliver, Leigh Oncale, Jeff O'Neil, Denny Organ, David Paris, Don Paul, Lorrie Paulus, Keith Pelfrey, Nathan Pelletier, Hemant Pendse, Joe Perotto, Wendel Peters, Maggie Slovonic Pfeifer, Maria Picher, Don Pital, Jane Portman, Doug Potter, Helen Potter, Brian Powell, Chris Powell, George Prince, Rick Prugh, Steve Puryear, Hannah Putnam, Ilene Quilty, Mel Radford, Rose Randolph, Dwaine Raper, Mike Raymond, Jennifer Reagan, Cathy Renault, Tim Riker, Larry Robinson, Jason Roche, Susannah Rockman-Lee, Laura Rolfes, Laura Lee Rose, Edward Rosenfeld, Clara Ross, Paul Ross, Rick Rothwell,

Sandy Rozecki, Kevin Sari, Abel Saud, Patric Sazama, Tim Scarpa, Rebecca Scherff, Eric Schulz, Paul Schurke, Michael Schutzbank, Randy Schwartz, Sheldon Scott, Michele Setzer, Erin Sharp, Kate Shore, Pat Shore, Terry Siddens, Mike Simpson, Mike Sirois, Tracy Jo Small, Allan Smith, Martin Smith, Conrad Soltero, Zach Sorrells, Andrew Southerland, Corie Roudebush Spialek, Elizabeth Staino, Jeffrey Stamp, Tara Stand, Brian Stautberg, John Steele, Janet and John Steves, Larry Stewart, Chris Stormann, Joey Suntken, Brian Sweeney, Ed Tazzia, Nicole Teeley, Rob Terry, Dileep Thatte, Dave Thomas, Jason Thompson, Robert Tomlinson, Pam Twist, Kara Valz, Lorie Van Gerwen, Andy VanGundy, Vandy Van Wagener, Dean and Karen Violetta, Chris Vogt, Ron Walters, Jake Ward, Jon Washington, Michael Washington, John Waters, Chris Wayne, Ryan Wayne, David Wecker, Bubba Weir, Richard Wells, Scott Wells, Brian Werneke, Walter Werner, Matt West, David Wheeler, Julie Phillippi Whitney, Nate Wildes, Robert Widmer, Jacob Wieneke, Don Wiesenforth, Jim Williams, Katie Williamson, Tom Wilson, Kara Stumpf Winterrowd, Anita Wood, Janet Woolman, Jaclyn Gardner Wyatt, Jill Youland, David Younge, Carrie Zapka, Bob Zider, and Mark Zieff.

It would be irresponsible of me to not make special mention of a handful of people who have gone above and beyond what is reasonable in their support of me and this movement.

Debbie Hall My friend, wife, and love of 40-plus years. Her wisdom shapes my thinking and makes me smarter every day.

M. Bradford "Buzz" Hall My dad. He taught me what Dr. W. Edwards Deming taught him. I will never forget his passion when talking about how leadership needs to focus on fixing the system, not blaming the workers.

Dr. W. Edwards Deming I never met Dr. Deming in person. I've learned about him from having discussions with those who worked with him and from reviewing his writing, videos, and audio recordings. My favorite Dr. Deming quote was his reaction to someone who was complaining that he had changed something in his teaching. His response was simple: *"I will never apologize for learning."*

Maggie Nichols The CEO of the Eureka! Ranch. Maggie was the first person to articulate the vision that we could enable everyone to be able to innovate.

My Mentors on Dr. Deming and System-Driven Leadership Kevin Cahill, Walter Werner, Bill Conway, Claire Crawford-Mason, Bob Mason, and Barry Bruns. I treasure every meeting, email, and phone conversation with each of them.

Robert Kennedy Retired president of the University of Maine. Before Innovation was popular, he saw that it was a critical life skill that all students would need to learn.

Roger Kilmer and Aimee Dobrzeniecki Retired from the US Department of Commerce. They were among the very first to see that innovation was not going to be optional for US manufacturing companies.

Jesse Bechtold, Larry Stewart, and Bob Zider Three pioneers who gave me strength when I needed it.

The Eureka! Ranch and the University of Maine Innovation Engineering Teams My dad taught me that smart people always hire and/or work with people who are smarter than they are. Innovation Engineering exists because the following people are smarter than I am: James Beaupre, Lydia Carson, Chris Coleman, Scott Dunkle, Bruce Forsee, Joe Girgash, Brad Hall, Debbie Hall, Margaret Henson, Renee Kelly, Corie Roudebush Spialek, David Lafkas, Jeremy Lancaster, Greg Lemmon, Margo Lukens, Angela McCue, Jesse Moriarity, Maggie Nichols, Hemant Pendse, Maggie Slovonic Pfeifer, and Jake Ward.

Richard Hunt My good friend and the best book publisher an author could ever have.

Special thanks to **Maggie Slovonic Pfeifer** for her help with editing this book. Her wisdom and sharp eye made it smarter and sharper.

TABLE OF CONTENTS

Introduction

System-driven innovation, like the System of Profound Knowledge that my grandfather taught, is a new mindset that you have to commit to.... Your market's going to change, your business is going to change. It gives you such an amazing advantage, because it teaches you how to look at and deal with those changes by thinking differently.

—Kevin Cahill, from the interview in the appendix
Executive Director of the Deming Institute
Grandson of Dr. W. Edwards Deming

The aim of this book is to teach you how to create a Meaningful Difference with your career, team, company, and community. This is accomplished through the Innovation Engineering system for thinking smarter, faster, and more creatively.

The need to think smarter, faster, and more creatively is broadly accepted in today's fast-changing world. What is not understood is how to do it. Innovation Engineering teaches you and everyone you work with a reliable system for creating fresh ideas and, even more important, how to turn them into reality more successfully. And, as you will learn in chapter 13, when just 10% of your team, company, or community has UNSHAKABLE belief in their ability to innovate a culture of innovation is created.

Innovation Engineering defines innovation in two words: Meaningfully Unique. When a product, service, work system, or job candidate is Meaningfully Unique, customers are willing to invest their time, energy, and money into it.

The never-ending quest for meaningful uniqueness is at the heart of this book, my life, and the Innovation Engineering movement.

Each of our students defines meaningfulness differently. Some find meaning in improving manufacturing, government, or even junior high school teaching systems. Others find meaning from creating smarter methods for rehabilitating prison inmates, caring for nursing home residents, anchoring North Sea oil rigs, or growing the impact of a non-profit. Some students find meaning in the invention of amazing new food products, medical devices, internet services, financial services, or industrial equipment.

The breadth and depth of application we are observing, from employing the Innovation Engineering mindset and methods, are both amazing and humbling.

Innovation Engineering

Innovation Engineering is a new field of academic study and management science. It reimagines how change is led, managed, and delivered. It accelerates the creation and development of more profitable and successful products and services. However, **new products and services are just 10% of the innovation opportunity; 90% of the innovation opportunity lies in systems for working smarter.** These include operational systems, production systems, sales and marketing systems, finance and legal systems, strategic alignment systems, idea decision systems, rapid research systems, and the list goes on and on.

Ideas for growth and efficiency implemented successfully are the outward manifestation of Innovation Engineering. The more meaningful impact lies in the transformation that occurs within each person. When employees and leaders are confident that they can innovate, a chain reaction of positives occurs. They feel good about their jobs, companies, and careers. And, they have hope for the future, as they know they can change and adapt as the world around them changes.

What makes Innovation Engineering reliable is that it's grounded in data, backed by academic theory, and validated in real-world practice. Collectively, it's the number-one documented innovation system on Earth. More than 35,000+ people have been educated in Innovation Engineering classes, and over $16 billion in growth and system improvement projects are in active development.

Innovation Engineering Case Study

One small example of Innovation Engineering effectiveness is Brain Brew Custom Whisk(e)y. It's a collaboration between my Eureka! Ranch team and Edrington Distillers of Scotland (distillers of the Macallan, Highland Park, and other super luxury spirits).

Using the Innovation Engineering system, we have invented and patented a Time Compression technology that crafts amazing whiskies and bourbons in 40 minutes (not years or decades).

The technology enables such richness of flavor with easy drinking smoothness that our products win 2 to 1 and 3 to 1 in head-to-head taste tests versus luxury scotches and bourbons. Two of our bourbons won top honors—double gold medals—at the North American Bourbon and Whiskey Competition, and one was a unanimous choice Double Gold at the San Francisco World Spirits Competition.

Even more exciting, the new technology enables the creation of custom whiskey. As we say, **"The world doesn't need another whiskey, but everyone needs their own whiskey."** Time Compression technology makes it possible for everyone to create their own unique mash bill and then apply a blend of Old World, New World, and craft aging styles for a one-of-a-kind original taste. To learn more, visit brainbrewwhiskey.com.

We understand that traditionalists may see Brain Brew Custom Whisk(e)y as being disrespectful to "the way it's always been done." However, the target audience for our innovations consists of forward-thinking craft spirits enthusiasts who are more interested in taste than tradition. Brain Brew is the ultimate demonstration of the Innovation Engineering mindset—traveling from invention and through development to test market in 10 months and winning top honors in international whiskey competitions in 18 months. Our marketing slogan is a variation of the famous

Apple commercial: "Some call us the crazy ones . . ." It articulates our courage and commitment to our mission.

Some call us the crazy ones . . . and we're OK with that.

Pedigree

Innovation Engineering was developed through experiences, ideas, and advice from innovation leaders at corporations such as Toyota Manufacturing, Trek, Procter & Gamble, The Macallan, The Walt Disney Company, American Express, Schlumberger, AT&T, Nike, Nestle, Humana, Kimberly-Clark, GOJO Industries, Cintas, Daimler, HoneyBaked Ham, Dunnhumby, and thousands of other companies that are less well known.

The development of Innovation Engineering also includes experiences, ideas, and advice from leaders of nonprofits such as March of Dimes; National Wildlife Federation; Alliance for Strong Families and Communities; College Board; Student Conservation Association; Earth Share; CoreChange; and INPEACE; the governments of the USA, Canada, Ireland, Scotland, and South Korea; and dozens of colleges and universities.

The impact on nonprofit organizations was confirmed by research by a team from Stanford University. They studied various innovation methods across a range of nonprofits. They found that most "innovation methods" don't actually result in innovative solutions. Most simply result in "innovation as usual." However, Innovation Engineering was found to be unique. The researchers concluded that it resulted in true breakout innovations. This validates that system-driven innovation is not just for commercial companies. Nonprofits that measure results based on delivery of their mission can also realize dramatic gains from it.

The Importance of Engaging Everyone in Innovation

When employees are enabled to innovate, they are more engaged. Gallup reported that only 31% of employees feel engaged; 69% feel nonengaged. This breaks down to 38% of management and 29% of Millennials. Both of these numbers are horribly low. Millennial disengagement is particularly concerning when you look at demographic trends.

Innovation Engineering provides a system that enables all employees (Baby Boomers, Gen Xers, and Millennials) to think, create, AND take

Annual Population of Baby Boomers and Millennials: 2000–2060

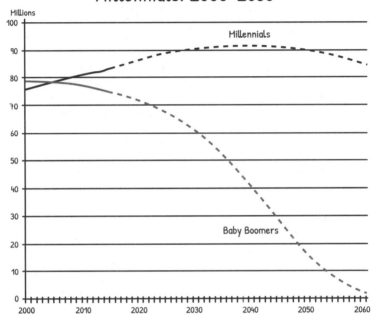

Note: Dashed lines represent projected years.
Source: U.S. Census Bureau, Population Division.

action on their ideas. When you enable employees to use their brains and imaginations, a cultural transformation occurs. In just six months, our tracking studies find measurable improvements on factors such as "the courage to take action," "optimism," "quality of work," and the organization being "a great place to work." Basically, work is fun again!

How Innovation Engineering Engages Everyone

Virtually every existing innovation/creativity program preaches the importance of embracing a childlike, extroverted, creative spirit. This works for the 15% of the population who have a right-brain creative thinking style.

However, it doesn't work for the 85% of the work population with a logical left-brain thinking style.

Asking left-brain logical thinkers to let loose makes them uncomfortable. It often causes them to disengage or, even worse, become active resisters. And, without the 85% who are logical, there is virtually no chance that a Meaningfully Unique innovation will become reality. That's because left-brainers are critical to accomplish the engineering, finance, production, and operational work that is required to make meaningful change happen.

Innovation Engineering methods and tools are designed to engage both left- and right-brain thinkers. Projects are focused with clear and motivating strategic missions that speak to both project vision and boundaries. Idea-sparking stimuli feature both right-brain trends/insights and left-brain technologies/patents. Decisions are grounded in data as opposed to corporate politics. Math and writing are both used to enable deeper thinking about ideas. Feasibility challenges are openly confronted not ignored. Key issues are tagged as "Death Threats" and resolved through disciplined and documented Fail FAST, Fail CHEAP cycles of learning.

The result is an unleashing of a culture of whole-brain thinking. The 15% who have a right-brain thinking style have new hope with Innovation Engineering, as there is a system for turning their ideas into reality. The 85% who are left brain are more engaged because for the first time, for many, they see an innovation system with structure, clarity, and discipline.

Quick Backstory on System Thinking

Innovation Engineering applies the system thinking of Dr. W. Edwards Deming to innovation, strategy, and the way we work together. For those who don't know of Dr. Deming, here's a quick overview.

After World War II, the Japanese economy and manufacturing base were in shambles. The country had a negative net worth. To rebuild it, American General Douglas MacArthur supported a program to educate business leaders in smarter ways of working. In 1950, Dr. W. Edwards Deming, a statistician from Powell, Wyoming, conducted a series of seminars in Japan. His mission was to teach system thinking to Japanese business leaders. He showed them how to approach manufacturing as a system of interconnected parts—instead of as a series of silos—to increase quality while also reducing costs.

The leaders of Japanese companies embraced the message. Japanese industry was so thankful for Dr. Deming's contribution to the rebirth of their economy that they named their national quality award the Deming Prize. The Japanese emperor awarded him the Second Order of the Sacred Treasure in recognition of his contributions to Japan. Shoichiro Toyoda, the first president of the Toyota Motor Corporation, described Dr. Deming's impact on Toyota this way:

> *Every day I think of what he meant to us. Deming is the core of our management.*
>
> —Shoichiro Toyoda, first president,
> Toyota Motor Corporation

I believe that the key to Dr. Deming's success was that he blended logical, rational discipline with emotional, soul-inspiring hope. He used his statistical science to enable the human spirit. At many of his four-day seminars he would start by saying: "Why are we here? We are here to come alive, to have fun, to have joy in work."

In the early 1980s, as Dr. Deming predicted would occur, the Western world faced the invasion of higher-quality products from Japanese manufacturers at better prices. It was called the Japanese miracle. In just 30 years they had risen from the ashes of war to challenge the world.

Dr. Deming's role in the Japanese transformation was "discovered" in the USA with the airing of an *NBC White Paper* documentary by Clare Crawford-Mason titled "If Japan Can, Why Can't We?"

The television special featured Dr. Deming and the story of Nashua Corporation, where the CEO, Bill Conway, had hired Dr. Deming to help him transform his company. The TV special discussed Nashua's success with applying Dr. Deming's mindset to the company's carbonless paper division. It was a story I knew well, as my father, M. Bradford "Buzz" Hall, had helped lead that project as director of central engineering.

The TV special made Dr. Deming, at the age of 80, the management rock star of the 1980s. He led up to 40 (four-day) Deming Seminars a year, well into his nineties. His teaching of system thinking ignited the greatest change in how companies are managed in 100 years or more.

More on the history of Dr. Deming's work can be found in the back of this book, along with an interview with Kevin Cahill, president and executive director of the W. Edwards Deming Institute and grandson of

Dr. W. Edwards Deming. Additional information, including a link to the original NBC documentary, can be found at the Deming Institute website: deming.org.

The Factory Represents Just 3% of the Opportunity

Derivatives of Dr. Deming's teachings are classically packaged today under names such as Total Quality, 6 Sigma, Lean, and the Toyota Production System. Each has had, and continues to have, a transformational impact on factories.

However, the factory was and is but a small part of Dr. Deming's vision. In his book *The New Economics,* Dr. Deming wrote that **the factory represented just 3% of the opportunity for company improvement from applying system thinking:** *"The shop floor is only a small part of the total. Anyone could be 100% successful with the 3% and find himself out of business."* He felt that 97% of the opportunity for improvement from applying system thinking lay in applying it to innovation, strategy, and the way we work together.

Just as Dr. Deming taught leaders how to transform **manufacturing** quality from a random act to a reliable science, Innovation Engineering teaches how to transform **innovation** from a random act to a reliable science.

> *To survive, companies need a durable competitive advantage. No technology, plant, product, or market will ever be that. The only durable competitive advantage is your people and their ideas.*
>
> *Yes, Innovation Engineering takes its founding principles from Deming, and I am sure Deming would have loved it. I am also quite confident that Juran, Crosby, and Taguchi would approve. The key issue to me is that Innovation Engineering creates a repeatable process that leads to a durable competitive advantage.*
>
> —Walter Werner, Deming Master

What Held Back the Application of System Thinking to Innovation?

Applying system thinking to innovation struggled because of a lack of data. In a factory, it's easy to gather data from production equipment.

Innovation is more difficult because it involves "human systems," which are classically unstable and unmeasured.

To paraphrase Dr. Deming: Much of what matters about innovation has been immeasurable, unknown, and unknowable. The good news is that, today, innovations and the impact of various innovation methods are measurable.

For more than 30 years, client projects at the Eureka! Ranch have served as a "laboratory" for innovation measurement experiments. PhDs and statisticians have run experiments and analyzed data from thousands of real innovation projects. To develop a significant database from idea to creation to eventual marketplace success took a lot of time and patience. Fortunately, the corporations mentioned previously—and others—were willing to participate in experiments and data collection requests over many years.

Statistical analysis of the database enabled us to identify what separates successful from unsuccessful innovations. The analysis also identified principles and methods for helping everyone think smarter, faster, and more creatively.

Thanks to the support of organizations large and small, we have the world's first and only complete database from idea creation, week by week through development, and all the way to market. It is this quantitative database that makes it possible to apply system thinking to innovation.

The Mission of the Innovation Engineering Movement

The Innovation Engineering movement is a global community of innovation pioneers dedicated to system-driven innovation. Our mission is . . .

> *To change the world through systems that enable innovation by everyone, everywhere, every day, resulting in increased speed (up to 6x) and decreased risk (up to 80%).*

Systems that Enable Innovation by everyone, everywhere, every day is the core of our mission. It's also the right thing to do.

> *William Hopper, coauthor of* The Puritan Gift, *explained to me that enabling employees was the key to the Japanese Miracle: "In 1961 when Sumitomo Electric Industries won the Deming Prize, they did it in a totally different way. Before their victory*

the winner's quality efforts were driven by experts. Sumitomo enabled all of the workers to be a part of the process of quality."

The Deming prize committee in 1961 wrote of the win by Sumitomo:

One of the most important differences between Sumitomo Electric and other companies which have been awarded the Deming Prize is that in Sumitomo people from the top down to foremen worked together. This was an important difference from what happened in previous winning companies and may have contributed much to success.

A newspaper story in Japan on Sumitomo's success told how they enabled frontline employees:

Foremen were trained to prepare control charts and became fully able to use them themselves. They then changed working methods so that younger workers could make products at a high yield. Before this quality-control method was introduced, only some highly trained technicians, with special skill and experience, could make products at a high yield. Afterwards, foremen were able to change the production method so that high yield was attained.

Sumitomo spent several million yen to introduce the new quality-control procedures, but the profit from them was in the hundreds of millions. The experience of Sumitomo is that if all employees cooperate to improve the method of manufacturing the product, a very high standard can be achieved.

—shared by Kenneth Hopper

As Japanese companies enabled frontline employees, industry gains from Deming's teachings grew exponentially. Kenneth Hopper created the graph of productivity gains (shown on the following page) for an article he wrote in 1979. Note the dramatic growth in Japan starting in 1961 with the win of the Deming Prize by Sumitomo.

Innovation Engineering is dedicated to the same kind of shift—from innovation being the job of a small group of "gurus" to enabling innovation by everyone, everywhere, every day. The result is a transformation in innovation results.

The Impact of Enabling Employees on Productivity Gains

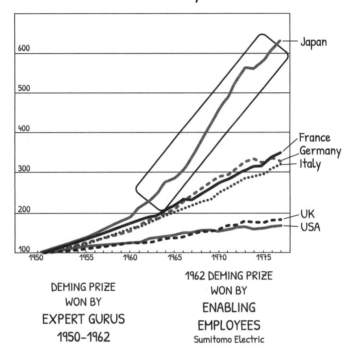

Increased Innovation Speed: Increased Speed is important if we are to take advantage of the opportunities created by today's digital and global economy. The good news is that order-of-magnitude increases in speed are possible. Digital tools and modern work systems make it possible to create, validate, manufacture, and make real new products, services, and internal ways of working faster than ever before.

Decreased Innovation Risk: Decreased Risk is important, given the epidemic of innovation failure that exists around the world. Research finds that just 5% to 15% of innovations are successful at large companies. Most business leaders would have greater odds of success if they went to a Las Vegas casino and gambled their innovation investment on one big bet. A slot machine would give them 32% odds of winning, blackjack 45%, and roulette 47%.

It's easy to realize increased speed by accelerating projects without regards to risks. Similarly, it's easy to reduce risk by slowing down all innovations and subjecting them to never-ending analysis.

What's needed is the *combination* of Increased Speed and Decreased Risk. This can only be accomplished by changing the system of how we think, lead, and work.

Why Call It Innovation Engineering?

The name Innovation Engineering precisely defines our purpose and mindset.

Innovation is about ideas that matter. Creativity is the creation of the new and novel. Innovation is about ideas that make a difference. The difference can be new products/services, how we do our work, or even how we ignite social change in our communities.

Engineering is about applied science. Many books and classes preach the virtues of innovation. Innovation Engineering is different—it details the big-picture leadership principles plus practical and proven "how to" methods for increasing innovation speed and decreasing risk.

We teach theory to provide a background understanding. However, our education programs are primarily focused on how to innovate. We sweat the details. We work and rework each element of innovation until it is reduced to a reliable and reproducible process that can be documented in writing in an operational manual. We tell students to start their innovation efforts by doing exactly what we teach. When they develop confidence in their capability, they then have a responsibility to help the Innovation Engineering community discover and validate even more effective ways to innovate.

An Academic/Industrial Partnership

Early on we decided to create Innovation Engineering in partnership with the University of Maine. They lead the Innovation Engineering movement on college campuses around the world.

Today, Innovation Engineering is recognized as a new field of academic study. It's offered as an undergraduate minor, a graduate certificate, and as an off-campus executive education program. A PhD program is also in development.

On college and university campuses we educate students on how Innovation Engineering will enable them to take advantage of the tremendous opportunities in the new economy. We explain how it will help them: 1) get a job, 2) get promoted, and/or 3) turn their ideas into reality faster and with less risk.

The Innovation Engineering courses enable the personal passion of students. A student graduating with a degree in history or English or business, with a minor in Innovation Engineering, or the graduate certificate, has the skills and confidence to apply, activate, and make a meaningful difference leveraging what they learned in their major field of study.

Studying Innovation Engineering on or off campus does not make you an "engineer," as that is a title reserved for those who have passed the requirements set up by engineering trade associations for certification as a professional engineer. However, it does teach key elements of the engineering mindset: curiosity, discipline, experimentation, problem solving, and how to use writing and math to think deeper about challenges you face.

Systems That ENABLE instead of Control

The word *system,* especially in connection with innovation, creates a vision of being controlled, constrained, and restricted. That is NOT the purpose of Innovation Engineering systems. We design and develop systems that ENABLE innovation by everyone.

The difference between systems that "enable" versus "control" is one of intent. In both cases the goal is the same—reliable delivery of desired results. As Graeme Crombie, an Innovation Engineering Black Belt (the highest Innovation Engineering certification) and an early supporter in Scotland, says:

> *When the system is designed to Enable then it allows employees to take ownership for desired results, thereby delivering a higher degree of certainty that desired results will be delivered. The old form of Control requires that leaders and managers use micromanagement, direct supervision, and overexerted influence on events that really they should be leaving to the worker.*

Empowerment gives people authority to change. However, this will have no impact if people don't know *where* to innovate, *why* to innovate, or *how* to innovate. Enabling is about providing the training, tools, and leadership coaching to make innovation practical, possible, and easy.

Dr. Deming famously declared, *"I should estimate that in my experience most troubles and most possibilities for improvement add up to the proportions something like this:* **94% belongs to the system (responsibility of management), 6% special causes (responsibility of employees)."**

Common Cause Error = Systemic errors of the system

- 94% of problems
- Management is responsible for making the improvement of the system a priority.

Special Cause = Random or fleeting events

- 6% of problems
- These are primarily the responsibility of employees.
- Note: Employees are also responsible for helping management improve the system.

The simple way to state the Deming quote is the way my dad always said it to me: *"94% of problems are caused by the system—6% by the workers."* Throughout this book, this is the version of the quote that we will use, as it is more directly relevant when applying system thinking to innovation.

Dr. Deming was a tireless advocate for enabling workers to have pride in their work. As he wrote:

> *A bad system will beat a good person every time. . . . A basic principle presumed here is that no one should be blamed or penalized for performance that he cannot govern. Violation of this principle can only lead to frustration and dissatisfaction with the job, and lower production.*

> —Dr. W. Edwards Deming

Improvement of a system involves reducing common cause variation. However, you can't improve a system that doesn't exist. And frankly, **more than 99% of companies have no system for innovation.** Now if you reject the idea that you don't have a system for innovation, you are in good company. Every week, when business leaders tell me they already have a system for innovation, I ask to see it. A moment of confusion then occurs. I follow up by asking to see the operations manual for it, the training program curriculum for teaching new employees and new managers. Confusion is now replaced with bewilderment. I then explain that if you can't write it down, you don't have a system. This also means that you can't blame employees for not following the company system for thinking smarter and more creatively when you don't have a system.

Why Should You Care?

Innovation Engineering will help you increase innovation speed and decrease risk. However, that's NOT the most important benefit of Innovation Engineering. According to Sheldon Scott, CEO of the Whitney Blake Company, the most important benefit is to **"Make Work Fun Again!"**—a close variation to Dr. Deming's promise at the start of seminars, stated earlier: **"Why are we here? We are here to come alive, to have fun, to have joy in work."**

By "fun" we don't mean frivolous play. We're talking about the joy that comes from doing something that makes a difference in the world. Said another way: In the irreverent manner of members of the Innovation Engineering movement on and off campus . . .

The fundamental aim of Innovation Engineering is to enable people to do COOL SH*T THAT MATTERS.

The simple fact is—when you spend your time and energy on projects, products, or services that matter to YOU, your ORGANIZATION, and to CUSTOMERS, then you experience a chain reaction of Pride of Work, increased sales, and profitability.

Pride of Work was a very important concept for Dr. Deming. He was once asked how he would summarize his overall message in a few words.

> *I'm not sure, but it would have something to do with variation.*
> Later he added, *I said earlier that my message had to do with variation. I've given it some more thought, and I would say it has to do with Pride of Work.*

—Dr. W. Edwards Deming

Whatever Happened to Pride of Work?

In my opinion, one of the greatest benefits of the internet is that it has enabled the "craft" movement, from distilleries to breweries to farm-to-table restaurants to Meaningfully Unique tools and toys. When you visit a new city, it's commonplace to search for real craft experiences.

What separates craft companies from mass-market companies is Pride of Work. Leading a team of young people, crafting Innovation Engineering courses and tools, and starting our Brain Brew craft distillery has provided me with a first-person understanding of the new way of business. At its core, it's about doing meaningful work. We aren't just doing our job. We are creating whiskey, classes, and internet tools that we are deeply proud of. We sweat details that our competitors ignore.

Steve Jobs' success with Apple and Pixar was due in large part to his commitment to maintaining a craft mindset despite being one of the largest companies in the world. His biographer, Walter Isaacson, told CBS News that Jobs learned this from his adoptive father, Paul Jobs: "Once they were building a fence. And he said, 'You got to make the back of the fence that nobody will see just as good-looking as the front of the fence. Even though nobody will see it, you will know, and that will show that you're dedicated to making something perfect.' "

I believe that the source of the wide range of positive and negative feelings toward Steve Jobs is this craftsmanship mindset. To those who get craftsmanship, fanatical passion is part of the process. To those who are practical and prudent, it's craziness.

Pride of Work is enabled when you are working on **Cool Sh*t That Matters!**

> *Some folks talk about innovation being constrained by the worker's fear of failure, laziness, or short-term targets driven by greed. The cause for this runs deeper. We have lost the joy of work for work's sake. It takes very little additional effort to do something right than it does just to do it. Don't make excuses, because ultimately the only person that will know if it's great work or not is you.*

> —Ken Grier, creative director
> The Macallan Scotch whisky distillery

Never-Ending Innovation on Innovation

We practice what we preach—never-ending continuous innovation of our training and tools.

We don't claim to know all the answers. We regularly upgrade our best practices with: 1) ideas from users, 2) academic research discoveries, and 3) licensed content from commercial experts.

We are very disciplined in what we add to the Innovation Engineering curriculum and tools. Our upgrade process involves a small team of volunteers adapting and applying the new approach to their work. Their focus is an "engineering" mindset of finding the 20% who give 80% of the benefit. They are relentless in simplifying and streamlining new systems and methods. When innovation system improvements or tools are validated as reliable, they are incorporated into our best practices.

We aggressively embrace new methods, systems, and tools. As I write these words, members of the Innovation Engineering movement are gathered at the Eureka! Ranch to innovate on our project management system. They are using stimulus from experiences, academic research, and other systems to ignite ideas for how we can further accelerate development projects.

We believe that learning how to innovate smarter and faster is not a competition. We encourage our students, both on and off campus, to experience every innovation class and tool they can find. **We have designed our innovation systems to make them work well with others.** Within our community we have many organizations that have painlessly integrated Innovation Engineering with 6 Sigma, Lean, Lean Start Up, Design Thinking, Business Model Programs, and Phase Gate systems. We believe in collaboration. As Ben Franklin said, **"We must all hang together or most assuredly we will all hang separately."**

Never-ending, continuous innovation on Innovation Engineering systems means that, while this book details the state of the art at this time, I anticipate that this book will be regularly updated with the latest learning. In the short term, you can keep up with new learnings by signing up to receive our blog. You can find it by going to innovationengineering.org/news.

The Organization of this Book

This book provides a beginning understanding of the six college courses that make up the Innovation Engineering curriculum. It begins with a discussion of the Innovation Problem and Solution. It then details how Innovation Engineering came to be born, developed, and validated. Chapters 3 through 8 outline systems for how to Create, Communicate, and Commercialize innovations. Chapters 9 through 12 review principles for how you can upgrade your internal innovation systems to be faster and more effective. They include a collection of four subsystems that are critical for enabling innovation: Alignment, Collaboration Cafe, Merwyn Rapid Research, and Patent ROI.

The book closes with a chapter on how to create an innovation culture within your team, company, or community.

How Could They Know?

As you embark on this journey, you will quickly see the world in a new way. Problems will be seen as opportunities to 19. A mindset of "If it's not broke, don't fix it" will be replaced with a never-ending passion for discovering ideas, methods, and tools for working smarter.

As your mindset changes, you are likely to find that your new thinking conflicts with others. You will become frustrated that they don't embrace and celebrate your new courage and confidence to use innovation to work in smarter ways.

A fundamental belief within the Innovation Engineering community is that people are fundamentally good. We believe that the naysayers you interact with are not against change or Innovation Engineering. They just don't understand it. They can't imagine that innovation could be a reliable science instead of a random gamble. It was the same with Dr. Deming's efforts in the 1980s. When asked if executives were doing enough to apply his teaching, his response would be loud and on the verge of belligerent:

> *Managers don't know about it. How could they know? How could they know there was anything to learn? How could they? How could they? How could they know there was any other way to manage?*

Quite simply, most adults think that ideas are magical and only randomly reveal themselves to so-called special people. How could they know that everyone can add value and make a difference if they are simply taught how to think quicker, faster, and more creatively.

How could they, or you, know? Until recently there were no courses available in system-driven innovation. The good news is that now you can learn how to use system thinking to enable yourself and your organization to innovate faster and with less risk. Not only can you learn it—you can master it.

However, before we get started, I want you to pause and reflect.

What Did You Learn?

If you attended an Innovation Engineering class on campus or off, or were working with some Innovation Engineering Pioneers on a project, you would hear this question often.

The question is designed to cause you to stop, think, confront, and explore what you've experienced from a "bigger picture" system perspective.

The best way to explore what you have learned, what confirms as well as what contradicts your preexisting thinking, is through conversation with your coworkers, family, or friends. Speaking what you learned out loud makes a difference. Research finds that when we speak our thoughts in a full voice so that our ears hear the idea, a different part of the brain becomes engaged, resulting in new levels of understanding.

The second best way is to have a conversation with yourself in writing. Write what you've learned in a journal, a notebook, or on your computer. The written word also has a way of bringing out truths that we aren't at first fully conscious of.

Each chapter ends with a section called **What Did You Learn?** You are free to utilize this prompt or to ignore it. Research finds that those who do—who consciously reflect—will realize a much greater return on their investment in reading this book.

> Rock & Roll!
> Doug Hall
> Springbrook, Prince Edward Island, Canada
> Cincinnati, Ohio, USA

You Have Two Choices to Make

1. **If you fully "buy in" to the need for Innovation Engineering,** skip ahead to Chapter 3 and get started. If you have some reservations, the next two chapters are for you.

Chapter 1 outlines the innovation problem and why innovation is no longer optional.

Chapter 2 outlines the Innovation Engineering solution, history, and pedigree.

I've included these two chapters because it's only with a total commitment to the new mindset of system-driven innovation that you will realize the potential of Innovation Engineering.

2. **If you are someone who values the PEDIGREE behind what you are being taught, flip to the back of the book and read the Backstory chapter on Dr. Deming.** It lays out the foundation that system-driven innovation is based on. If this is not important to you—simply go ahead to Chapter 1 or 3 as detailed above.

1

PROBLEM:
Innovation Is No Longer Optional

The way we live—and the way we do business—is changing like never before. Our growing interconnectedness is transforming the way the world works. As power shifts from the hands of central authors to the hands of the people, movements are becoming more powerful and moving more rapidly than ever before.

—Richard Branson, CEO of Virgin

It's a Dickens of a Time

Those organizations that are leading change in their industries are winning. Those that are "reacting" to the forces of change are losing.

During a recent speech at the UK Marketing Society's annual conference in London, I thought it would be funny to loosely recite Charles Dickens:

It is the best of times, it is the worst of times. It is the age of wisdom, it is the age of foolishness. It is the season of light, it is the season of darkness. We have everything before us, we have nothing before us. We are all going direct to heaven, we are all going direct the other way.

A few laughed, but most didn't. I would learn later that most saw it as confirmation that these days are indeed the worst of times.

The life cycle from monopoly to commodity used to take decades. Today, because of the internet, it's often measured in less than a year. The consequence is acceleration of Joseph Schumpeter's Creative Destruction—organizations that don't innovate are destroyed by those that have **embraced a mindset of never-ending, continuous innovation.**

The new reality was made clear following the recession of 2008, when the marketplace didn't bounce back like it had in the past. The good news, from my perspective, is that the world as we knew it is NEVER coming back. The world has changed, rewarding those who innovate and destroying the profitability of those who don't.

In 2011 we conducted a survey of CEOs for the US Department of Commerce, the results of which quantified the gap between those who innovate and those who don't. The survey found that those who had an innovation mindset following the recession realized significantly better business results three years after the recession of 2008.

SALES GROWTH: +84% for innovators versus +4% for noninnovators

PROFIT GROWTH: +96% for innovators versus +13% for noninnovators

EMPLOYEE GROWTH: +64% for innovators versus +1% for noninnovators

A similar study with CEOs of companies in Ireland found nearly identical results. I've found similar patterns in qualitative interviews in Korea, Vietnam, Turkey, Mexico, Spain, and Italy. Today, we live in a global economy. And, no matter where you live, **if you're not meaningfully unique, you'd better be cheap.**

The root cause for the differences in results was that, when the recession hit, those who embraced innovation quickly pivoted. They changed their offerings, realizing nearly double the percentage of company sales in products or services that they didn't offer three years before (37% versus 19%). They also went after new customers, nearly doubling the percentage of sales from new customers (domestic and export) versus three years before (43% versus 23%).

It's Not a Theory—The Pace of Business Has Really Changed

In the past, there was little urgency to change what we offer or how we work. It was possible to create a for-profit or nonprofit company based on an innovative service or product and to market it to the same customers for years.

Over the careers of most senior leaders, the life cycle of profitability for new products and services has been long. It has not been uncommon for a company founder to innovate and for the life cycle of their offerings to last for two generations. Children of innovators, if they managed the family business right, could have great careers. By the third generation, the marketplace usually changes such that it needs to be reinvented if the organization is to survive. Sadly, most don't—and only 3% of family businesses make it to the fourth generation.

In the past, it has been possible to succeed even with an inferior product or service in your region. This was because customers didn't know that there were other alternatives available in their towns or countries (or the world) that offered greater value for the money.

The internet has changed everything. Today, customers have the ability to know more about what alternatives exist in the world. It gives them the ability to painlessly compare value for the money. It also gives them the ability to share their experiences with other buyers, making it hard for companies to make false promises. For example, **when you put a new "design skin" on the same old product, customers quickly figure out that your "improvement" is just skin deep.**

Today, a business doesn't last for a generation. In many industries, product or service life cycles are now months or years.

Timed Out

A friend of 25 years told me recently that he has "Timed Out." He went on to explain, "The world has changed and I'm no longer relevant or respected."

Timed Out is a concept that the Innovation Engineering Pioneers and myself just don't get. Timed Out is something that happens to you when you stop learning and growing. **Timed Out is something that happens when you're dead!**

With the Timed Out mindset, great wisdom is prematurely lost to the organization. Yes, the world has changed. However, what's needed is for those with 30-plus years of experience to fully engage in gaining a working understanding of the new opportunities that technology makes possible. Then they need to commit themselves to mentoring the next generation of leaders, just as they were taught when they were younger.

A mindset of Timed Out is sad. Worse than that is the SELFISH mindset. It exists across all industries—for-profit, nonprofit, large companies, and small ones. It goes something like this: **"I have two/four years until retirement. I think I can make it without changing."** Or: **"I am close to being eligible to take early retirement. I don't want to do anything that will risk it."**

This mindset is SELFISH. It causes deep, deep resentment among younger workers who still have marriages, young children, and/or big college bills to pay off in the future. They feel betrayed as the older workers, whom they have looked up to for years, suddenly are exposed as frauds in their minds. Hmmm . . . **and we wonder why younger generations are not engaged?**

The Innovation Engineering Pioneers believe that the internet, with its transparency and increased cycle speed, is a GREAT THING. It creates separation between those who are dead and those who are alive. It rewards those with the courage to create differences that matter. It makes it easier to connect with new customers around the world.

Today Is a Repeat of History

The internet has created exponential growth in our ability to exchange information. On a much smaller scale, a similar increase occurred at the turn of the century before last in the USA.

From 1870 to 1910, there was explosive growth in the ability of the marketplace to exchange information. During this time period, 5.1 million phones were installed, railroads developed into an efficient national network, and the concepts of "brands" and national advertising were born. In just four years, from 1871 to 1875, the number of brands with registered trademarks grew nearly tenfold, from 121 to 1,138.

The consequence of this increased exchange of information was a marketplace that was closer to a true free market economy. As customers had more information, they could compare the value they received for their money. Those merchants who didn't offer a meaningful point of difference (i.e., value for the money) soon lost sales and died.

Because the change in exchanging information came faster than most companies were ready for, the impact on the economy was deflation, as companies had to cut prices to win back sales. In total, there was a 30% decrease in the consumer price index during this time period.

The internet has created a 1,000X greater disruption than the introduction of railroads and national advertising. Everyone can know everything about a product. Differences that are marketing "smoke and mirrors" are quickly exposed. Having lots of money to spend on marketing is no longer a cure for mediocre nonprofit services or commercial offerings.

TODAY'S Growth in Our Ability to Exchange Information Is Exponential

The internet really is the biggest innovation in history. It's more important than the computer, even more important than the transistor. The internet came and everything became for everyone. We were set free.

—Steve Wozniak, cofounder
of Apple Computer Company

Today, around 40% of the world's population has an internet connection. In 1995, it was less than 1%. Today, there are 250 million registered domain names. The impact of the internet is greater than simply the ability to text or look up information. It's igniting new infrastructures and systems.

As an example, having something shipped to my rural farmhouse on the north shore of Prince Edward Island, Canada, historically took up to two weeks. Today, I can have almost anything I want shipped to me by Amazon Prime with free delivery in two days. For the first time, there are even UPS brown trucks and FedEx trucks traveling the island.

I think Prince Edward Island will find, in time, that the exchange of information and infrastructure systems like shipping will have a greater impact on the economy of the island than the 12.9-kilometer bridge to the mainland that opened in 1997. The impact will be positive when they learn that, like the bridge, change goes both ways. The new marketplace makes it possible to live in a paradise like Prince Edward Island and do business across planet Earth.

David Carr wrote in *The New York Times,* "Change comes very slowly, but then happens all at once. The future, as it always does, sets its own schedule."

HINT: If Your Goal Is to Make Money, Innovation Is the Only Choice

Recently, a CEO I know told me: "We're conservative. We're slow to change." Or as another CEO told me: "Doug, I don't get it. I don't know how to innovate, my team doesn't know how to innovate, and, frankly, my customers have never asked us to innovate. Why the focus on innovation?"

If a purpose of your company is to make money, or if a desire of your nonprofit is to survive and sustain, then innovation is your only choice.

Researchers at Georgia Tech have compared companies' self-reported strategies for success versus the profit margin they realize. As the chart that follows shows, the conclusion is simple—if you want to make more money, innovation is the only strategy. Companies pursuing innovation as their core business strategy realize 50 to 100% higher profit margins than those that pursue "low cost, high quality, fast delivery, or voice of the customer (doing whatever the customer says)."

Meaningfully Unique Is More Profitable

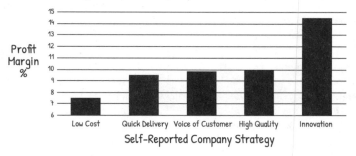

Basic economic theory predicts these research results. When you offer something that is meaningful and that no one else offers, you have a monopoly, resulting in higher profitability.

It's the Best Time to Be in Business!

The interconnected marketplace is creating exciting opportunities for increasing innovation speed. Just as it's empowering customers, it's empowering companies. Proactive leaders can discover and develop breakthrough technologies with faster speed and less risk if they upgrade their management and innovation systems to leverage the opportunities present in the new marketplace.

Evidence of the rising ability to innovate is the number of patent filings in the USA. The USA is a great barometer, as the market is big and many of the world's patent offices use the US filings as benchmarks.

Historically, patent filings have grown at a slow and stable rate. However, as the chart that follows shows, as the number of internet users around the world has grown, so, too, has the number of patent filings. The internet has enabled inventors and entrepreneurs to make technical connections, conduct patent searches, and find opportunities faster than ever before. It has made it the best of times to be an inventor.

Growth in Patent Filings

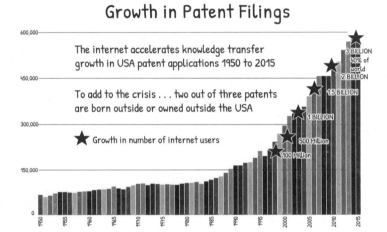

The internet accelerates knowledge transfer growth in USA patent applications 1950 to 2015

To add to the crisis . . . two out of three patents are born outside or owned outside the USA

★ Growth in number of internet users

Interestingly, two out of three patents filed in the USA are granted to someone either born outside the USA or to a company from outside the USA. To borrow a line from Bruce Springsteen, "Born in the USA, owned in the USA" is not the way with technology anymore. The internet is making it easy for everyone everywhere to innovate. In fact, somewhere in South Korea, Northern Ireland, or South Africa, there is someone with an idea, some education, and a ton of motivation to disrupt your company, industry, and career.

The Classic Management System Can't Keep Up with the New Rate of Change

When the pace of change was slower, it was possible to treat strategy, innovation, and the way we work together as independent functions, just as Henry Ford segmented work on the production line. However, as the world moves faster, we don't have the time for the inevitable meetings, communications, miscommunications, and rework that are created by the classic command-and-control management system.

The challenge today's leaders face is that, as the life cycle has accelerated, their method of management has not adapted to the new pace of change. The classic method of managing innovation as a department, or as something led by specialists, is just not fast enough anymore.

What's needed is a culture in which innovation is the mission of everyone, everywhere, every day—a culture in which innovation is enabled through scalable education systems and tools. The result is an amplification of the effectiveness of employees just as a tractor amplifies the amount of land a farmer can work versus with a horse and plow.

To restart success for organizations that are the victims of change: **Cost cutting won't solve the problem. Working harder won't solve the problem. Beating the workers won't solve the problem.**

The ONLY sustainable solution to the accelerated pace of change is to create a culture of innovation.

The Five False Innovation Cures

Growing an innovation culture is hard. It's really hard. The existing infrastructure has evolved over time to be 100% focused on decreasing risk. And, as the marketplace changes faster, the culture responds by amplifying its avoidance of risk.

Worse yet, we are organized in companies the same way we were in universities—in departmental silos. Each worker reports to a head of a silo—be it manufacturing, marketing, product development, finance, legal, market research, or sales. The corporate system rewards loyalty to the silo more than to the organization. It is the silo that gives us a pay raise. It is the silo that prevents us from being laid off or downsized.

It is very easy for every silo to do a perfect job, but collectively we are not effective. Dr. Deming spoke about how everyone applying their best efforts, working with diligence, can still result in the company going out of business. The reason is that the success of an organization lies in the interactions between the people, processes, and departments.

Getting the system to work is so difficult that most leaders are not willing to take on the challenge. As the CEO of a Fortune 50 company told me: "I don't have the energy to change the system. When it comes to innovation, our system is broken—that's why I set up these special teams working outside the system."

When leaders are ready to confront the reality that: 1) they need to innovate to compete in today's marketplace and 2) their current system for innovation management doesn't work, they frequently seek out one or more of what the Innovation Engineering Pioneers call "False Cures." These are simplistic management fixes that sound promising but, in the long term, often cause more damage than good.

FALSE CURE 1: MORE INSPECTION, METRICS, AND BIGGER REWARD.
The hypothesis is: If management reviews the development of innovations more frequently and diligently, then innovation success will be realized. The truth is that inspection of quality doesn't work. Just as in the factory, innovation quality must be built into the organization's work systems and tools.

A related hypothesis is that if we manage by metrics and reward people for hitting the numbers, then innovation success will be realized. The truth is that metrics without a method simply creates stress that ignites the "gaming" of the system to hit the numbers.

Metrics are invaluable when used as a tool for improving the system. They are destructive when used as a means for motivating. Metrics are the outcome of the system. Sustained improvement in metrics only occurs with improvement in the methods and tools that make up the work system.

Success with innovation requires intrinsic passion and dedication. The promise of extrinsic rewards will not sustain innovators through the inevitable ups and downs that occur when trying to discover and develop a Meaningfully Unique innovation. As Dr. Deming and others have taught, extrinsic "beating of workers" and "bribery of workers" only serves to increase fear and decrease intrinsic motivation.

With Innovation Engineering, we have two measures that we use to quantify progress.

Our **INNOVATION SYSTEM** measure is the weighted value of the innovation pipeline. This is a measure of the value of all organizational projects for savings and growth that are in development. Each project is aligned to a strategic priority, called a Blue Card, in the language of Innovation Engineering. The value of each project is weighted based on where it is in the development process versus historical norms of what value will be realized when the project is made real and/or ships into the marketplace.

No metric is more important to your future bottom line than the weighted value of all the ideas that are in your innovation pipeline.

Our **INNOVATION CULTURE** measure is what percent of the time employees are engaged in proactive versus reactive work. When employees are 100% reactive, their days are spent "fighting fires" and in wasteful "rework." When employees spend a high percentage of their time being proactive, their days are focused on anticipating the future. When a culture is proactive instead of reactive, employee engagement, productivity, and effectiveness are much higher. This is because employees feel a sense of control over their future instead of feeling they are simply victims of external circumstances.

These two measures—Innovation Pipeline Weighted Value and Proactive Culture—are the foundations of Innovation Engineering. There are other metrics, independent variables, that are predictive of these two measures, such as: average cycle time for learning, time to development decisions, collaboration levels, data-based decision-making, training levels, and patent filings.

FALSE CURE 2: THE BIG IDEA HUNT. The hypothesis is: If the organization just had more big ideas going into the organization's innovation pipeline, then all would be great. In truth, more stuff going into the front end of a broken system doesn't result in bigger ideas becoming reality. Most development systems reduce all ideas, no matter how big they start, into the same old stuff. As one company leader who is part of the movement said, "Every 'big idea' that we put into our system comes out looking like a minor variation of something we currently offer. We need to fix our system."

The foolishness of the "big idea hunt" was made clear in a famous study of technology transfer by the Massachusetts Institute of Technology (MIT) over 16 years. It found that when a large company licensed a "big idea" technology from MIT and put it into their existing development system, 80% of the time they ended up failing. Most MIT innovations died in development and never made it to market.

FALSE CURE 3: SKUNK WORKS TEAMS. The hypothesis is: The only way to make sure that real innovations survive is to manage them outside of the existing culture. The truth is that, in most cases, the innovations will eventually need to use the infrastructure—and when they do, **the culture strikes back,** resulting in disruption, chaos, and the eventual failure of the Skunk Works. Skunk Works is the name for Lockheed Martin's Advanced

Development Program. It was responsible for a number of famous aircraft designs. The name "Skunk Works" is thought to have come from the moonshine factory in the comic strip *Li'l Abner*. Lockheed Martin's team was successful because they operated 100% outside of the organization from idea through production to sales and delivery to customers. They were a complete, freestanding business operation. This was easier for them to do as they sold to one customer—the military.

For much of my career, I was a vigorous advocate for Skunk Works teams. I've led or helped coach hundreds of these teams around the world. However, after 40-plus years of experience, I've come to the conclusion that my mindset was wrong. I now believe that working with and upgrading the existing culture—by enabling the leadership and employees with system-driven innovation—is the only sustainable and reliable path that a company can use to create a never-ending stream of innovations.

Initially, the Skunk Works teams generate the perception of success. This is because they spend the majority of their time on the innovation as opposed to "the system." However, eventually the success vaporizes, as an open or passive-aggressive civil war occurs when the new innovation needs to access resources within the existing organization. At around 18 months, the team ends up spending more time trying to convince those in "the system" to support their breakthrough innovation than they spend on the idea itself. As momentum stalls, those within the system point out the waste of time and energy, and slowly but surely the leadership gives up on the venture and/or the team members give up and quit the company.

The failure of Skunk Works projects is regrettable. However, my bigger reason for no longer supporting this approach has to do with basic human rights. It's not fair to allow some within the organization the freedom to think and create cool stuff outside the system, using advanced tools and methods, while at the same time shackling others with working within a bureaucratic prison.

When the CEO stands up and celebrates a team that innovates outside the system, what message do you think it sends to the others? Those in the existing system have ideas too. They can make the ideas happen too. They could do amazing things as well . . . *if* they had the same training and tools as the innovators.

FALSE CURE 4: BUY AN INNOVATION CULTURE. The hypothesis is: If we just acquire a small entrepreneurial company, a miracle will occur to transform our culture. This is a more expensive variation of the Skunk Works approach. And like many of these approaches, it gives a message to the culture that they are "stupid" and the new company team is "smart." This creates discontent and disengagement within the existing culture. The result is often conscious or subconscious resistance to the new ideas. This is one of a number of reasons why independent research and a *Harvard Business Review* article finds that 70% to 90% of mergers and acquisitions fail financially. In addition, there is no real opportunity for learning when you buy a successful company. The biggest learning has already happened—it was the startup years of trying, pivoting, learning, and pivoting.

FALSE CURE 5: BE A FAST FOLLOWER. The hypothesis is: If we give up being first to market, we can reduce our risk. The problem with this approach is that, if the pioneer is really good, then, as a provider of copycat products, our only choice is to sell our offerings at a lower price. Multiple research studies documented in my book *Meaningful Marketing* finds that, on average, fast followers generate half the profits of the pioneer. And it's not very motivating to be an employee of a company that dedicates itself to being a follower. Great people want to do great things. They want to be part of an organization that leads change instead of simply reacting to others.

Innovation Requires a Flip of Mindset

It is rare that anyone loves their existing innovation system. Despite what some may think, no one gets up in the morning and says, "I love to work in an inefficient bureaucracy." Rather, they feel they have no choice because they don't feel they can change the system. They follow the rules of the system because, frankly, they see that as less painful than trying to work outside the system.

What's ironic is that while companies are addicted to cost cutting, **there is probably no greater waste of time, energy, and money than inefficiencies within the existing systems regarding how new ideas/innovations are supposed to occur.**

Upgrading an innovation system requires a flip of mindset. It requires an acceptance of the basic Deming premise that **94% of the challenges lie in the system, and 6% are the result of the worker.**

Upgrading an innovation system might well be the greatest legacy of a leader. Retired CEO of Procter & Gamble A. G. Lafley, in his book *The Game-Changer,* puts the new mindset toward innovation this way:

> *My job at Procter & Gamble is focused on integrating innovation into* **everything** *we do.*
>
> *Every business has some central organizing principle that people use as the basis for making decisions, meeting challenges, and creating opportunities. For P&G, it is innovation.*
>
> *Innovation must be the central driving force for any business that wants to grow and succeed in both the short and long terms. We live in a time when the rate of changes is such that today's unique product or service becomes tomorrow's commodity. Winning—playing the game better than your competitors and changing the game when necessary—requires finding a new way to sustain organic revenue and profit growth and consistently improve margins.*
>
> *This means seeing innovation not as something left to the R&D department, but as the central foundation in the way you run your business, driving key decisions, be they choice of goals, strategy, organization structure, resource allocation, commitment to budgets, or development of leadership.*
>
> *All too often, managers decide on a business strategy— what markets to pursue and what products to make—then turn to innovation to support it.* **This is the wrong way around.** *Innovation needs to be put at the center of the business in order to choose the right goals and business strategy and make how-to-win choices. It is the central job of every leader—business unit managers, functional leaders, and the CEO. The CEO, in fact, must also be the CIO—the chief innovation officer.*
>
> *Innovation is the foundation for controlling your destiny. It was for P&G (in my experience) the real game-changer—the real source of sustainable competitive advantage and the most reliable engine of sustainable growth. Innovation is the answer.*

What Did You Learn?

- Step back and THINK.
- What did you learn from this chapter?
- What confirmed what you already thought?
- What challenged your preexisting beliefs?
- As the world has changed, how have you changed?
- For your organization, is today the best of times or the worst of times?
- For your career, is today the best of times or the worst of times?
- Are you optimistic or pessimistic about your ability to face the new realities in the marketplace?

2

SOLUTION: Innovation Engineering Pedigree

We want sales and profits to GROW FOREVER. To do this, we need to innovate to meet changes in the market, with customers and competition. However, innovation requires CHANGE and entering the UNKNOWN. We HATE CHANGE and the UNKNOWN. We avoid it until we MUST DO IT. However, when we MUST do it—it might be too late. I wish there was a way to make innovation projects as reliable as cost-saving projects.

—Patricio Morales
Monterrey, Mexico

Definition of a System

The Innovation Engineering movement defines a system as Dr. Deming did: *two or more independent parts with a common aim.* In the case of an organization, this means two or more departments (parts) that work together toward a common organizational mission.

Sadly, the average organization realizes **less than the sum of its parts**— they realize less than what each department delivers independently. This is because, rather than optimizing their interaction with other departments for the good of the organization, each department's primary focus is on delivering their departmental metrics, no matter the consequences to the organization as a whole.

Good organizations are the **sum of their parts**—they realize an additive impact from the interactions of their departments. There is cooperation and collaboration between departments. The management of each department reacts to issues rapidly. **They readily sacrifice short-term department results** for the accomplishment of the overall mission of the organization.

System Versus Process

"A <u>SYSTEM</u> is two or more parts that work together to accomplish

a SHARED AIM"
Dr. W. Edwards Deming

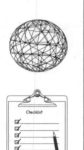

A <u>PROCESS</u> doesn't require different groups or departments to work together.

Great organizations are the **product of their parts**—they realize a multiplicative impact from the interactions of their departments. Employees anticipate customer needs and the needs of other departments. Good organizations innovate to problem-solve challenges when they arise. Great organizations **anticipate issues and proactively innovate** to take advantage of opportunities, lead market change, and prevent problems from developing.

To move from an average or good organization to a great organization requires the engagement of leadership. This is because only the leadership of a team, department, division, or organization has the bigger picture understanding of today and tomorrow.

Dr. Deming wrote of the need to replace management with leadership. To paraphrase Dr. Deming: **The job of management is one of prediction. It's about finding out what will help the customer in the future. It's about finding how to get ahead of the customer.**

Leadership is about leading a team, department, or organization into the future. It's about making strategic choices on what products, services, and markets to invest resources in. It's also about investing in capability building, such as employee education, tools, and systems to enable team members to work smarter.

In 1954 Peter Drucker wrote in his management classic *The Practice of Management:*

It is not enough for the business to provide just any economic goods and services; it must provide better and more economic ones. It is not necessary for a business to grow bigger; but it is necessary that it constantly grow better. . . . Every managerial unit of a business should have clear responsibility and definite goals for innovation. It should be responsible for its contribution to innovation in the company's product or service; and it should in addition strike consciously and with direction toward advancement of the art in the particular area in which it is engaged: selling, accounting, quality control, or personal management.

More recently, Kouzes and Posner wrote in their leadership classic *The Leadership Challenge:*

Innovation and leadership are nearly synonymous. Leaders are innovators; innovators are leaders. The focus of a leader's attention is less on the routine operations and much more on the untested and untried. Leaders are always asking, "What's new? What's next? What's better?"

Full Stop
Predicting the Future is Really HARD

The paragraphs above make it seem easy to lead an organization into the future. It's not. It's very hard to set strategy for the future. That's because the future is unknown.

When setting strategy, leaders always work with imperfect information. They make decisions on where competitors and customers are going to be in the future. I say this in my own defense. The students on campus like to remind me of the interview I did in 1999 for *Inc.* magazine. In it, I was asked what I thought about the internet. My response was:

The internet is a library. Before it existed, I didn't go to the library that often. Now that it exists, I don't go there any more than I went before. It's a great place to find eclectic facts, but its practicality and functionality are limited.

It's fair to say that I totally missed that one. And the internet's "memory" is very unforgiving.

It's not possible to predict the future with precision. Fortunately, there are Future Mining tools that we teach, such as if/then scenarios, patent mining, and lead user immersions, that can help leaders think smarter about the future.

The Idea for Innovation Engineering Was First Sparked on December 19, 1979

I had just returned home for the Christmas holiday from the University of Maine, where I was in my junior year studying chemical engineering. With a sense of urgency, my father, Merwyn Bradford (Buzz) Hall, sat me down in our family living room.

"I learned something amazing this fall from a statistician named Dr. Deming," he explained. "With manufacturing, it is well understood that you have a choice. You can either have high quality or low cost. You can't have both. This fall I've learned that you can have both if you apply system thinking to manufacturing."

To be honest, my mind at the time was more on spending time with my high school girlfriend, whom I would soon marry and spend my life with, than on hearing about some statistician.

But Dad was not to be stopped. With an uncharacteristic passion he said, "Doug, this is really important for you to understand. It's going to change the way companies are run. Deming's done it. He is the reason why the Japanese cars are so much better quality and Detroit is having so much trouble competing with them."

The conversation with my dad got my attention. It made sense to me logically. But what really caught my attention was the emotion my dad expressed. As an engineering physics major, he was not prone to being emotional.

Over that holiday we talked more about what he had learned. He taught me the difference between special cause and common cause errors. He taught me about "Plan, Do, Study, Act" cycles of learning. I didn't know it at the time, but that conversation would change the trajectory of my life and how I looked at the world.

Applying Dr. Deming's teaching would be the secret to the success of my work at Procter & Gamble, my companies, my books, and even my approach to philanthropy.

Years later, thanks to Larry Stewart, one of the earliest Innovation Engineering Pioneers, I would have the honor of teaching Innovation

Engineering in Powell, Wyoming, Dr. Deming's hometown. In Powell, I told the story of how my dad had taught me that you didn't have to make a choice; you could have high quality and low cost if you changed your system. I added, "I am here to teach you that, when it comes to innovation, you also don't have to make a choice. You can have both increased innovation speed and decreased risk, if you change your system of thinking."

Procter & Gamble Was the Research Lab for the New Way of Thinking

The country of Japan was where Dr. Deming's teachings were developed, refined, and made real. For Innovation Engineering, Procter & Gamble served a similar role.

It started when, after graduating from the University of Maine, I took the path less traveled by chemical engineering graduates. Instead of taking an engineering job, I went to work for P&G in their brand management department.

As I look back on it, it's a miracle that Mark Upson hired me. I did not have the experience to do the job. Fortunately, Mark took a gamble on me because of my entrepreneurial energy. I'd created and sold learn-to-juggle and magic kits as a teenager—and founded a promotional products company on six campuses when I was in college.

Being a chemical engineer in a marketing job, fresh out of college, was a major shift in mindset. I found myself relying on the system-thinking principles my dad was continuing to teach me. When I got tired of reworking budget charts, by hand, for the hundredth time, I changed the system. I found a new computer program called VisiCalc—the first major spreadsheet. I wrote a one-page memo and got the first personal computer on a P&G Brand Group—an Apple IIe. It enabled me to do budget chart changes in 95% less time than by punching a calculator. It also allowed more advanced statistical analysis of business data. At the time, the office manager actually said to me, "One day I can imagine one of these computers on every floor." I replied, "I can see one on every desk." He just shook his head.

I applied system thinking to strategy, finance, product development, packaging design, and promotion design.

To the leadership of P&G, my nontraditional system approach was both exciting and frustrating. Fortunately, most of the people I worked for were by nature system thinkers who evaluated the whole and not simply the parts. My first boss had this to say about me:

Were there times I wanted to strangle Doug? Absolutely. He
was what I call a 'high-maintenance subordinate.' You had to
watch him like crazy. He'd be nodding at what I was saying,
but his mind would be somewhere else. Linear, he's not. He's
more like a helicopter pilot—he sees the same thing you see,
but from a different perspective. . . . Doug's divergence paid
off a number of times in the context of inventions that would
not have been discovered simply by taking incremental steps
forward from where we were.

—Barb Thomas, my first boss at P&G

I was quickly promoted to brand manager. In the 1980s, the P&G brand manager job was like the chief engineer role at Toyota. I had the responsibility to lead the business of my brand; however, I had no authority over any of the departmental silos. As the brand manager I was the "hub of the wheel," leading the inevitable trade-offs required to move business-building innovations from idea to reality.

Being a P&G brand manager was the greatest job I've ever had. It is the inspiration for the project leader role designed into Innovation Engineering and explained in Chapter 8. The only difference is that, today, anyone in the company can take the role, whereas at P&G in the 1980s it was filled exclusively by those in the marketing department.

After a few years, I was offered the opportunity to be either the brand manager of Tide or to be brand manager of a struggling (and, frankly, failing) innovation group in the food & beverage division. For me it was an easy decision—innovation was my passion.

Soon Eric Schulz joined the team. He fully bought into the idea of changing the world by changing the innovation system. He had faced the pain and suffering of the existing P&G innovation system that was designed to control rather than to enable innovation.

Our starting place was to learn everything we could about innovation. We interviewed top experts. We read academic articles and ran lots of experiments. We quickly learned that if it took three months to execute a learning cycle—concept, package, customer research, and analysis—we could only do four cycles in a year. So we changed the system. We invented a new system we called Rapid Test that enabled us to create, test, and report results from four cities in seven days. Today, that Rapid Test system is even faster. As you will learn in Chapter 10,

companies today can simultaneously test in four countries and painlessly get results in hours.

And thus was born the P&G Invention Team. I was soon promoted
to associate advertising manager (director of marketing at other companies). I insisted that we have no budget. We would cross-charge business
units for our work. The result? We ended up making quite a profit, which
was a real problem for the finance department, as staff groups were not
supposed to be profitable.

Demand for our services was greater than Eric and I could provide.
Instead of hiring more people, we became very good at collaborating. You
will learn more about how to accelerate collaboration in Chapter 10. We
worked with partners who understood system thinking—big companies,
small companies, citizen inventors, and university professors. These external collaborations multiplied our capacity and were a raw and rough version of Connect and Develop that P&G would make famous in later years.

The finance department did an audit of our effectiveness. They compared projects of similar complexity. They found that our P&G Invention
Team took a product to market with 10% of the staff, in 16% of the time,
and at 18% of the cost of a similar project using the traditional system.
It wasn't that we were any smarter. We upgraded the existing system to
enable us to work faster and more effectively.

Sadly, the person responsible for managing me at the time didn't get
it. Incorrectly, he wrote in my last personnel review that I had a special
gift. I didn't. The secret to my success, then as now, was system thinking.

> *Doug brings an extraordinary degree of creativity, entrepre-
> neurial instinct, and energy to his work. He has brought eight
> product concepts from invention to shipping, all within the past
> year . . . with a ninth project soon to follow. This has to be
> something of a record.*

The next part of the review was not so positive.

> *Doug has just one key opportunity for improvement: He needs
> to treat the "system" with more respect. . . . [He] takes almost
> malicious pleasure in "beating the system" by developing
> new product concepts faster and cheaper than if work were
> done through traditional channels. . . . It does not help to rub
> people's noses in their inefficiencies, their cost of operation or*

their tortoiselike speed. . . . Finally, and of much lesser impor-
tance, Doug has a too-low tolerance for paperwork, memo writ-
ing, budgeting, and similar administrative errata which, until
successfully addressed, will limit his effectiveness in conven-
tional management assignments.

It would take me another 20 years to realize that the most valuable advice in this review was the second part. I was using upgraded systems to beat the system—but not treating the existing system with respect. The art department wasn't wrong when they protested my renegade actions, nor was the product development, regulatory, or legal departments when I broke existing rules.

What I didn't understand was that true system thinkers work within the system to improve the system. Rubbing people's noses in their inefficiencies, their cost of operation, or their tortoiselike speed is not appropriate. The problem is the system, not the people.

Eric has gone on to do amazing things at Disney, Coca-Cola, and other places. Like me, he has moved to teaching. He currently teaches marketing at Utah State University, where he has incorporated system thinking into solving marketing problems. His students have no idea how lucky they are to have him teaching them.

The Creation of an Innovation Guru

After 10 years at Procter & Gamble, I looked up one January 1st and realized my growth had stopped, so I decided it was time to retire from corporate life and start my own company.

With three credit cards for financing; our family basement as the office; and my wife, Debbie, five months pregnant with our third child,

I founded what is known today as the Eureka! Ranch. The company's purpose was to turn innovation from a random gamble to a reliable system. However, in the 1990s, the business world was not ready for system-driven innovation. Innovation was the practice of Creative Gurus.

So, in a fraudulent move, I marketed myself as a guru. I say *fraudulent* because the truth was that my so-called expertise was actually powered by smarter systems for finding, filtering, and fast-tracking fresh ideas. Marketing myself as a guru worked. The media and clients bought it:

>*"America's #1 Idea Guru"* —A&E Top 10

>*"America's #1 New Product Idea Man"* —*Inc.* magazine

>*"Former Procter & Gamble marketing whiz Doug Hall goes to any length to encourage a fresh perspective . . . clients say it works."*
>—*Wall Street Journal*

>*"[Doug Hall is] an eccentric entrepreneur who just might have what we've all been looking for—the happy secret to success."*
>—*Dateline NBC*

>*"When Doug meets Disney, creativity ne'er wanes; our team explodes when he jump-starts our brains!"*
>—Ellen Guidera, VP, Disney

Clients came from around the world to work with the "guru" at the Eureka! Ranch just outside of Cincinnati, Ohio. The majority (88%) of our business was repeat. We worked with the best and brightest at innovation at the time: Procter & Gamble, Nike, Disney, American Express, Hewlett Packard, Ford, Pepsi-Cola, Frito-Lay, Schlumberger, as well as thousands of other consumer and industrial companies around the world.

We worked with companies that were desperate. Sadly, when they reached out to us, it was often too late. That was the case with AT&T (the original), Blockbuster, Circuit City, Maytag, Chrysler, and Gillette. We worked with each of these companies within a year of them ceasing to exist as independent companies.

Data Drives Success

Working with clients at the Eureka! Ranch provides a real-world laboratory for further developing and refining the application of system thinking to innovation. Every Eureka! inventing project is a live R&D experiment that adds to our wisdom. Our research is not always as controlled as academic research. However, what we lose in controlled experimentation we gain in marketplace "realness." We measure real people working on real projects that are really important to them and their organizations.

The result is the largest database of real-world data on innovation in the world. This hard data, statistically analyzed, is the reason the Innovation Engineering System can promise increased innovation speed up to 6X and decreased risk by 30% to 80%.

The data includes: 1) innovation perceptions and beliefs from hundreds of thousands of adults, 2) real-time quantitative data on more than 15,000 innovation teams in the process of innovating, 3) quantitative research on over 25,000 innovations, and 4) comprehensive project data (idea, forecast, learning) on over $75 billion worth of innovations as they travel the journey from idea to market.

Learning from this research, plus reviewing more than 2,000 academic articles, was the basis for my books: *Jump Start Your Business Brain, Meaningful Marketing,* and *Jump Start Your Brain 2.0.* Together, these books lay out the research methodologies and the foundational principles of Innovation Engineering.

New Learning Opens New Doors and Lays the Foundation for Innovation Engineering

The quantitative research improved the effectiveness of Eureka! Ranch client projects. It also opened up new opportunities.

In May 2001, Graeme Crombie, from the consultancy group Matrix in Glasgow, engaged Maggie Nichols and myself to teach our system approach to innovation in Scotland. Today, Graeme and his team use Innovation Engineering to help companies across Scotland and Ireland.

On a less significant note, it opened up opportunities for me to serve as a judge on the first season of ABC TV's reality program *American Inventor.* And, in Canada, I hosted another reality TV program with Maggie Nichols and Maggie Pfeifer of the Eureka! Ranch called *Backyard Inventor.*

The rigor and originality of the research also caught the eyes of the leadership of the University of Maine and the University of Prince Edward Island, each of whom presented me with honorary doctorate degrees.

The University of Maine was so excited that President Bob Kennedy, with the support of Hemant Pendse, Jake Ward, and Renee Kelly, committed to an experimental course in Innovation. During the fall of 2005, the first Innovation Engineering course was taught at the University of Maine with Margo Lukens, Darrell Donahue, and Liz Downing teaching nine pioneering students.

In 2009 I took a sabbatical from the Eureka! Ranch and lived on campus to help build version 1.0 of the Innovation Engineering courses. On December 10, 2009, following an event in Freeport, Maine, with business owners, it became clear that Innovation Engineering had to move from the campus to the business world. On a conference call with Renee Kelly of the University of Maine and Maggie Nichols and Scott Dunkle of the Eureka! Ranch, the Innovation Engineering movement as a commercial leadership science was born. During January of 2010, at the Sugarloaf Ski Resort, we ran the first three-day Innovation Engineering Leadership Institute. The program was raw and rough. Despite that, the reaction from CEOs of large and small companies in attendance was overwhelmingly positive.

The response we received at Sugarloaf indicated that the world was ready for system-driven innovation. To be honest, I also think we got lucky, as the recession of 2008 had opened up leadership to the need to do something different. They knew they needed to innovate, and, frankly, the "guru" approach wasn't working for them with its 5% to 15% success rate.

INNOVATION
ENGINEERING®

The Innovation Engineering Curriculum

With the support of what would become known as the Innovation Engineering Pioneers, a full body of knowledge was defined that was both academically rigorous and industry relevant. There are 48 critical skills, each with 2 to 4 subskills. Today, six courses are taught: 1) Fundamentals, 2) Advanced Create, 3) Advanced Communicate, 4) Advanced Commercialize, 5) System-Driven Leadership, and 6) Innovation Engineering Experience. The Innovation Engineering logo includes an icon for each of the key skill areas: Create, Communicate, and Commercialize.

Details on the current curriculum can be found at innovationengineer ing.org (I haven't included it here, as it undergoes never-ending innovation, as all college courses should). We upgrade and improve each course each year, based on new data, analysis, and the frontline experiences of the Innovation Engineering community.

Scheduling issues and the high cost of college courses can make it challenging for students to complete the six courses. To reach the maximum number of students, the first course, Fundamentals, was designed to provide a functional knowledge of the three fundamental skills of creating, communicating, and commercializing innovations. Students completing the fundamentals course at a high standard are certified as Innovation Engineering Blue Belts.

Upon completing all classes on campus, students graduate with an Innovation Engineering minor or a graduate certificate. They also have the option of becoming a Certified Innovation Engineering Black Belt.

Off campus, frontline employees, managers, and executives are taught the same content as on campus—but in a compressed format that integrates the learning with direct application to their real-world work. The Innovation Engineering Network offers two programs of training, application coaching, and certification:

Innovation Engineering Blue Belt enables fundamental understanding. It teaches employees, managers, and leaders how to apply the Innovation Engineering mindset and methods to their personal and professional lives immediately.

Innovation Engineering Black Belt enables mastery of the Innovation Engineering system-driven innovation mindset. It enables them to bust bureaucratic systems and enable big ideas. Classically, Black Belts focus their work on leading very important projects or teaching other employees, managers, and leaders.

A New Way of Learning—Cycles to Mastery

Jake Ward of the University of Maine first identified that we needed to develop both a great curriculum and a new way of learning. Creating a new way of teaching was especially important because, as a new field of study, there was not a base of faculty who had the breadth and depth of experience with system-driven innovation.

Two years of R&D later, a new system of teaching was born and branded as Cycles to Mastery. Its purpose is to enable all who are willing to achieve mastery of Innovation Engineering. It's based on iterative cycles of learning. It blends: 1) the work of Benjamin Bloom on the 2 Sigma Problem, 2) formative assessment, 3) Deming PDSA cycles, 4) quality control charting, 5) flipped classroom, and 6) competency-based learning. It involves five different types of classes:

DIGITAL CLASS: These classes involve five- to seven-minute videos that cover the core content of each of the Innovation Engineering subskills. Interactive quizzes feed forward what students have learned and not learned to the instructor, so that adaptations can be made in the next class.

LAB CLASS: The digital content is made real through group and individual assignments in which students get hands-on understanding of the content. Feedback loops provide grading of each assignment. Each student is given the opportunity to resubmit till they achieve success. The percentage correct on each assignment is fed forward to the instructor, so that the next class can be modified appropriately.

APPLICATION CLASS: Students are challenged to put the subskill learning into a broader context. Students apply the new learning plus prior learning on realistic scenarios or challenges.

REFLECTION CLASS: Students write a reflection on what they have learned and how they can apply it in their lives. This solidifies the learning at a deeper level.

EXPERIENCE CLASS: These are real-world challenges. They are used to bring the learning to life. Off campus, the experience class involves coaching the student in applying the learning to their daily work. On campus, the experience is flexible. It can be part of an internship. It can be creating a new invention, starting a company, or leading an innovation project for the university that the student attends.

Cycles to Mastery has been shown to generate 200% to 400% increases in the number of students achieving mastery levels versus the classic teaching approach. Multiple learning experiences take the student from intellectually knowing to deeply understanding the skills.

When we teach Innovation Engineering on college campuses, the students get rich repetition. Off campus, we accomplish repetitions by coaching the students as they apply the learning to their projects. Ken Grier, creative director for the Macallan and an Innovation Engineering Black Belt, feels that applying his learning to his work was the most valuable part of the process: **"The forced rigor of actually doing it, practicing it, getting coaching feedback was 70% of my learning."** Ken's observation of the importance of hands-on application was confirmed by Deming Master Walter Werner: "Education begins when you leave school, not while you are there. The classroom is not the hard part, not even close."

The most exciting aspect of Cycles to Mastery is that it includes a system for never-ending increases in the mastery standard. Control charts identify when the classes are so effective that student learning has risen above control limits. This signifies that it's time to increase the difficulty of assignments and therefore raise the mastery standards. In effect, Cycles to Mastery delivers "Learning Inflation" instead of "grade inflation."

On campus, students give enthusiastic support for the Cycles to Mastery teaching method.

> *How is this better? Less stress. This approach allows the information to stick in your head so you don't forget it. The applying is the important part that makes it stick. No more information regurgitation.*

> *Failing isn't a bad thing here. You lose your fear of failing here, because it's okay. Because you are doing live grading, it's like [the instructors] are working with us, not against us.*

> *I've always struggled with regular lectures and I am always wondering if I'm really learning, but with this I feel like I am actually learning and actually building skills.*

> *Compared to old classes, here you are learning a new way to think, not just the content. Working on changing the mind instead of cramming it with information.*

> *This is the best thing that ever happened to any college.*

In retrospect, the decision to invest the time, energy, and money to invent a new system of teaching is probably the most important decision we have made. It has enabled us to have a scalable system for truly democratizing innovation across entire companies, countries, and cultures.

Quite simply, if you are willing, you will be made able to master the Innovation Engineering body of knowledge. We have successfully taught artists, scientists, engineers, economists, politicians, lawyers, accountants, musicians, and poets. We are so confident in the teaching system that we offer an ironclad guarantee—IF YOU ARE WILLING, YOU WILL BE MADE ABLE. You are guaranteed achieving mastery if you put in the time and follow the Cycles to Mastery methodology.

Innovation Engineering 1.0, 2.0, 3.0, and 4.0

The development of the Innovation Engineering system has followed the same principles we teach. It's been an iterative process of experimentation, learning, adapting, and improving. The support of thousands of managers has made it possible.

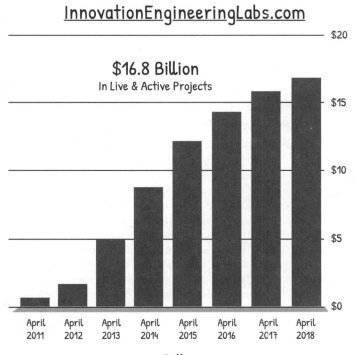

InnovationEngineeringLabs.com

$20

$16.8 Billion
In Live & Active Projects

$15

$10

$5

$0

April 2011 · April 2012 · April 2013 · April 2014 · April 2015 · April 2016 · April 2017 · April 2018

In Billions
(Discover – Develop – Deliver)

The graph on the previous page details the growth of live and active projects in the Innovation Engineering portal.

To help you understand how Innovation Engineering got to where it is today, I've included below a quick history of the major upgrades to Innovation Engineering (IE). As I said earlier, if you have already bought in, feel free to jump to the end of the chapter.

IE 1.0: ACCELERATING THE FRONT END OF INNOVATION. The first version of education and tools was a system focused on discovering and selecting smarter innovations to put into the organization's existing development system. Students were supported by IELabs.com, a cloud-based internet portal that, in the case of IE 1.0, helped them create and communicate bigger and smarter ideas. The most valuable section of IE Labs 1.0 was:

Tools and Documentation: This was a toolbox of Create, Communicate, and Commercialize Tools plus step-by-step how-to guides for how to run projects. Today, this section continues to be one of the most popular parts of IE Labs.

With IE 1.0, organizations quickly went from having a lack of ideas to overflowing with ideas for growing their businesses. This created a backlog of projects. To deal with it, business executives challenged us to find ways to apply the system mindset all the way to market. This led to...

IE 2.0: A COMPLETE SYSTEM FROM IDEA, THROUGH DEVELOPMENT, TO REALITY. The move from simply idea creation to the actual work of commercializing innovations required significant upgrades in education and tools. To ensure fast startup, IE 2.0 software tools were designed to work "outside of the box" with no setup required. Then, as teams work with the software it becomes more intelligent and customized. Major IE 2.0 upgrades included:

Innovation Pipeline: A next-generation project management system was created based on rapid cycles of iterative learning instead of command and control. It's a "smart" system that painlessly enables strategic alignment, deeper thinking, and fact-based decision-making.

Merwyn Rapid Research: A suite of research tools that result in 10X faster testing at 7% of the cost of classic research methods. This means project leaders can make smarter decisions based on hard data instead of judgment. The suite includes an artificial intelligence coaching app, risk adjusted sales forecasting, and a smart idea screener that's been validated as being seven times smarter at evaluating innovations than business leaders at Fortune 100 corporations.

Collaboration Cafe: A digital suggestion box system that leverages the latest in psychological understanding of what ignites and constrains collaboration. The result is smarter ideas and decisions because more people are sharing more ideas and advice.

Patent ROI: A collection of tools that enable project leaders to mine 9 million public domain patents for idea inspirations, to find 250,000 flea market patents per year that can be bought cheaply, and to write a provisional patent application in about an hour.

Create, Communicate, and Commercialize Tools: Nearly 100 tools that enable everyone to think smarter, faster, and more creatively about new ideas.

IE 3.0: A SCALABLE SYSTEM FOR ENABLING A CULTURE OF INNOVATION.
With IE 1.0, we were primarily enabling specialist innovation managers. With IE 2.0—taking ideas to market—we quickly found that we were touching many people across the company. And, if they didn't have the new innovation mindset, they didn't always understand why we were pushing for innovations that often change what they do and how they do it. What was needed was a system for enabling a culture of innovation.

With IE 3.0, we developed programs that enabled managers to quickly apply Innovation Engineering to their daily work. For example, if they are team leaders, we encourage them to innovate on ideas for helping their team work smarter immediately. IE Labs 3.0 added other important upgrades:

Innovation Metrics: This is a dashboard of real-time innovation metrics. They help leaders identify the output of their innovation system and the status of their innovation culture. New survey instruments enable leaders to understand how "future proofed" their organization is for the new world. Diagnostic data helps identify where to focus energy to improve the innovation system and culture.

Classroom Upgrade: New Innovation Engineering Blue Belt (Quick Start) course was added to the curriculum. Dozens of How-to in 2 Hours workshops were added to provide functional "how-to" learning to help people on a real-time basis.

System-Driven Leadership Course: This advanced course was totally rebuilt to greater leverage the Deming System of Profound Knowledge. A new four-step process for busting bureaucratic systems was developed from Dr. Deming's work to help leaders deal with complex system challenges.

IE 4.0: A PERSONAL VERSION OF INNOVATION ENGINEERING. Our hopes are to engage an entire department, division, or organization in the new mindset. However, often the broader organization is not ready to change. IE 4.0 is about enabling each individual to use the tools and systems of Innovation Engineering to amplify their dreams, aspirations, and careers. A new software platform named ThinkStormer enables individuals to apply the IE mindset and methods very quickly with near-instant results.

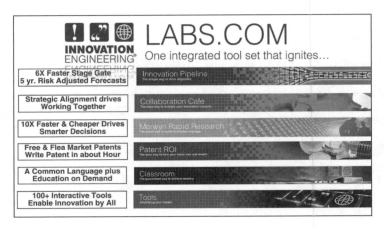

Changing the World

We are confident that we will change the world by enabling innovation by everyone, everywhere, every day. What we don't know is how long it will take. It took 30 years for Dr. Deming's teachings in Japan to be recognized in the Western world. No matter how long it takes, we—the Innovation Engineering Pioneers, the Innovation Engineering Institute organizing body, and myself—are in for the duration.

The reason we are confident that we will change the world is that we have a Plan A and a Plan B. Plan A is to teach Baby Boomers and older Gen Xers, who are currently in positions of authority, the Innovation Engineering mindset of system-driven innovation. Plan B is to teach undergraduate and graduate students on college campuses around the world. As I tell them, *"If Plan A doesn't work, you are my backup plan—you're just going to have to do a takeover."*

I'd love to be able to say Innovation Engineering was the result of a grand vision. But that's not how it happened. It was created by a group of pioneers with a feeling that there had to be a better way to innovate. The movement was helped by the availability of massive volumes of quantitative data on innovation. However, the real key to success was a never-ending curiosity to learn more. And it is this passion for learning that is the key to our past and current success. As Dr. Deming said:

> *It's so easy to do nothing. It's a challenge to do something. Learning is not compulsory; it's voluntary. Improvement is not compulsory; it's voluntary.*
>
> *But to survive, we must learn. The penalty for ignorance is that you get beat up. There is no substitute for knowledge. Yet time is of the essence.*

Turn the page or flip the screen, and let's get started with education on some basic innovation definitions. But first . . .

What Did You Learn?

- What systems do you work with that are world class?
- What systems do you work with that are barriers to your speed and success?
- How focused are you and your organization on the future?
- What is likely to happen in the future that you are not confronting reality on?
- What stops you from using data to help you make smarter decisions?
- What is the learning process that your company uses to train people?
- In what areas are you smarter today than you were a year ago?
- What should you focus your learning on right now?

3

Innovation Agreement

Innovation is the ability of an organization to change as its outside world changes. You've got to have that in an organization.

—Sir Terry Leahy,
retired CEO of Tesco

A Major Mistake

As we embarked on bringing system thinking to the world of innovation, we made a major mistake. We assumed that everyone understood what innovation was and why it was important.

The mistake was discovered and quantified during a quarterly review of data from our Innovation Culture survey. The survey measures employee and management perceptions and their mindsets toward innovation. We have fielded this survey before every innovation project the Ranch and the Innovation Engineering community have run since 1995. What we learned was shocking.

**7 out of 10 managers DON'T AGREE
that there is a need for their organization to innovate!**

**8 out of 10 managers see NO URGENCY
for their organization to innovate!**

It was an embarrassing moment for me. For years, I had mistakenly thought that everyone saw innovation as I did. The reality is that the majority of managers and business leaders don't see innovation as needed or urgent.

As an aside, we missed this data insight because of the way we had been reporting the data. For 20 years we reported results relative to a world-class standard. During this analysis we looked at the data in the absolute, not on a relative basis. The result was an entirely new insight.

A New Beginning

To address the lack of agreement and urgency that we had discovered from our analysis, we implemented a program of beginning all of our conversations and classes with a discussion on:

WHAT is an innovation?
How do you know one when you see one?

WHY innovate?
Explain in a way that would motivate workers and leaders.

If you can't agree on WHAT an innovation is or WHY it's important to innovate, then the rest of the conversation on HOW to innovate is irrelevant.

WHAT Is an Innovation?

If you want to be entertained, ask five people in your organization how they define an innovation. More specifically, how would they know one when they saw one? The word innovation has been used and abused to the point where there is little agreement on its definition.

Our Definition of Innovation

The Innovation Engineering community's definition of innovation is precise.

Meaningfully Unique

MEANINGFUL in that it has an obvious value to the customer. That is, the idea is so meaningful that customers would willingly give up their existing behaviors for it. Importantly, it is also instantly understandable as to "Why should I, the customer, care?"

UNIQUE in that it is a genuine original. It's a nonobvious leap that doesn't exist in the world. Often it offers a quantifiable advantage such that you can put a number on how much better it is versus the existing alternative, if there is one.

How to Evaluate if Your Innovation Is Meaningfully Unique

The simple way to identify if your new or improved product or service is innovative is to ask the question: **"Are customers willing to pay more money for it?"** No customer wants to pay more money for anything. If they

A Product or Service is

Meaningfully Unique
when . . .

Customers are willing to pay <u>more money</u> for it.

are willing to pay a premium, then the offering must be both meaningful and unique.

Conversely, if they are not willing to pay a premium—because they can achieve essentially the same benefit or effect elsewhere—then it's a commodity. It's not a requirement to charge a higher price for an innovation. It's also possible to charge the same as competing offerings and use the increased demand to drive increased sales volume.

For system improvements or nonprofit causes, the equivalent question is: **"Does the innovation offer a value that is so meaningful and unique that other stakeholders (departments, employees, partners) are willing to invest their time, energy, and/or money into changing from what they are doing now to the new approach?"**

You can quantitatively assess your Meaningful Uniqueness by asking potential users, customers, and stakeholders for their ratings of Purchase Intent (Meaningfulness) and New and Different (Uniqueness) each on a 0–10 scale. Then you weight the average ratings 60/40 (60% Purchase + 40% New and Different). Our research has found this is the single most predictive measure of marketplace success with an innovation. Details on the data behind this can be found in the academic research article, "The real-time response survey in new product research: it's about time," published in the *Journal of Consumer Marketing*. I wrote it with Lynn Kahle of the University of Oregon and with Mike Kosinski.

Other qualitative ways to identify if an idea is meaningfully unique include:

Is the idea so surprising, so original, so newsworthy that it will generate word-of-mouth? Ideas that offer real news spread by word of mouth. Is your idea so original that customers would share it with others and on the internet via their social media outlets? A common question I ask is: "Would a customer post this innovation on Facebook, and, if so, what would they write?"

Does the idea instantly spark additional ideas? Great innovations set off a chain reaction of ideas because they open our minds to seeing the world in a new and different way.

Is the idea patentable? This is my personal favorite. Patentability is arguably the most clear and specific definition that exists for what is a true innovation. To be patentable, the innovation has to be a "nonobvious leap" for someone who has ordinary skill in the field. And, frankly, an idea that is obvious to someone like your competition would be hard to defend as a real innovation, wouldn't it?

An innovation is also genuinely Meaningfully Unique when you just can't stop thinking about it. When an idea is a real innovation, you have an urgency to get started on making the idea real as soon as possible. This is especially important with today's Millennial generation. They rightly give an even greater importance to working on things that matter. Richard Branson of Virgin put it this way in *Screw Business as Usual*:

> *These days I think you've got to talk about your value proposition—why are you so proud of your product? And you've got to communicate that pride in ways that add up to a young generation that's very well informed and very idealistic. The young care about where products come from. They care about what the company that makes the product actually does in the world—or not. But you can't fake it. You have to say, screw business as usual and just do it.*

The Three Dimensions of Meaningfulness

For innovative ideas to go from idea to reality, it takes energy. The more meaningful they are, the easier it is to gather the energy required to make them happen. There are three dimensions of meaningfulness:

1. Meaningful to CUSTOMER is a given. The innovation must matter to customers. If the customer doesn't see the innovation as offering greater benefit value relative to the price charged, then they will demand the benefit of a lower price.

2. Meaningful to the COMPANY is a given. If the organization cannot profitably develop, produce, and deliver the innovation, then there will be no energy to pursue it. And, if the innovation is not aligned with the leadership's vision of where the company needs to go in the future, then the idea will not happen, no matter how potentially profitable it is in the short term.

Meaningful to customer and company are classic requirements for innovations. However, they are not enough. Making meaningful change happen is hard work. In order to generate the energy needed for change, the idea must have a third level of meaningfulness.

3. Meaningful to WORKERS is critical. For ideas to happen, they must be meaningful to those who are working on the project. Academic research on innovation success confirms that for meaningful change to happen it must be driven by intrinsic motivation.

Quite simply, you can't "bribe" people to change. They must want to make the change happen themselves. They must love an innovation to see it through from idea to reality.

As Wilbur Wright, one of the Wright Brothers, wrote to his father: "It is my belief that flight is possible, and while I am taking up the investigation for pleasure rather than profit, I think there is slight possibility of achieving fame and fortune from it."

Meaningfulness Is More Than Skin Deep

A classic mistake is to believe you can take the same old product or service and dress it up with a new "skin" and see dramatically different results. The reality is that, with the internet, your "smoke and mirrors" will be found out very quickly. A bad painting in a fancy frame is still a bad painting.

A classic example of this is the horse carriage business in Cincinnati. In its day, Cincinnati was one of the world's leaders in the manufacturing of horse-and-buggy carriages. One of the leading companies of the day was the Alliance Carriage Company. As the automobile developed, they rejected it. Instead of innovating their carriages by adding a motor, they turned their energy toward design and marketing—investing in massive variations of design and the mailing of a "successful salesman" brochure that enabled

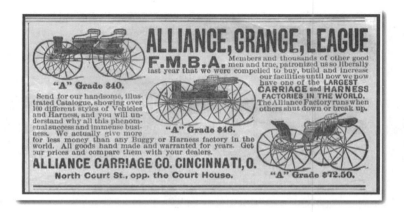

endless choices and a new direct-sale business model. In the end, they resorted to price as their point of difference. As the advertisement above indicates: "We actually give more for less money than any other Buggy or Harness factory in the world."

The owners of the Alliance Carriage Company were optimizing a product whose life cycle was coming to an end. They tried to use the decline to their advantage. In the advertisement they write about their buying up of other factories: To paraphrase, "We now have one of the largest carriage and harness factories in the world. The Alliance Factory runs when others shut down or break up."

Hmmm . . . Sound familiar? Industry in decline . . . Mergers and acquisitions create larger failing companies . . . Existing players resort to marketing and design gimmicks . . . Industry eventually dies as new technology makes it obsolete.

The right choice for the Alliance Carriage Company was to restart their business by leveraging their skills and resources. Interestingly, they were offered the opportunity to become part of the automobile industry. Both Henry Ford and P. W. Packard came to Cincinnati to find financing and to acquire a license to use patents owned by the city's carriage makers. However, the owners of the many carriage-making companies in Cincinnati were loyal to the horse. They saw no need to change. Eventually, Ford and Packard both found investors living in Detroit; thus, the automotive capital of the US became Detroit not Cincinnati.

Meaningful Uniqueness Creates a Chain Reaction of Positives

Meaningful Uniqueness grows sales from both new and established customers. Tracking research studies confirms not only higher rates of new customer trial but also higher repeat purchase rates when an offering is meaningfully unique versus competitive offerings.

Just as important, when your offerings are Meaningfully Unique, a new energy is ignited among suppliers, employees, managers, owners, and customers. They have a sense that they are a part of something that makes a difference—a real difference in the world. They have a sense that they are doing something that matters—something that makes a meaningful difference in their souls. The poet David Whyte, in his book, *The Three Marriages: Reimagining Work, Self and Relationships,* defines good work this way:

> *Good work like a good marriage needs a dedication to something larger than our own detailed, everyday needs; good work asks for promises to something intuited or imagined that is larger than our present understanding of it. We may not have an arranged ceremony at the alter to ritualize our dedication to work, but many of us can for a certain work, a certain career or a certain future: a moment when we held our hand in a fist and made unspoken vows to what we had just glimpsed.*

A common reflection from those who have embraced the Innovation Engineering mindset is: "For the first time, I am doing the kind of meaningful and creative work that I imagined I'd be doing when I started my career."

Two TYPES of Innovations—Customer Opportunities and Internal Systems

Innovation is about new products and services, but it's also about changing how we work. It's about how everyone does their jobs, from the receptionist to the production line employee to the accounting department. We group new innovations into two types.

VIO—VERY IMPORTANT OPPORTUNITIES: These are innovations for growing sales and/or profitability from new or current customers/ markets. They are externally focused. They include ideas for new or improved offerings.

VIS—VERY IMPORTANT SYSTEMS: These are innovations for working smarter. They are internally focused. They include ideas for enabling growth, cost savings, performance, quality, or productivity. It is not uncommon for system innovations to be enablers of new opportunities.

VERY IMPORTANT is added as a descriptor to Opportunities and Systems to make it clear that they are a priority. Every organization has things that must be done to keep the current business operations going. The Very Important designation provides clarity on what things people should be working on that are beyond their day job.

Why Innovation?

When price is the primary driver of customer purchasing decisions, your offering is a commodity. Throughout the ages, profitability has been determined based on where an offering exists on the continuum from commodity to monopoly. Most new businesses start out as monopolies; over time, competition copies, and what was once a monopoly is soon a commodity. The difference today is that the internet is accelerating this process as consumers are able to learn the truth, the whole truth, about your offering faster than ever before.

To make it worse, internet price shopping and bidding systems make it easy for everyone to buy cheaper. And, when there is no difference between offerings, the discounting systems become the true drivers of sales volumes.

The impact of being the pioneer versus the follower with a technology can be seen in research on order of entry into the marketplace. On average, net profitability goes down by 50% or more for those who follow versus those who pioneer.

Innovation Is the Only Way to Beat the Business Life Cycle

All organizations, products, services, and careers follow a life cycle, moving from:

- **Birth,** where the Meaningfully Unique offering comes to market. Profitability and optimism is high.

- **Growth,** where profitability grows as we become more efficient at producing the new offering.

Why Innovation?

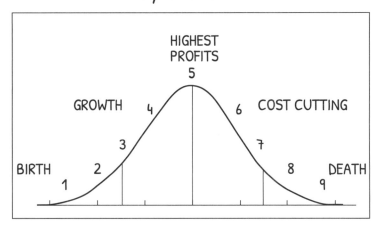

- **Highest Profits,** where we hit maximum efficiency as a result of our efforts.

- **Cost Cutting,** where competition has matched, we are becoming a commodity and are in a fight for our lives.

- **Death,** where it's just not worth the effort anymore.

There is no fountain of youth for humans. But for organizations there is, and it's called innovation. Innovation allows corporations, nonprofits, governments, and societies to restart and be reborn. With innovation, commodity products, services, and companies can be reborn as monopolies.

Ben Franklin once said, ". . . nothing can be said to be certain, except death and taxes." And if you don't innovate, he's right. All products, services, companies, and even careers eventually die. The key is to reinvent yourself before the decline occurs. Once negative momentum starts, it takes tremendous time, energy, and money to turn it around.

With innovation, the business life cycle is restarted. For example, P&G's Tide laundry detergent still maintains a premium profit margin, even in Walmart stores. The reason is simple: 61 innovations in 61 years.

Innovation Restarts the
Business Life Cycle

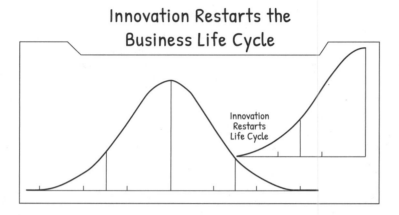

At P&G we were taught that there is no brand "life cycle"—only brand managers who did not do their job leading their businesses into the future.

A. G. Lafley defined the importance of innovation this way, in his book *The Game-Changer:*

> *Winning is pretty much the same in today's business world as it has been for decades: Create new customers, new products, and new services that drive revenue growth and profits. What's different is how to do it.*
>
> *The acceleration of change today is unprecedented. It creates opportunities as well as the threat of obsolescence.*
>
> *The best way to win in this world is through innovation. But innovation has often been left to technical experts or perceived as serendipity or luck. Lone geniuses working on their own have, indeed, created new industries or revolutionized existing ones. But there is a problem. You can't wait for the light bulb to go off in someone's head. The fruits of innovation—sustained and ever-improving organic revenue growth and profits—have to become integral to the way you run your business. That means making innovation central to the goals, strategy, structure, systems, culture, leadership, and motivating purpose and values of your business.*

Companies led by great leaders never reach maturity and decline. Instead, these leaders proactively reinvent their organizations and their offerings on a never-ending basis. John Muldoon, Innovation Engineering Black Belt and innovation leader at the Edrington Group in Scotland, described the challenge this way: *"The real determining factor is having a leader and a team that have the courage to determine their own future, not becoming a victim of someone else's future."*

Never-Ending Cycles of Cost Savings and Growth

A misperception is that the Innovation Engineering movement is against cost savings. That is incorrect. Cost savings are critical to innovation and company success. That's because whenever something new is developed it's inefficient because it's new. Researchers Gottfredson and Schubert, in their book *The Breakthrough Imperative,* on the impact of experience, report that with every doubling of experience costs go down an average of 25%.

The impact of experience is a key reason why profits grow as you go up the left side of the life cycle curve. It's also the reason why those who innovate continually get farther and farther ahead of those who don't. The innovators start out with offerings that are less efficient; then, as they gain experience, they get smarter and smarter at driving down costs. Those that copy are always behind on the experience effect, as they are challenged with sales and profitability disadvantages.

World-class innovation companies are also world class at reducing costs after they ship innovations. At Procter & Gamble, when a new product was recommended, a key part of the approval process was the pricing recommendation. This document would outline why the product could sell at a premium (Meaningfully Uniqueness) as well as the costs of production both today and over the next five years. The estimates would include cost savings over the next five years—both identified and unidentified but known based on the experience effect.

Sadly, at many companies this is not understood. When the financial forecasts are done wrong, the new idea is compared versus the existing offering that has been produced and optimized for many years. The result is that good ideas get killed because of a lack of understanding that Meaningful Uniqueness means you can sell at a higher price and the experience effect means that costs will go down over time.

Cost savings are critical for helping innovations grow in profitability as they go up the left side of the experience curve. Conversely, cutting costs when a business is on the right side, the downward side of the life cycle curve, can be a big mistake. Leaders must ask themselves: Is it a better investment of time, energy, and money to reduce costs? Or would it be better to invest those resources in reinventing the offering to restart the life cycle curve?

A senior government statistician once shared with me a national study involving tens of thousands of companies. The study found that those manufacturing companies that did the most Lean Manufacturing work, to cut costs and increase capacity, were the companies that were most likely to go out of business. His conclusion wasn't that Lean was bad. In fact, he was a huge advocate for it. What he did feel was that it was being used at the wrong time. Instead of trying to "cost cut" to growth, these companies needed to focus their energies on reinventing themselves and then use Lean to optimize the profitability of the new offerings created.

Three LEVELS of Innovations: Working Smarter Ideas, CORE Projects, and LEAP Projects

There are three levels of Meaningfully Uniqueness when it comes to innovations.

WORKING SMARTER IDEAS: These are simple ideas that you should "just do." They are small, low-to-no-risk ideas for working smarter. They are often suggested by and enacted by employees to solve problems that they face during their day-to-day work. Collectively they can add up to amazing impacts. As you will learn in Chapter 10, academic research finds that, with the proper system, employee-driven cost-saving ideas can generate four times greater financial impact than formal cost-saving projects. They also transform the culture. Research by Dean Schroeder and Alan Robinson finds that companies can realize from 12 to 100 ideas implemented per employee per year. The goal is to create a system in which Working Smarter ideas can be suggested, approved, and executed quickly and efficiently.

CORE INNOVATION PROJECTS: These are incremental innovations to existing offerings or systems. They are low on risk and uncertainty; however, they have more complexity than "just do" ideas. They often require

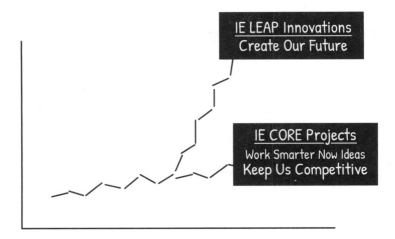

coordination across departments or the investment of time, energy, and/ or resources to implement them. To be implemented, they require a more formal project management approach requiring two to four phases, depending on complexity. They are critically important to the growth of

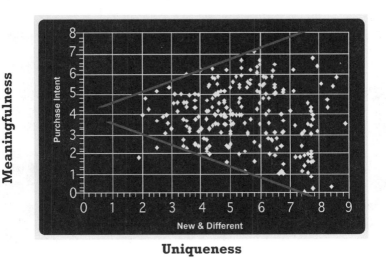

the organization. A balanced innovation pipeline has 85% of its innovation projects in this area. These projects generate about 50% of the profit growth for an organization.

LEAP INNOVATION PROJECTS: These are disruptive innovations. They have the potential for high reward, and, as a result of being very unique, they also have a higher risk of failure. They are ideas that change the trajectory of the organization. In a balanced portfolio they represent 15% of projects but about 50% of profit growth. These are the new business models, new technologies, and new market projects. LEAP innovation projects give your organization an "unfair" advantage versus the competition.

Note: Coca-Cola and Google both use a 90% CORE, 10% LEAP balance for how they focus their investments and workforce. I advocate a slightly higher percent for LEAP (15%) because, frankly, most companies overestimate what is a true "LEAP," and I find it results in a better balance.

The challenge with innovation is rarely a lack of CORE innovations. Most organizations are good at incremental change. This is fine so long as the innovation pipeline has a healthy level of disruptive LEAP innovations that can create a new future for the organization.

The following graphic provides a visual representation of the relationship between meaningfulness and uniqueness. Each point on the graph represents a new innovation. This graph was created from ideas across industries that were quantitatively tested with potential customers. It shows that the more unique your idea is as a potential LEAP innovation (on the right side of the graph), the greater the risk and reward. Conversely, CORE innovations that are less unique (left side of graph), offer less risk and reward.

Harvard Business Review reports there is a 5X greater chance of profitable success with ideas that are in the top right. We reduce the risk associated with ideas that are on the right through rapid "Plan, Do, Study, Act" cycles of learning covered in Chapter 8.

For most organizations, the challenge with Working Smarter ideas and CORE projects is not creating them. Rather, the challenge is that they take too long and cost too much to discover and develop. We need a faster and more efficient system for executing them.

Even Steve Jobs, cofounder of Apple, recognized the importance of CORE innovations. As he said, **"I have a great respect for incremental improvement,** and I've done that sort of thing in my life, but I've always been attracted to the more revolutionary changes. I don't know why. Because they're harder. They're much more stressful emotionally. And you usually go through a period where everybody tells you that you've completely failed."

The challenge with LEAP innovations is finding the courage to pursue them and, once you have found them, resisting the temptation to sandblast off all the originality to make them fit your existing business model, production resources, and/or marketing approach.

What Did You Learn?

- In your career, when did you work on a project that was Meaningfully Unique? What did it feel like working on that project?
- In your career, when did you work on a project that was NOT Meaningfully Unique? What did it feel like working on that project?
- When have you lived the various points on the life cycle curve? What did each feel like?
- What prevents you from pursuing ideas that are true LEAP innovations?
- CORE innovations should be fast and easy to execute. What makes them hard to do?
- Do you give time and energy to Very Important System innovations?
- What else did you learn?

4

Innovation System

If a factory is torn down but the rationality which produced it is left standing, then that rationality will simply produce another factory. If a revolution destroys a government, but the systematic patterns of thought that produced that government are left intact, then those patterns will repeat themselves. . . . There's so much talk about the system. And so little understanding.

—Robert Pirsig
Zen and the Art of Motorcycle Maintenance

94% Is the System, 6% Is the Worker

It is very frustrating to be the leader of a department, division, or company and not be optimistic or confident in the organization's ability to innovate. Or said another way—to not feel confident that your strategic plan to improve the organization's future can be executed.

When leaders don't believe that the people in their organizations can innovate, they usually blame their people, not their innovation systems, training, or tools. As a senior executive told me just six days ago in a meeting, "I just don't think we have the people we need to be innovative. My people aren't creative."

I responded with some simple questions:

- Do you know how to innovate? Were you ever taught how to innovate?

- Did you ever teach them how to innovate?

- Have you given them the training and tools to innovate?

- Do you have a documented innovation system—what to do, why to do it, how to do it?

- Do they have a way to test and experiment with their ideas quickly and at low cost?

- Can they collaborate inside and outside the company with no stress or fear?
- Do they have the time and resources to innovate?

The simple fact is that most innovation challenges are the result of a poor system, not poor workers. It is rare that workers consciously create failure. The desire to make a difference is core to the human spirit. Everyone has a personal desire to make a difference, to work smarter, and to improve their futures. The problem is they don't know how. They were never taught or provided the systems and tools to innovate.

When they are told to innovate, they are presented with what they perceive is a very risky situation. Without a reliable system or support, they see innovation as gambling with their career and reputation. Conversely, when they are provided with the education, systems, and tools needed to innovate, a new spirit takes root. Powerlessness is replaced with confidence. Fear of the future is replaced with a belief that no matter what the challenge is, we can solve it.

The Power of a Great System

When the culture believes in its system for innovation, a chain reaction of positives occurs. Bold ideas are encouraged and enabled. Problems are seen as opportunities for reinvention instead of frustration. Rapid cycles of experimentation are the norm. Collaboration is embraced.

When leadership has confidence in the capability of their innovation system, they pursue bolder strategies. When they are not confident, then they set strategies that are "practical," which means they are weak and suboptimum.

The old worldview of innovation systems was about control. The new worldview is about enabling everyone everywhere to innovate successfully. Taiichi Ohno, the father of the Toyota Manufacturing System, said it this way:

> *Brilliant process management is our strategy. We get brilliant results from average people managing brilliant processes. We observe that our competitors often get average (or worse) results from brilliant people managing broken processes.*

Did You Design Your Innovation System?
Or Did It Design Itself?

Gordon McGilton, one of the top teachers of the Deming philosophy, taught me to ask leaders if their organizations designed their innovation system or if it designed itself. He explained that, in most cases, when someone finds a way to get something done, it becomes THE WAY. However, there is often no system for vetting if THE WAY is the RIGHT WAY for the organization as a whole or just for that work team or department.

Gordon explained that in areas where the system doesn't work, we become efficient at explaining and compensating for the failures. For example, when our sales forecasting system is flawed, finance adjusts all forecasts downward. When innovations are not Meaningfully Unique, sales departments use price discounts to hit introductory sales targets. When management doesn't believe in their innovation system, they institute excessive testing, analysis, and approvals to reduce their fear.

Bureaucracy—the Easiest Way to Kill Innovation

Innovation equals change. Change means uncertainty. Uncertainty means fear. The best way to prevent innovation or change is through the implementation of bureaucratic systems. Bureaucratic systems, such as excessive rules, regulations, or reporting, create barriers to change, and these barriers protect the status quo.

Bureaucracy multiplies when organizations grow to a size where loyalty to department is greater than loyalty to the organization. Tom Peters once said something along the lines of: "After you get to a dozen people, you have a hopeless bureaucracy."

Recall, systems are defined as two or more independent parts working toward a common aim. In business and nonprofit organizations, this means divisions, departments, and/or teams focused on achieving the overall aim of the organization.

If a GOOD SYSTEM is "two or more independent parts working toward a common aim," then a BAD SYSTEM is "two or more independent parts working toward separate aims."

Bad systems are created for one of three reasons:

1. PROTECTIONISM: One department seeks to optimize its results/metrics, without thinking through what the impact is on interconnected departments. With innovation, this is often sparked by departments seeking to push work onto other departments. They do this because cost cutting has reduced their staff such that they can't handle their existing workload.

2. OVERREACTION: A random mistake happens and we overdo our rules and regulations. With innovation, this is often the result of a new product, service, or system failure. When a failure occurs, instead of focusing on fixing the root cause, the company implements excessive rules and inspections.

3. SUBVERSION: Someone wants to prevent change from happening. This person uses a passive-aggressive approach of installing "rules, regulations, and inspection" to slow down or kill the change. Ego, jealousy, and/or fear are often the root motivations. With innovation this can be caused by "not invented here" syndrome or the feeling that "I've got three years to retirement and don't want to mess up."

Sadly, once created, bureaucratic systems self-multiply. One act of protectionism, overreaction, or subversion creates equal and opposite acts of protectionism, overreaction, or subversion from other departments. Fortunately there is an antidote.

Bureaucracy Busting—A Four-Step Antidote for Ending Your Suffering

I believe the most powerful thing Dr. Deming created was the four steps for improving any system. He called them the System of Profound Knowledge. Dr. Deming's four principles are simple to understand. However, it takes decades to fully appreciate their consequences. A full explanation of the System of Profound Knowledge would fill a book longer than this one. On campus, it's taught as a semester-long course titled System-Driven Leadership.

The four principles are independently valuable. Together, they form a simple four-step process for diagnosing and improving any system.

Step 1: Appreciation for a System—Make the system visible.

Step 2: Knowledge About Variation—Separate special from common cause errors.

Step 3: Psychology—Identify positive versus negative psychological forces on the system.

Step 4: Theory of Knowledge—"Plan, Do, Study, Act" cycles of learning.

STEP 1: APPRECIATION FOR A SYSTEM. This starts with recognizing that there is a system of interconnected and independent parts. The diagnosis process starts with making the system(s) visible on paper. When you define the system clearly, then everyone can see how their efforts fit into the bigger framework. They can also see the interactions in the system.

The process of making the system visible begins with defining:

  a. The aim of the system—what its purpose for existence is

  b. System boundaries—where the system begins and ends

  c. System stakeholders—who are most impacted by the system

  d. The one-system metric—the primary output the system is designed to deliver

  e. Enabling metrics—variables that help predict the one-system metric

  f. Broader, superstructure systems like innovation have enabling subsystems to help the system achieve its aim. The five most important subsystems for innovation include: Education, Alignment, Collaboration, Rapid Research, and Patent ROI. Each of these is defined in greater detail in future chapters.

The last step in making the system visible is the creation of a simple flowchart. The chart can be linear or nonlinear, simple or very complex. With human systems, like innovation systems, we find it best to start with a simple four- to seven-step flowchart that defines the "bigger picture" system phases.

STEP 2: KNOWLEDGE ABOUT VARIATION. With our system made visible in Step 1, we now identify areas of high variance caused by the system itself (common cause errors). Everything has variation. People have variation. Projects have variation. Every measurement has variation. When we understand and appreciate variance, we make smarter and more meaningful decisions. Instead of beating the employees to work harder, we enable the employees through systemic improvements. We use training, tools, and systems to amplify employee impact and reduce variation.

Much of the frustration in life is when we don't understand when the variance is common cause (part of the system) or special cause (an error by the employee). Sadly, when it comes to strategy, innovation, and how we work together, the systems are often so far out of control it's hard to even get started with identifying special or common cause. The good news is that, in these situations, even a small application of system thinking can generate tremendous improvement.

One of the early Innovation Engineering companies had a totally random approach to selecting what innovation projects to work on. By instituting a disciplined system at the front end of innovation projects, they improved their speed to market with innovations by 40% in just 12 months.

Most innovation systems have extreme variance. A primary reason for the variance is the lack of clarity on how the organization innovates. There is no agreement on what an innovation is. There is no education or systems for creating, communicating, or commercializing ideas. A simple test of clarity for a human system, like innovation, is: Can it be defined in writing? When the system is so clearly defined that you can write an operations manual or a series of checklist steps and tasks, then you have a defined system.

Innovation projects within an organization have variance in their level of risk and reward. LEAP innovations have higher risk than CORE innovations. Innovation projects focused on the company's largest profit center are different from minor requests from customers. Sadly, most organizations don't recognize these differences. They apply the same system to every innovation project, causing needless bureaucracy and frustration. The solution, as detailed later, is to have separate innovation systems for each of your common types of projects.

Variation can be **common cause** (errors of the system) or **special cause** (random events usually due to humans). The following excerpt from a speech my dad wrote on Dr. Deming's work outlines the differences between common cause and special cause problems.

> *One of the most important methods for identifying who and what is responsible for your problems is what Dr. Deming calls special causes and common causes. Special causes are problems that can be controlled by the workers and supervisors, and these, according to Dr. Deming, from historical samples, are 6% of the problems we are involved with.*
>
> *Common causes are problems that only management can solve. These are faults of the system which make up 94% of all of our problems. Now, in a lot of companies, this will be quite a revelation because most managers sit around saying, "Hey, if the workers would only do a better job, we would be much better off."*

> *In fact, some of the management people in the automobile industry say, "Yes, but Japanese workers are much more dedicated than American workers and American workers may have too many pleasures, too many things to be able to do a good job." Dr. Deming says this is all wrong; 94% of our problems are faults of the system that only management can solve.*
>
> *Examples of special causes or worker-solvable problems are: absence from the job, using wrong materials, negligent handling of goods. Examples of common cause or only-management-solvable problems are: poor product design, poor machine maintenance, poor training and tools to do the job.*

Dr. Deming was very clear that it was the job of leadership to understand the difference between the two types of errors. I believe that much of the friction between leadership and employees is a result of a lack of understanding of the differences between the two. With human systems, the variances are often so large and obvious they can be identified easily through simply visualizing data in a simple graphic.

As systems become more defined, quantitative control charts can help us define opportunities for improvement with statistical precision. The chart on the next page shows an example of a control chart. Measurements that are between the Upper Control Limit (UCL) and Lower Control Limit (LCL) boundaries are common cause errors caused by the system variance. Errors outside these ranges are special cause errors. Our goal with system innovations is to improve the average output from the system while also reducing variation in results.

STEP 3: PSYCHOLOGY. Having made the system visible and identified areas of high common cause variance, we next identify areas of negative psychology. Human systems have elements that create positive and negative motivation to those who interact with and within the system. Positive psychology dimensions are motivating to those involved in the system. Negative psychology dimensions are demotivating.

The most powerful psychological tool for enabling innovation is to leverage intrinsic as opposed to extrinsic motivations.

Intrinsic motivators include a sense of purpose, pride in work, and personal engagement. These are the most powerful drivers of positive psychology.

Control Charts

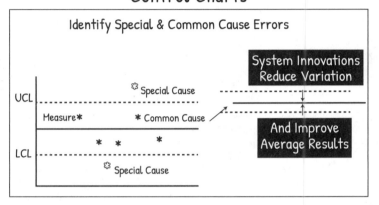

Identify Special & Common Cause Errors

Extrinsic motivators include intimidating people into innovating or bribing them to think creatively. If they work, they only work for a short time. Evidence of this is the classic suggestion box with a "prize" for the best idea. The contest works once or twice, but participation dies off as the purpose is the prize, not pride of work—and only one or two ever win.

Over 100 years of academic research finds that intrinsic motivation is far more powerful. Intrinsic motivation means that those who innovate do so because of an internal belief that the new idea or method is meaningful to them (Cool Sh*t That Matters!). Intrinsic motivation is a key reason why entrepreneurs are up to 10X more successful with innovations than large corporations (50% success versus 5%).

STEP 4: THEORY OF KNOWLEDGE. Having made the system visible and identified areas of variation and of negative psychology, we now seek to improve the system. We take an action to reduce variation or remove negative psychology. The action is done using a disciplined approach known as the Deming Cycle. It's a version of the scientific method that is also known as a Cycle of Learning—"Plan, Do, Study, Act," or PDSA. Or in the irreverent way of Innovation Engineering Black Belts, it's called "Fail FAST, Fail CHEAP" cycles of learning.

The PDSA approach provides a disciplined structure for improving the system. When we come to resolution with the first learning cycle, we then begin another PDSA cycle to improve the system.

A Story of the Power of Intrinsic Motivation

The most remarkable innovation successes that I have observed over my career have been driven by intrinsic motivation.

Some time ago, I was working on a new product for a major beverage company. We were at a market research location where hundreds of consumers tasted our final options for the test market. Two of the products did well. The third failed. The answer seemed obvious: It was time to kill the failed product.

Then the product developer spoke up and said, *"I really believe in the product that failed. And I think I know how to fix it. Could I have the weekend to work on it before we make a final decision?"*

On Monday morning we gathered on a conference call. The product developer reported that she felt the product was fixed—and that she could have it perfected by the end of the week when we had to go into small-scale production for the test market. At this point we had three options: 1) delay production and run another consumer test, 2) drop the product, or 3) trust the product development person and go for it. Given that it was a small-scale test market, and the risk was low, I recommended that we trust the product developer and go for it. Her response was magic: "I won't let you down. It will be great."

Her internal motivation to "do something great" had an impact. **In market, her product had nearly twice the repeat purchase rate of the other two products.** Trusting in intrinsic motivation, and trusting in her, resulted in a product going from worst to best.

When employees have a sense of intrinsic meaning and purpose, they commit themselves in a boundless way that is awe-inspiring. When their motivation is "bought" through extrinsic rewards, though, it is transactional motivation that has clear and constraining boundaries. And with each transaction, the level of reward needed to motivate goes up.

> *Some extrinsic motivation helps to build self-esteem. But total submission to extrinsic motivation leads to destruction of the individual. . . . On the job, under the present system, joy in work, and innovation, become secondary to a good rating. Extrinsic motivation in the extreme crushes intrinsic motivation.*
>
> —Dr. W. Edwards Deming,
> *The New Economics*

A Story of the Importance of Knowledge About Variation

Great leaders think and dig for root causes when defects, mistakes, or problems occur. They know that if they can discover the root issue, they will solve instead of patch the problem.

Poor leaders often embark on a search for the guilty instead of taking responsibility for mistakes that are a result of the system. In most cases, the failures will repeat themselves. When a negative event occurs, the question leaders should explore is: Is the mistake a result of a special cause (system) or common cause (worker) error?

A story of the power of identifying special cause and common cause errors comes from my dad's work at Nashua Corporation. He was working on carbonless paper production. Carbonless paper is writing paper or forms that have one coating on the top and another on the bottom of the sheets. When you put them together and mark the top sheet, the mark shows on the sheet below.

Nashua Corporation was having problems with the quality of carbonless paper from its Merrimack, New Hampshire, plant in the USA. The process involves carefully coating the paper stock with the special CF and CB coatings, as they are called.

Before Dr. Deming, it was thought that workers were to blame for the poor quality. In fact, data showed that, during some shifts, the workers created great quality products, while during other shifts they made poor quality products. Even worse, it seemed that the workers didn't concentrate very well. The same people who would make products of good quality on one shift would make bad ones on their next shift.

The existing solution to this variance in quality was to increase the amount of toner put on the paper. Doing so ensured that the paper would always have enough toner to transfer the writing to the next page. The problem is this added significantly to the cost.

About this time, my father met Dr. Deming. He asked him for advice. Dr. Deming had my father create run charts on the system. They tracked various variables over time. A printout of the actual charts my dad created is shown on the following page.

The graphics made it easy to see that the pH and temperature of the coating were very stable. However, the viscosity, or thickness, of the toner supplied to the workers to use at the plant varied wildly. The workers

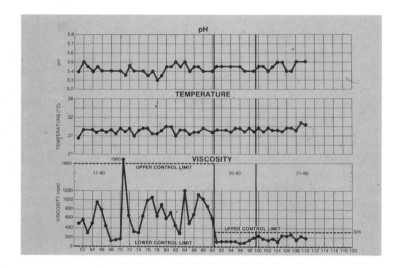

would pour each drum of toner into the coater, and if it was too thin or thick, no matter what they did, the carbonless paper they produced would be poor quality, as there would be "skips" due to a lack of even coating.

No amount of beating the workers, bribing the workers, or inspecting their work could resolve the quality problem. Even the worker had no ability to improve quality, as the variance in product quality was built into the system. The quality of the workers' output was controlled by the viscosity of each barrel of coating they poured into the coater.

My dad worked with the toner supplier to control viscosity. The right side of the chart shows the reduction in variance. With viscosity stable, the company could reduce the amount of toner being applied. The result was a savings of $750,000 (in 1980 dollars).

This project was one of Dr. Deming and Bill Conway's early case study examples of the power of applying system thinking to manufacturing.

A New Leadership Mindset

System-driven leadership is a new mindset. It starts with the leadership, with their broader knowledge, setting the aim for the overall system. When there is no clear strategic aim for where the company is going . . . where it is innovating . . . then individual departments create their own vision for optimizing their areas of responsibility.

> *Every system is perfectly designed to get the results it gets.*
> —Dr. W. Edwards Deming

The new mindset focuses the organization on optimizing the outcome of the "whole" system, then the properties of the parts. This is the reverse of the classic approach, in which the parts—of departments, divisions, teams—are defined first, then derive the whole.

I can't say what business was like 100 years ago; maybe it was so simple a leader could know everything. I can say that, at the speed the world is changing today, there is NO CHANCE that a leader can have total knowledge. A retired West Point–educated army officer told me:

> *Today's technology is changing so fast and is so specialized there is no way I can understand what my frontline troops can do. As an officer I need to set the commanders intent then listen and learn from my troops. If they've been trained properly and have the right resources they will be far smarter on how to execute than I ever could be.*

The greatest benefit of the Deming principles is that leaders get to be true leaders. When you have a system that's reliable, that adapts for variation, that is built on cycles of learning and intrinsic motivation, then employees are enabled to be great. The result is joy in work for both the leadership and employees.

At the Eureka! Ranch, I know we are living the system-driven principles when, after a robust discussion on an issue with the team, I feel confident to say in conclusion, "Do the right thing!" It's a phrase that Ranch staff love to hear, as it enables them to use their judgment. Importantly, it's not meant as do the "correct" thing but rather the "right thing" based on their judgment, their training, and our shared cultural values.

After I moved to saying, "Do the right thing," I soon faced a situation in which employees made decisions that turned out badly. This was the key test of my confidence in system thinking. In each case, I asked, "What did you learn?" They explained, and value was realized from the failure.

To be fair, I can't always say, "Do the right thing." As the CEO, I have to have the final say on company values and on some legal and financial issues. However, my feeling is that every time that my team can make decisions, it is a win.

> *Psst . . . company, division, or department leaders—imagine a world where decisions are pushed down in the organization. Where you or your employees are enabled to do the right thing. Your time is freed up to think on important and meaningful issues. From personal experience, I can tell you it feels awesome!*

As I became aware of the power of system thinking, I soon observed that others were living it as well. Bill Belichick, head coach of the New England Patriots football team (the most successful North American sports team over the past 10 years), is a believer in system thinking. Once the training and game plan is done, he tells his team, **"Do your job."** Christopher Price of WEEI radio station explained it this way: "'Do your job' cuts to the heart of Belichick's coaching style. The hint is a simple one: If you execute the game plan that I laid out for you as a coach—do your job— then the whole team will benefit as a result."

In a similar vein, 15-year Army Infantry Captain Eric Curtis (an Innovation Engineering Blue Belt and CFO for WorkSite Lighting, LLC) is a believer in system thinking. After briefing his troops on the strategic mission, he enables them by telling them to "do great things!" As he explained to me, they have the training to do the job; they understand the Army core values and policies. It's his job to enable them to . . . Do Great Things!

"Do the Right Thing," "Do Your Job," "Do Great Things" are mantras that enable employees. They are trusted to do the right things in the right ways, based on the situation and a combination of what they observe on the frontline, plus the training, systems, and tools they've received.

What Did You Learn?

- What in this chapter surprised you?
- Reflect on a time when you approached a challenge as a system challenge?
- Explore challenges you face at this moment in time. Are your challenges due to special cause or common cause errors? Are you unfairly blaming employees when the real issue is the system—training, tools, and methods—that they have been provided?
- Does your formal or informal innovation system enable or control?
- Is your formal or informal innovation system grounded in intrinsic or extrinsic motivational factors?
- What do you think are the top three improvements in your innovation system over the past year?

5

LEARNING MINDSET: The Three Innovation Principles

Essentially what you want to do in business is to be able to go in every morning and say, "Today I can do better than I did yesterday." And, the only way you are going to do that is if you know more.

—Drayton Bird, retired vice chairman, Ogilvy Direct

Innovation requires a learning mindset. You can't create a new idea without learning. When learning is a priority, you have hope, along with faith in the future. A learning mindset is engaged 24-7 in seeking out new stimuli and diversity of thinking.

Learning and its cousin, curiosity, are the fuel that enables innovators to never give up. The personal motto of Admiral Robert Peary, the first person to reach the North Pole, was a quote from the Roman philosopher Seneca: *"Inveniam viam aut faciam"*—Latin for *"I shall find a way or make one."* Peary made a way by inventing new systems for arctic travel. He pioneered new cooking systems, relay supply systems, dog sledding systems, and management systems. He achieved his North Pole mission through a commitment to never-ending learning.

Education "Best Practice"

The best practice for instituting Innovation Engineering is to start by educating the leadership of the company. In the military this is called "leading from the front." When leadership makes the commitment to embrace learning, it sends a signal to the employees that "this time" the company is serious about change.

Leaders who are transparent in their desire to learn send a message to their organization to do the same. Conversely, leaders who resist getting involved in learning also send a message to employees.

Bill Conway, the CEO of Nashua Corporation who ignited the Quality movement in the USA with Dr. Deming, told me that for nearly five years he spent 50% of his time educating managers and employees in the new system mindset. Think about the impact it had on employees when Bill was asking about variation and what experiments they were running to improve the system. Lawrence C. Hornor, who worked for Bill, described his commitment in the foreword he wrote for Bill's book, *The Quality Secret.*

> *It seemed that Bill was everywhere. He coached, cajoled, exhorted, and even threatened until it became obvious that to work at Nashua Corporation, you would have to learn and practice the "new way" of working.*
>
> *He was personally very visible to all the employees. With the chief executive involved to such a degree and exhibiting a detailed understanding of what could and should be accomplished, it was impossible not to join him in the effort. People also began to understand that he respected their opinions and was looking for their help and suggestions. He was never satisfied and was persistent in looking for an even better way— continuous improvement, he called it.*

While leadership from the top is the best method, it's not the only method to ignite a system mindset. In fact, we find that leadership of culture change, by top leadership, occurs less than 5% of the time with large companies. With small companies, it's higher, around 50% of the time.

The majority of the time, the ignition of an innovation culture begins with an innovation pioneer inside the organization applying the methods personally. They attend a public training program to learn or read a book. Then they use these skills to enable those within their sphere of influence. They use the Innovation Engineering mindset, tools, and systems to improve how they lead their own projects, team, department, or division.

The pioneer's success attracts the attention of other employees and teams. They, too, want to make work fun again. They want to work smarter, not harder. They want to unleash their curiosity and creativity. They want to do Cool Sh*t That Matters. Basically, the new mindset makes too much sense to be ignored. As detailed in Chapter 13, diffusion of an innovation mindset across a culture becomes self-sustaining when just 10% have unshakable belief in it.

Sometimes the new mindset diffuses quickly across the organization. Sometimes it takes a long time. We have observed that no matter how long it takes, the new mindset rarely dies. Once a leader's eyes are opened to understanding that 94% of innovation is the system and 6% is the worker, it's impossible for them to embrace the old way.

Education of Pioneers and Leaders

Forty-eight skills make up the Innovation Engineering body of knowledge. The most effective executive method we have found to start the education experience is to use highly compressed courses: IE Blue Belt Quick Start Course and IE Black Belt Mastery Course. Prior to attending, participants gain an understanding of the mindset from videos covering key skills and subskills.

During the in-person experiences, they are immersed into the new way of thinking through a series of very fast hands-on experiences. The speed and immersion help participants make the flip of mindset to using systems, instead of egocentric experts, to enable innovation.

Following the course, their eyes are opened to a new way of working. However, they won't fully trust it until they have experienced it themselves in their work. Without this trust they will "talk the talk," but when faced with a business stress they won't "walk the talk." Instead, they will resort to their historical ways of working.

Colin Guthrie, CEO of Mental Performance Consulting Group, who is also an Olympic sailing coach, describes the performance-under-stress phenomenon this way:

> *Olympic excellence is more than simply having world-class physical abilities and technique. There are many great athletes. Gold Medal performances are achieved when you are able to focus, analyze, and think as clearly when the starting gun goes off as you are able to in practice. Learning to do the right things under pressure is an intellectually stimulating experience that includes assessment, self-awareness, coaching, and practice to fully trust in yourself.*

Applying the new mindset to their projects, participants build confidence. Basically, it means getting your hands dirty by seeing, feeling, and experiencing what it takes to take an innovation in the organization's systems or offerings from idea to reality. This is why we have designed 80% of Innovation Engineering education to be focused on frontline coaching of direct application.

I believe that you cannot lead a company's innovation systems effectively if you don't know the strengths and weaknesses of the company's innovation methods and tools that employees currently have available to them. I've found that the best way to get leadership to support innovation system and tool development projects is to have them personally experience the frustration of working with a bureaucratic system for projects, collaboration, research, patents, etc.

The Three Principles That Help Make Some of the Unknown Knowable

As explained earlier, Dr. Deming felt that the factory offered 3% of the opportunity for company improvement. A challenge with applying system thinking to innovation, strategy, and how we work together has been a lack of data. Deming quoted Dr. Lloyd Nelson of Nashua Corporation: "The most important figures needed for management of any organization are unknown and unknowable."

New methods of data collection and analysis have enabled us to start to quantitatively understand how to turn innovation from a random gamble to a reliable system.

Research finds that three principles drive the discovery and successful development of Meaningfully Unique innovations. Together they make up a very simple equation.

These principles were identified through measuring and charting real projects at real companies. Measurements were made during the process, then compared versus outputs using multiple measurement systems. The details of the research are reviewed in my book *Jump Start Your Business Brain*.

1. EXPLORE STIMULI: The old approach to creating ideas is called brainstorming. However, it's usually more like "brain draining," as ideas are "sucked" from the brain. The new approach is to systematically use

$$MU = \frac{S^D}{F}$$

Meaningfully Unique ideas = $\dfrac{\textbf{Stimulus} \text{ Mining}}{\text{Drive Out } \textbf{Fear}}$

Diversity of thinking

stimuli to spark ideas. The stimulus can be related to the challenge, such as customer problem survey results, new technologies, or competitive actions. Or it can be unrelated, such as analogies, visualizations, and cultural excursions. The stimuli set off a chain reaction in your brain that brings fresh ideas to life.

The process is systematic, in that, prior to creating ideas, we do what we call Stimulus Mining. It's a process of finding facts, insights, and inputs that can open the mind. The most useful Stimulus Mining areas are: 1) Wisdom Mining, 2) Patent Mining, 3) Market Mining, 4) Insight Mining, 5) Future Mining, and 6) Unrelated Mining. These are reviewed in greater detail in the next chapter.

A simple tertile analysis documents the impact of stimuli on Meaningfully Unique idea development as part of Eureka! sessions. The greater the stimulus the greater the number of high-quality ideas that still existed after the raw ideas were defined in greater detail, edited, and evaluated.

	# of Meaningfully Unique Ideas Invented
High-Stimulus Groups	47
Medium-Stimulus Groups	38
Low-Stimulus Groups	22

2. LEVERAGE DIVERSITY: Stimuli spark the reaction that ignites fresh ideas. Diversity is the fuel that amplifies ideas from good to Meaningfully Unique. The greater the diversity of opinions the more effective you will be, not only at creating ideas, but also at problem solving and making your ideas real.

No matter what your challenge, there is someone inside and/or outside your organization who can help you think smarter, faster, and more creatively about it.

Asking for help, listening to the advice, and being willing to change our minds are probably the greatest challenges with adopting the new mindset. Research with over 12,000 managers finds that 95% of companies don't collaborate very well. A team that doesn't collaborate is like a poor football, hockey, or basketball team. Players are focused on individual achievement as opposed to helping the team win. As the formula and data modeling indicate, diversity has an exponential impact on the quantity of high-quality ideas created.

As you would expect, research conducted during real-world innovation projects finds that the greater the diversity of thinking, the greater the number of high-quality ideas that remain after the raw ideas have been defined, edited, and evaluated.

	# of Meaningfully Unique Ideas Invented
High-Diversity of Thinking Groups	46
Medium-Diversity of Thinking Groups	30
Low-Diversity of Thinking Groups	18

3. DRIVE OUT FEAR: Stimuli and diversity ignite ideas that are Meaningfully Unique. But they come alive only in proportion to the extent that you are able to drive out fear. Fear directly destroys the ability of individuals and cultures to discover, develop, and deliver ideas that are Meaningfully Unique.

Our research finds that as fear increases, the number of big ideas generated decreases. Fear of the unknown, fear of rejection, and fear of exposure kill idea creation.

There are two fundamental ways to reduce fear.

Method 1 is to make the unknown known. We do this by defining the whole idea from a customer and company perspective. For the customer, this means defining: Customer, Problem, Promise, Proof, and Price. For the organization, this means defining the Math Game Plan (sales forecast or savings), Death Threats, and why we are Passionate about the idea.

At an early stage, all of these definitions are more hypotheses than certainties. Thus the need for the second method of driving out fear.

Method 2 involves adopting the Deming Cycle, also known as "Plan, Do, Study, Act," as the method we use to manage our projects.

"Plan, Do, Study, Act" (PDSA) is a mindset where rapid experimentation is used to enable data-aided decision-making. Politics and opinions are replaced with facts and data. Importantly, PDSA is done quickly, with cycle times of one hour to a maximum of seven days. It's used to both resolve early-stage project Death Threats and to provide structure to project management and the innovation development process. It's used for Very Important Opportunities and Very Important Systems. With VIOs, the quantitative research is with current or new customers. With VISs, the quantitative research is with internal stakeholders. With "Plan, Do, Study, Act," the egocentric "declare and defend" is replaced with a curiosity to discover, experiment, and learn.

The data shows that as we drive down fear, the number of Meaningfully Unique ideas created goes up. And this data is only at the start. Continued tracking of ideas through the development process finds that driving out fear is critical if teams are to have the courage to problem solve instead of compromise when they come face to face with inevitable development challenges.

	# of Meaningfully Unique Ideas Invented
Low-Fear Groups	42
Medium-Fear Groups	34
High-Fear Groups	31

A system mindset, exploring stimuli, leveraging diversity, and driving out fear are simple principles. Their application is anything but. To develop them as a new mindset across a culture, to build confidence in them, takes education and repetition.

When we really live these principles, problems become opportunities to improve your innovation.

Recently, a new product team I was coaching ran into two serious development challenges. Specifically, two regulatory barriers prevented us from being able to scale up test products. We didn't feel the regulations were reasonable; however, the rules were the rules. And, as a multinational company, changing rules would take years.

The team assessed the situation. The option of giving up or compromising on the product was discussed. Clearly neither was an option. Not only did customers love the product—as evidenced by high Meaningful Uniqueness scores—but the team loved it as well.

The only option was to reinvent how the product was made to avoid the regulatory barrier. Instead of whining, compromising, or giving up, the team went to work. A problem-solving session identified a dozen theories on ways to address the problem. Fail FAST, Fail CHEAP (Plan, Do, Study, Act) experiments were run.

Within a week, the team had identified a new raw material and a new patentable method of production that overcame both issues. Most important of all, the result was a product that was preferred versus the old product, 72% to 28% in paired comparison testing.

As the project leader said in a text to me after he validated both changes in scaled-up production: "This rocks! Reinventing to address what I believe are stupid regulatory rules actually leads us to a better product. Never again will I let a team compromise their product to mediocrity."

What Did You Learn?

- What have you learned in the past six months? How are you smarter?
- Other than reading this book, what are you actively trying to learn right now?
- What do you want to learn more about / get better at?
- What sphere of influence do you have where you could apply the new mindset?
- Think back to a time when a stimulus in the form of new knowledge or learning helped you spark a new idea.
- Think back to a time when diversity and interacting with others helped spark a new idea or make an existing idea better.
- What fears prevent you from creating fresh ideas?
- What fears prevent you from experimenting with fresh ideas?

6

LEARNING MINDSET: Create System

There is no such thing as a new idea. It is impossible. We simply take a lot of old ideas and put them into a sort of mental kaleidoscope. We give them a turn and they make new and curious combinations. We keep on turning and making new combinations indefinitely; but they are the same old pieces of colored glass that have been in use through all the ages.

—Mark Twain
Mark Twain's Own Autobiography:
The Chapters from the North American Review

Create, Problem Solve, Re-create

The Innovation Engineering course titled CREATE should be called CREATE, PROBLEM SOLVE, and RE-CREATE.

For successful innovations, 10% of a project's creativity is used to spark the starting idea. The remaining 90% is used to improve and reinvent the idea as it's made real. Thomas Edison felt the ratio was even higher. He famously said, "Genius is ninety-nine percent perspiration and one percent inspiration."

The HARD Way to CREATE = Brain Draining

The hard way to create ideas is to sit in a room and attempt to "suck" ideas from your mind. It's a process of poking and prodding your brain to think up ideas. This process is called brainstorming. However, the effect is more like brain draining. I call it the "suck method" of creativity. It is grounded in the belief that ideas come from inside us. This is an egocentric view of the world of idea creation. Brain draining is not effective, efficient, or fun. With brain draining, the brain is considered the source of all ideas, a sort of idea library ready at all times for any withdrawals its owner may wish to make.

The SMART Way to CREATE = Stimulus Response

The smart way to create ideas is to feed your brain stimuli—sights, sounds, learning, facts. Then, have your brain react to the stimuli to create Meaningfully Unique ideas. Stimuli spark ideas, setting off a chain reaction of idea associations and creations. Stimuli can take many forms—from sights, sounds, and scents to customer data and firsthand experiences.

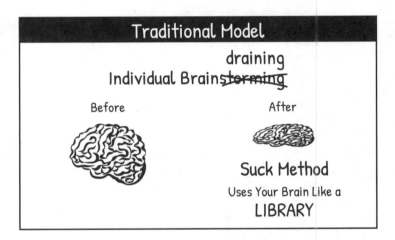

Diversity of perspectives multiplies the sparks from the stimulus through the different ways that each person perceives and interprets the stimulus.

Those whom society considers to be creative geniuses are simply those who have learned how to open their minds to stimuli. They have an overwhelming curiosity to learn more about their problems, possible solutions, and life itself. They have an openness to fresh ides from themselves and others. They embrace a new world of "curiosity and change" when it comes to ideas instead of the old "declare and defend" approach.

As an example, many years ago, I was working with a team of very fluid innovators whom we called Trained Brains. We were in the Netherlands on

behalf of the Van Melle candy company. The event was being filmed by *Dateline NBC.* I should warn you that today what I'm about to describe would be considered politically incorrect. The Mission was to invent new candies for children. The initial stimulus used to invent ideas was **A TOY GUN.** This example is particularly useful when explaining how stimulus and diversity work because it is so outrageous.

Here's the Actual Conversation That It Set Off . . .

"Make candy you can shoot."

"Make bullets kids can bite with red blood inside."

"Make silver bullets like the Lone Ranger had."

"Make little candy bullet wounds that bleed."

"Make candy named after famous assassins."

"Make a gun that shoots sometimes and other times it doesn't."

"Make a Russian Roulette candy with surprises inside."

"Make candies that are like FireBalls or Fruity Fruit."

"Make it so you can't tell if it's hot or fruity."

Ordinarily you would never assume that something like a toy gun could be useful to create ideas for a children's candy. In this case, it ended up sparking the idea for a candy called G.U.T.S.—Great Unbelievable Tasting Sweets. It was a hard candy with a powder inside. Inside was either a sweet cherry center or a hot "cherry bomb" cinnamon center.

The Classic Way Children and Most Adults Problem Solve

When we are young in age or new at a job, our mind is open to many options. When faced with a problem, we can see many possible solutions.

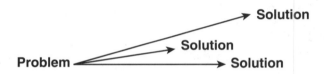

As we age, we learn that not all of these solutions are perfect. We soon start to edit our ideas before we even give voice to them.

As we age, we develop patterns of thought. When we see a problem, we see only one answer. In fact, even when the problem is a variation on an old problem, we actually transform the problem into the old problem so that we can then use the same solution.

A. Problem ⟶ B. Solution

This linear reaction to problems is a very efficient way to live. Life would be chaotic if every time we faced a situation we had an unlimited number of possibilities for what to do next. To compensate for the multitude of possibilities, our brain develops reactionary behaviors. When we see a lion, we think fear. When we see a kitten, we think cute. A linear response to stimulus makes life efficient. However, it's not helpful when we are looking for fresh ideas.

The More Effective Way to Problem Solve

The more effective approach is to use a stimulus as a spark to disrupt your normal thinking pattern. In my first book, I called this system for creating ideas and problem solving Stimulus Response. Creativity expert Dr. Edward de Bono named this approach Lateral Thinking. An artist might call it an inspiration. When Robert Frost sees two paths in the woods, it becomes the inspiration for poetry: "Two roads diverted in a wood, and I—I took the one less traveled by, And that has made all the difference."

Combining the stimulus response wording with Dr. de Bono's classic drawings, the process can be easily visualized. To create fresh ideas, a stimulus is used to disrupt our normal thinking patterns. In Dr. de Bono's words: It gets the brain to think "laterally." "A" to "B" is disrupted by the stimulus interaction at "C," sending the mind to Response "D."

A. Problem   C. Stimulus

D. Response = "Fresh Solution"

The Stimulus Response method makes it easy to craft fresh solutions to your problems. If you want more solutions, you simply fill your brain with more stimuli. Your mind is then used to associate, connect, and piece together the stimulus into fresh ideas for solving your problem. Fresh ideas don't appear "magically." Rather, your mind connects and processes each stimulus into new ways of looking at solving your problem.

The Stimulus Response method of discovering solutions is like working out—the more you do it, the stronger you become. Every time you create ideas, you fill your brain with more stimuli and connections. When you least expect it, an old connection will provide the link you need to solve a problem.

> *Creativity is just connecting things. When you ask creative people how they did something, they feel a little guilty because they didn't really do it, they just saw something. It seemed obvious to them after a while. That's because they were able to connect experiences they've had and synthesize new things.*

> —Steve Jobs
> cofounder of Apple

Another Example of Stimulus Response

As another example, say you are in the business of selling Christmas trees. However, because of new competition you end up this season with 300 trees that you haven't been able to sell. You need ideas for ways to make money on these trees.

With Innovation Engineering, before you start to create ideas, you do what we call Stimulus Mining. You read, you search the internet, you talk to experts, you post on social media asking for things to do with pine trees. From this you get dozens of stimulus sparks related to uses for pine trees, including:

- Pine is very high in vitamin C.

- An academic study in Japan found that depression levels went down when people walked through a pine forest for 15 minutes twice a day.

- Extracts from pine have been found to be a cure for jet lag, circulatory problems, and knee pain.

- Extracts from pine have been found to improve memory in the elderly.

- There are lots of recipes for pine teas, martinis, and other foods and beverages.

You gather a group of friends together to think about ways to use your leftover trees. You show them the stimuli you've found and ideas are sparked . . . some wild, some with potential . . . all that are fresh versus what you would have thought of by yourself.

- Create a portable pine forest for people, consisting of pieces of chopped pine that click onto a necklace to wear when walking for exercise.

- Create a travel package of pine oil and extracts for when you fly.

- Create super pure pine needles that are specially processed to maximize health benefits for use as a tea and as a gin and tonic, as pine is an evergreen like juniper.

The idea of using a stimulus as inspiration is not new. Artists have borrowed from the natural world to inspire their works for centuries. Thomas Edison was a great believer in the power of using stimuli to spark ideas. He said once, "Make it a practice to keep on the lookout for novel and interesting ideas that others have used successfully."

The greatest barrier to using stimuli to spark ideas is the ego. Instead of letting the ideas flow by responding to stimuli and sharing ideas with others, we attempt to control, direct, and declare solutions. **When we shut our minds down from stimuli, learning, and sharing ideas with others, we paralyze our ability to ignite fresh ideas.**

You Already Know How to Use Stimuli

Practice is required to build your confidence in your ability to identify fresh solutions. This is not because stimuli are difficult to find or use but because you will need to retrain your brain to think differently. The good news is that you are probably using Stimulus Response in your daily life without even being conscious of it.

- When you wander around the kitchen pantry looking at what's available to make dinner or flip through recipe books, you are using stimuli to spark ideas.

- When you wander around the mall at holiday time, thinking about what to get for a gift, you are using stimuli to spark ideas.

- When you pull information from a weekly sales letter, you are using stimuli to spark ideas.

- When a baby empties a cupboard on the floor and starts playing the drums with the pots, she is using stimuli to spark ideas.

- When the singer hears the rhythm of the train over the tracks and is inspired to write a song, that's using a stimulus to spark ideas.

- When the product designer gathers military gear to serve as inspiration for a new line of outdoor gear, she's using stimuli to spark ideas.

As your brain fills with stimuli, you immediately start to make connections. You literally can't stop yourself, as the human brain is wired to find order in the jumble of ideas that are being fed into it.

Without even thinking about it, your brain will search for patterns that will ignite within you fresh insights and ideas.

You already know how to use stimuli. What's needed is to build your confidence in it by making it a conscious practice. To do this you need to start practicing and applying it. As Copthorne Macdonald, scientist and scholar on wisdom, wrote in *Toward Wisdom,* "Before we can deal with the considerable trials of practice, we must first overcome our fear of starting."

Don't tell me you are too old to learn a new way of thinking. Many of the greatest breakthroughs in science come at later ages, as older people actually have more experiences/stimuli to pull from, if—and it's a serious *if*—they still have the energy and desire to open their minds to fresh ideas.

Stimulus Mining

Stimuli can be gathered from a random walk, gathering sights, sounds, and perceptions. It can also be gathered through the disciplined Stimulus Mining approach.

Stimulus Mining is so important that we spend nearly half of the Innovation Engineering CREATE course on it. It's a disciplined process of gathering facts, insights, sights, sounds, and even ideas that we mix, match, and rearrange into fresh ideas to solve our challenge.

The process of gathering stimuli often sparks initial ideas. We write them down to keep them safe, as these initial ideas become additional stimuli on our quest to find Meaningfully Unique ideas.

Having gathered the stimuli, the ideal approach is then to share them with others to multiply our diversity exponentially.

Stimulus Mining Depth

There are three levels of Stimulus Mining: **Exploring, Experiencing,** and **Experimenting.**

Exploring is the gathering of the facts, data, and findings. It's about sifting through the multitude of information to find pieces of stimuli that can disrupt traditional thinking and spark fresh ideas. If you were working on inventing a new type of pizza, it could involve gathering data on pizza-purchasing trends, regional variations, or even pizza taste preferences around the world. It could involve gathering pricing on various pizza ingredients and details on different cooking systems.

Experiencing is about taking a deep dive into your object of inquiry. It's about seeing, feeling, experiencing from the inside out. For example, if you were working on inventing a new form of pizza, it could involve gaining deep knowledge into the chemistry of pizza crusts and sauces. It could also involve tasting lots of pizzas. It could also involve enrolling in a professional pizza college or working the line at a pizzeria. Experiencing could also involve a deep statistical analysis of pizza purchasing, attitudes, habits, and practices. Deep experiences help you identify unexpected insights and idea starters that are not visible on the surface.

Experimenting involves Fail FAST, Fail CHEAP experiments. The tests are sparked by "connecting the dots" between facts, insights, intuition, or experiences. It involves creating new "What if" hypotheses. In the case of pizza, it might mean using different types of grain to create pizza dough. It might involve trying to create a cracker crust and topping recipe that cuts calories in half. Or it could be connecting declines in red meat consumption and the trend of raw food to invent new types of cold or raw pizza options.

With both Experience and Experiment, the findings are often shared with others through photos, audio, video, or a re-creation of a portion of the immersion experience.

Stimulus Mining Breadth

There are six forms of Stimulus Mining. We organize them into three groups: Classic Mining (Insight and Market), Tech Mining (Patent and Wisdom), and Stretch Mining (Future and Unrelated).

CLASSIC STIMULUS MINING is the most common method used today when creating ideas. It includes Insight and Marketing Mining. It is ideal for the generation of incremental CORE innovations.

1. INSIGHT MINING (VOICE OF THE CUSTOMER): Insight Mining involves understanding what customers and potential customers perceive and believe. With internal system innovations, Insight Mining is focused on connecting with those who are responsible for the system and who are affected by it.

Insight Mining involves having direct conversations with customers or potential customers. It also includes customer observation, or as market researchers call it: ethnography. The internet provides a powerful method of conducting Insight Mining. Reviewing social media, blogs, etc. for comments provides insights. Posting questions on the same internet sites can spark a chain reaction of Insight Mining feedback.

The odds of getting great value from Insight Mining go up when you ask questions that go beyond problems with the existing offering and focus on wishes. Classic questions that can be asked include:

- What would be such a WOW for _____ that you'd be willing to pay more money for it?

- If you could wave a magic wand and wish for anything other than lower price, what would you wish for from _____ ?

Qualitative opinions are a valuable method for sparking ideas. However, care must be taken, as they could be random opinions that are not broadly shared by others. To enhance reliability, various methods are used, including InterAct Sessions and quantitative research.

InterAct sessions are advanced forms of focus groups. They involve three to six simultaneous mini-groups of customers who are provided stimuli to recall and react to. This ignites up to 6X more fresh ideas from customers.

Quantitative research is the only statistically reliable system for gathering Insight Mining. Classic Insight Mining surveys include:

- **Problem Surveys:** Customers are asked to rate various problem statements relative to a product, service, or system on how "big" of a problem the stated issue is to them and how "frequently" they experience the problem. This provides valuable stimuli for sparking fresh ideas.

- **Idea Starter Surveys:** Customers are asked to rate one-sentence statements of possible ideas. They rate how much they "like" each statement and how "new and different" each is. These results provide insight into what ideas are perceived by customers to be Meaningfully Unique.

A classic workflow would be to use qualitative conversations with customers to identify possible problems or idea starters. This is followed by quantitative research to quantify on a broader basis. The research is then used in a Create session to spark more ideas.

2. MARKET MINING (BENCHMARKING): Market Mining involves looking at competitive offerings and solutions to the problem you seek to solve. At its most basic, it's about creating a chart showing the advantages and disadvantages of your offering versus others. The most experiential form of Market Mining involves seeing, feeling, and experiencing firsthand key competitive alternatives.

With Market Mining it's important that you look at the whole story of the competitive offering. Otherwise, it's easy to disregard the approach that competitors use because it's different from what you do. For example, when you look deeper, you often find that while they might be virtually giving away one part of their offering, they are making more money on another part that you are giving away.

The internet also provides new options for Market Mining. It makes it easy to find spec sheets on competitive offerings and to see how the competitor is positioning their offering. It also makes it easy to find how competitors in other countries and cultures are approaching your challenge. For example, a simple search for "Best Pizza in Iceland" takes you on a global Stimulus Mining journey.

Somewhat more advanced Market Mining options include:

- Listening to the Q&A during quarterly earnings webcasts of publicly held companies

- Reviewing trademark filings by your competition

- Interviewing industry trade show executives on what the up-and-coming companies are

- Visiting the low-rent district at trade shows to see what entrepreneurs are doing

- Interviewing retired executives. LinkedIn and Facebook make this process easy.

A very powerful Market Mining method is to gather the problems and promises that competitors are making. Write them as simple statements without brand names. Then conduct quantitative problem surveys and idea starter surveys. Compare the results with the sales results of each. This identifies those products that are overperforming and underperforming versus their basic customer problem and promise.

TECH MINING is a more advanced form of Stimulus Mining. It includes Patent and Wisdom Mining. It is especially valuable when creating disruptive LEAP innovations.

3. PATENT MINING: Patents are arguably the world's most effective source for inspiring genuine innovations. Patents are blueprints for how to accomplish something that has been judged to be Meaningfully Unique in the world. They provide step-by-step instructions for how the invention works. That's because when a patent is filed, the inventor is obliged to make an enabling disclosure that can be executed by someone with skill in the art without excessive experimentation.

Patent Mining leverages the published inventions of others to inspire fresh ideas. At its root, it's one of the reasons that patents were created. In exchange for making your invention public so that others can build on the invention after its term expires, the inventor is rewarded with a government-supported commercial monopoly.

The easiest way to create a Meaningfully Unique innovation is to take one or more free patents that are in the public domain, making them free to us, and create an invention that builds on them or combines them.

Alternatively, you can purchase Flea Market Patents to use directly or build on. These are patents that can often be bought for a few thousand dollars as the inventor has decided to not pay maintenance fees to maintain the patent. Lastly, there are valid patents for inventions that can sometimes be licensed for use. More details on patents are provided in Chapter 12.

The two barriers to Patent Mining are the painful ways that patents are written, as well as the egos of technical people who feel they know everything. The first problem is easy to solve. There are technologies inside Innovation Engineering Labs and at other online databases that make it easy to find and filter patents.

- Filter to the 40 to 50 patents that matter quickly. You can do this by looking into the 150,000-plus classes that patents are categorized in.

- Carousel viewing systems allow you to quickly click through the key drawing, title, and abstract, saving patents that you might want to look at more deeply.

- Artificial intelligence systems allow you to type your idea in natural language, and the smart system then identifies patent classes to explore.

Somewhat more advanced Patent Mining options include:

- Exploring pending patent applications to identify the latest technology trends

- Using patents to point you to an inventor who often has additional technologies that have not been patented. A retired Procter & Gamble inventor told me, "For every patent I filed at P&G there were four to eight others that I thought of but didn't get the time or support to pursue." As with Market Mining, talking to retired employees can be an invaluable resource for fresh ideas.

4. WISDOM MINING: Wisdom Mining is the most powerful way I know to create a transformational LEAP innovation. Wisdom Mining involves reviewing academic articles for inspiration. Academic articles, like patents, represent a new contribution to the world as judged by those with skill in the field.

Academic articles disclose, at no cost, root technologies and understandings that are new to the world. Unlike industry, which tends to focus on applied product development, academic research tends to be more basic R&D—the type of exploration that has the potential to transform industries. However, academic research studies are foundational building blocks—that need to be translated, developed, and packaged to generate commercial value.

Note: Most free databases of academic articles only provide the abstracts of articles and require a purchase to see the full article. One way around this is to check with your local library. Many libraries provide access to full-text academic articles or have copies of the journals on site. Alternatively, InnovationEngineeringLabs.com offers, as part of membership, access to the most useful full text databases we've found for innovators.

As with patents, academic articles are written in a manner that makes them hard to comprehend. I find I often have to read them multiple times before I can fully understand them.

STRETCH MINING is a mind-liberating form of Stimulus Mining. It includes Future and Unrelated Mining. Like Tech Mining, it is ideal for the generation of both disruptive LEAP innovations and incremental CORE innovations.

5. FUTURE MINING: Future Mining stretches your mind by focusing you on the future. This focus on anticipating the future is a key theme in Dr. Deming's teaching. He explained, "Management's job is one of Prediction." When it came to research, he defined the goal as, "To try to learn what will help the customer in the future. To try to figure out what will get ahead of the customer."

Whereas Patent and Wisdom Mining are grounded in scientific fact, Future mining is grounded in theories about the future. The theories are not random. They are predictions about what could happen. Even a theory based on a consistent trend of data is not a certainty. An outside force could occur that changes the trajectory of the trend, making it happen faster or not at all.

The best way I've found to think about future mining is to use scenario planning. Scenario planning is a field of science that has a deep pedigree of successful applications. As practiced, it requires intensive research. A simple way to get started is to use an "if/then" approach. If _____ were to occur, then the consequence could be _____ . This would generate opportunities for _____ .

By stating "if a scenario were to occur," we are avoiding having to defend the stimulus. We are thinking about future possibilities, not certainties. The result is spending less time debating and more time thinking of fresh ideas for making a meaningful difference.

Advanced methods for Future Mining that we teach include:

- **Trailblazer.** A delphi system for quantifying future possibilities based on the instincts and wisdom of a diverse range of experts.

- **Mining those with the long view.** People retired from the industry often have a better appreciation for long-term trends. They also have no ego involved in defending today's approach.

- **Lines of evolution.** A systemic way of looking into the future. It is based on the work of Genrich Altshuller, a Russian innovation expert who spent years identifying reproducible patterns in innovation solutions and in the evolution of industries.

6. UNRELATED MINING: Unrelated Mining is about stretching the mind with a stimulus that is not directly related to the challenge. There is a broad range of options for Unrelated Stimulus from stories of successful innovations in unrelated fields to magazines, movie scenes, music lyrics, greeting cards, or simply highly provocative products.

When working with Unrelated Mining, a problem-solving mindset—and a playful mind—are necessary. Forced association is used to problem solve the riddle of how to make the unrelated stimulus relevant to the challenge.

Generally, an unrelated stimulus requires a level of trust, confidence, and playfulness among those utilizing it. The number of ideas generated is often lower than with a related stimulus, but at the same time they tend to be more dramatically different.

Advanced Methods of Unrelated Mining include:

- **Grab Bags:** This involves providing a small toy or product to spark ideas. The team is then challenged to deconstruct the item listing key components, functions, and benefits. The deconstructions are then used to inspire new ideas. We've found that putting each item in an individual brown paper bag provides focus to the thinking instead of a basket full of items to explore.

- **Expeditions:** I learned this from Jim Henson, inventor of the Muppets. When looking for inspiration on new characters, he and his team would tour art museums in New York or London. When you walk through a gallery, the images, designs, concepts, and even names of the art pieces can be invaluable to inspiring ideas. The Eureka! Ranch team has led innovation Accelerators at locations that provided unique opportunities for stimulus expeditions. We've held sessions and sent teams to explore Walt Disney World; Universal Studios; zoos; cruise ships; and the streets of London, Seoul, Toronto, and Portland, Maine. Years ago we used Polaroid cameras for participants to capture stimuli to bring back to the group. Today, we use a Collaboration Cafe app inside IE Labs, which sends images via smartphone to a private project digital workspace.

- **Take Over Time:** A very popular form of unrelated stimulus is called Take Over Time. It involves thinking about what other companies, brands, or famous or historical figures would do if they took over your challenge. Similar to Grab Bags, teams are challenged to deconstruct the stimulus into core values and principles inherent in the "take over" stimulus, then to apply them to the challenge.

A great unrelated stimulus sets off a chain reaction of ideas. My simple test for evaluating the potential for an unrelated stimulus is to "shake it"—that is, think quickly about it—I can quickly see a few ideas. If I can do it without much effort, I know that when a group of people are exposed, there will be even more ideas.

Leveraging Diversity

The stimulus gathered through one or more of the six minings is then used to inspire ideas. This can involve an individual simply using it. You simply sit down and start to fill your brain, with the stimulus sparking new ideas and twisting and turning your mind.

The most powerful method for processing the stimulus into ideas is to gather a group of people to help you. The stimulus you have gathered is multiplied exponentially by collaborating with others. Each person brings to the stimulus unique life experiences and knowledge that will spark unique ideas. The gathering can be a short idea-focused Create session. Or a multiday Accelerator session, in which cycles of creating are used to refine, reinvent, and optimize ideas.

Our initial reactions to stimuli are based on our experiences and expertise. Those in manufacturing review ideas and immediately think of production issues. Those in legal immediately look for possible legal risk. Those in sales search their minds for customers who would purchase the new idea. Research and development experts review for technical feasibility.

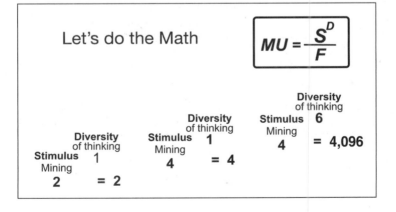

Let's do the Math

$$MU = \frac{S^D}{F}$$

Diversity of thinking
Stimulus Mining
2 = 2
Stimulus 1

Diversity of thinking
Stimulus 1
Mining
4 = 4

Diversity of thinking
Stimulus 6
Mining
4 = 4,096

Each viewpoint is invaluable in helping you develop a three-dimensional perspective regarding your idea. By listening to each person, and building on their thinking, you help your idea develop richness. Collectively, these perspectives can dramatically enhance your probability of executional success.

Diversity has an exponential impact on the number of high-quality ideas created. If one brain looks at a stimulus and creates 5 ideas, then two brains looking at the same stimulus can create not 5 but rather 25 ideas!

Here's the math on the power of diversity . . .

Stimulus-Sharing Methods

Stimuli can be shared informally, reviewing a few findings, and then, as a group, free-associating on the ideas that are sparked by the stimulus. Every perception by every group member becomes an additional piece of stimulus.

More formally, stimuli can be shared using what are called Spark Decks. These are presentations of ideas, images, video, and/or audio that are presented using presentation slides. We teach students to use a very disciplined format that is both **Disruptive** and **Divergent.**

The left side of a presentation slide communicates a disruptive fact or insight. The purpose being to cause the stimulus response or lateral thinking effect described at the start of this chapter.

Disruptive Fact
(quick research)

Divergent Prompt
(idea starter)

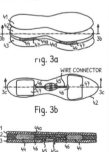

Built-in wear-indicator device with a sensor and microprocessor.

rig. 3a

It can measure and report the use history of the shoe and feature.

Fig. 3b

A display that shows the current point in the shoe's life cycle.

Fig. 3c

- What problem might we solve or prevent with the built-in sensors?

- What information could we promise?

- How could we offer the smartest shoes on Earth?

Source: US 6,578,291B2

The right side of the slide contains a few divergent prompts. The purpose of these is to provide a set of "nudges" to spark the creative thinking process.

Classically, 6 to 12 slides will be shown as a set. Participants are given a few moments after each slide is reviewed to think and reflect on thoughts. After the complete set is shared, the group breaks into groups of four to six people who then build on each other's ideas.

Spark Decks have proven to be one of the most effective methods for sharing custom stimuli with a group. In preparation for a very important project, we often work three to six work streams to explore and develop stimulus Spark Decks for sharing at the Create session.

Stimuli from experiences or experiments are shared using slides or by having participants experience the experience or experiment themselves. Over the years, people who sell paint have sanded and painted old furniture. Executives who make garden equipment have gardened. And executives who make surgical equipment have "operated" on stuffed animals. Each of these ignited fresh ideas and insights.

Stock Exercises for Leveraging Diversity

There are literally hundreds of stock stimulus exercises that don't require customization. For details on some of the most validated methods, see my book *Jump Start Your Brain 2.0*. The ultimate reference is *Techniques of Structured Problem Solving* by Dr. Arthur Van Gundy.

The Two Rules for Great CREATE and ACCELERATOR Sessions

Alex Osborn invented the word and concept known as brainstorming. He identified two rules of brainstorming that are as true today as when he first identified them in 1942 in his book *How to Think Up.*

SUSPEND JUDGMENT: The psychology of idea creation is very simple. Negative feedback loops stop creation. Positive feedback loops ignite creative momentum. To create fresh ideas, we need to suspend judgment on the value of each initial idea.

Suspending judgment separates the creation from the evaluation of early ideas. When you create and evaluate in one pass, a mindset of negativity develops. If every idea you have is shot down, soon you don't say ideas. Soon fresh ideas are withheld for fear of being shut down. If instead you simply create, create, and create, then a chain reaction of positives is evoked. All ideas, good or bad, serve as stimuli for even more ideas.

Over the years we've discovered many techniques for building positive momentum. For example, we offer what we call "thunderous applause" when people share an idea with the broader group. We also encourage senior leaders to set the standard. We encourage them to offer to the group a crazed or even "stupid" idea early in a Create session. When senior leaders do this, it frees up others to do the same, as it stretches the psychological safety zone for others. The thinking goes like this: "I hesitated to speak an idea for fear that it was too crazy. However, after the CEO said that stupid idea, I figured at least my idea wasn't as dumb as what he had said."

QUANTITY CREATES QUALITY: Research I conducted with Dr. Andy Vangundy, of the University of Oklahoma, confirmed what other researchers have found—that the more ideas you create, the more big ideas you end up with. It's believed that this is because initial ideas act as stimuli for more ideas. The more ideas you have, the more connections to bigger ideas can be made.

Contrast this with the approach of focusing on finding just the one big idea. In our classes it's common for some teams to follow the advice and create a lot of ideas before picking their best idea. Other teams attempt to simply create the answer, thinking it will be the shorter, easier path. Every time that I remember, the best ideas come from the team that took the time to create many ideas first.

Dean Keith Simonton of the University of California confirmed that quantity does indeed create quality. Simonton studied 2,036 scientists throughout history, and he found that the most respected scientists produced not only more great works, but also more bad ones. They produced. Period.

If I were helping lead your team in a problem-solving session, I would challenge you to create 20, 50, or 100 possible solutions, depending on how very important the problem is. My goal would be to ask for more than is reasonable. The team may well complain when I challenge them, saying it's unreasonable. However, when we are done, they will thank me. Osborn's research confirms what will happen. He found that the second half of brainstorming sessions generate 78% of the big ideas. In addition to generating more stimuli, the initial ideas that are generated are usually the obvious ones. When the obvious ideas are exhausted, then original ideas are developed.

Mind Mapping:
The Ultimate Stimulus-Processing Tool

With Innovation Engineering we take an engineering mindset to our tools and work processes. We take the work of others and distill it into the 20% that reliably delivers the bulk of the value. Our intent is not to diminish the research and development of others. Rather, given our focus on frontline application, our students can't afford to invest weeks or months learning one specific methodology. We do, however, encourage students and readers to learn more about each Create method from the creator's own work.

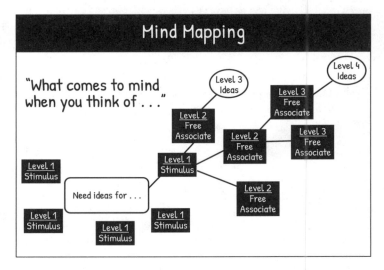

For example, if I were stuck on a deserted island and could have only two tools to create a solution to get me off the island, Tony Buzan's Mind Mapping is one of the ones I would want to have. Mind Mapping is a display thinking system. Instead of a one-dimensional list, ideas are displayed as a two-dimensional web of connections and associations. Tony Buzan has developed Mind Mapping into a rich and deep tool.

By the way, the other tool I would want to have is TRIZ, Genrich Altshuller's system of intelligent stimulus. With TRIZ, Maggie Pfeifer of the Eureka! Ranch took what is taught over weeks and simplified and automated it so that it can be learned and practiced by students and

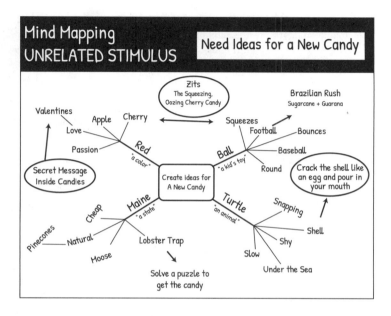

businesspeople in minutes. TRIZ is a system of smart stimulus based on an analysis of the key insights behind millions of patents.

We have simplified Mind Mapping to make it into a simple stimulus-processing tool that can be quickly used by individuals or groups. The process works like this:

STEP 1: TASK. In the center of the paper, write the task. Need ideas for . . .

STEP 2: STIMULUS. In the first spokes out from the center, detail the STIMULUS to be explored. These could be the stimuli from Spark Decks or ideas sparked by the Spark Decks.

STEP 3: FREE ASSOCIATIONS. In the second and additional spokes out from the stimulus, list whatever comes to mind when you think of the stimulus. These can be perceptions, beliefs, good ideas, bad ideas—anything and everything that comes to mind. The process of free associations should take less than a minute. It should be instinctive and not over-thought. The goal is to provide a number of "leaping off" points to work from so you don't become tunnel-brained and locked into a single dimension when you start creating ideas.

When a stimulus is multiplied in this manner, it takes on greater depth and character. It ignites many more sparks that can light new ideas. When working in a group, the multiplication of a stimulus lets everyone participate in the creation of ideas. When we don't multiply a stimulus as a conscious step, we end up creating far fewer ideas. Resist the temptation to leap directly from a piece of stimulus to an idea. The extra minute it takes to multiply stimulus is time well spent.

STEP 4: CREATE IDEAS. At the outside edges, list ideas. If they are particularly provocative ideas, good or bad, circle them so that you can find them again quickly. Here's the structure of a Mind Map as we use it.

This example of a Mind Map uses unrelated stimuli to invent ideas for a new candy.

As with all techniques, you are encouraged to learn more about the many other uses for Mind Mapping from Tony Buzan's books.

Innovation Is a Journey

To become great at creating ideas, you need to see the process as a journey. If you believe that your first idea needs to be brilliant, you will never be a great innovator.

The notion that you create great ideas by first creating lots of bad ones is a fundamental mindset that you must embrace, or you will get frustrated as an innovator.

Perfect, no-risk, mega-disruptive ideas are never invented in one pass. All first ideas, no matter how great you might feel they are, have flaws. All ideas go through "Plan, Do, Study, Act" cycles of learning—reinvention, reinvention, and reinvention to become awesome. The education pioneer Hamilton Holt said it well:

> *Nothing worthwhile comes easily. Work, continuous work and hard work, is the only way to accomplish results that last.*

Ed Catmull, cofounder and president of Pixar, arguably the most successful animation studio of all time, had this to say about how bad ideas are the key to great ideas: "Early on ALL of our movies SUCK. That's a blunt assessment, I know, but I make a point of repeating it often, and I choose that phrasing because saying it in a softer way fails to convey how bad the first versions of our films are."

Everyone Can CREATE

The good news is that no matter how "uncreative" you might think you are, you can create Meaningfully Unique ideas if you leverage stimuli, diversity, and cycles of reinvention.

Twenty-five years ago, Ralston Purina hired my Eureka! Ranch team to invent ideas for a new children's cereal. To gather stimuli, we invited two groups of students to invent ideas for us. Group 1 featured students who felt they were very creative. Group 2 featured students who felt they were not creative.

Both groups participated in separate sessions. For the first 30 minutes they were taught Osborn's two rules of brainstorming and how to leverage stimulus and diversity. The next 90 minutes were spent inventing ideas for a new cereal for children.

Content analysis of the students' ideas revealed that the students who believed they were NOT creative created over three times more Meaningfully Unique ideas.

We observed, in this small base study, that the first group of "creative" students created ideas, then stopped. The uncreative students started slowly, but having been taught a system for creating and given encouragement, they became even more creative. An amazing momentum developed. When the session came to an end, they didn't want to stop. We have experienced the same with adults. When you teach adults a system for discovering solutions to their problems and provide encouragement, their natural creative spirit is activated. And when it is activated, they experience true joy in work.

What Did You Learn?

The value of stimuli and diversity are obvious. However, their application is not. The natural habit is to declare and defend ideas based on your opinions. THINK.

- When in your life has a piece of stimulus (a learning, an observation, a fact) sparked a fresh solution to a problem you had?

- When in your life has diversity (a conversation with others) sparked a fresh solution to a problem you had?

- In your personal life, what are examples of where you use stimuli and diversity to create fresh ideas and/or solve problems?

- In your work life, do you use stimuli and diversity, or do you resort to brain draining?

- What prevents you from using it more?

- In the company you work for or the school where you learn/teach, what prevents the use of Stimulus Mining and diversity to solve problems?

- Which of the six types of Stimulus Mining (Wisdom, Patent, Market, Insight, Future, Unrelated) do you use? What stops you from using the others?

7

LEARNING MINDSET: Communicate System

If you can't explain it to a 6-year-old, you don't understand it yourself.

—Albert Einstein

Communicate Is the Secret to Being Great at Create and Commercialize

Create and Commercialize generate the most excitement when students learn about Innovation Engineering courses. However, among those who practice Innovation Engineering, Communicate is acknowledged as the most powerful way to improve their ability to Create and Commercialize.

- Communicate skills transform "Create" idea fragments into persuasive ideas and enable "Commercialize" teams to pivot, adapt, and align on clear and focused business opportunities.

- Communicate skills turn ordinary ideas into extraordinary concepts.

- Communicate skills give focus to rapid "Plan, Do, Study, Act" cycles of learning.

Communicate helps you clearly articulate the problem your innovation addresses, the promise you are making to address the problem, and the product/service/system proof that makes the promise possible. With this clarity we can then leverage Stimulus Mining to learn how to improve the idea. And, with our idea clearly defined on paper, we more efficiently leverage diversity and get help from others. We better sell our idea to ourselves, and in so doing reduce our fear. We create "pull" for our idea from customers and stakeholders. Most important of all, we help our customers understand how the idea will make a meaningful difference in their lives.

While other courses and programs teach useful methods of enhancing creativity and project management (Commercialize), we know of none that teaches the Communicate skills. Without the Communicate bridge between creating and commercializing, ideas are sparked but wasted—and teams often accelerate ideas not worth working on.

All elements of Innovation Engineering are grounded in data. However, the greatest volume of data supports the Communicate course. Tens of thousands of concepts have been evaluated over the years to identify the traits that have a statistically significant impact on your odds of success. This chapter contains an overview of the findings. To learn more, see my book *Meaningful Marketing* (titled *Jump Start Your Marketing Brain* in paperback.)

Our Destination: Turning Ideas Into Concepts

The Communicate course teaches you how to write a clear and complete description of your innovation that speaks to your customer's needs.

We call this piece of writing a concept. It's not a long piece. Ideally, it's a short and focused 50 to 100 words. It can be longer, but it's rarely more than 300 words. It's a blueprint of your idea. It's a manifesto for change.

A concept is not advertising, but it provides a framework for your advertising communications. A concept is not a business plan, but it gives definition to your business plan. A concept is not an R&D brief, but it does provide a vision for what you will be developing.

A great concept description communicates with clarity the Meaningful Uniqueness that your idea will offer to customers. The concept description ALWAYS changes and gets better and better during the development process as you learn more.

Concept Writing Can't Be Outsourced

Concept writing helps you think deeply about your idea. You have to do it. You can't outsource it. Concepts are the strategic foundation of your innovation. With the foundation clear, you can get help from others to craft your message more creatively. However, you and you alone must define your innovation.

If you're like most adults, you'll resist this, claiming you're not a writer, author, or copywriter. You don't have to be! I'm not asking you to write like Ernest Hemingway or Stephen King. All you need to do is take the idea in your imagination and define it on paper. When you do, others can then see your idea as you see it. And they can then help you improve your idea and make it into a reality.

Writing organizes your thinking. When you give words to your idea, it becomes real. Writing is a first prototype. When your idea is defined in writing, the strengths shine and the holes become glaringly obvious.

Great Innovations Start with a WHOLE Idea, Then You Derive the PARTS

Dr. Russell Ackoff of the Wharton School believed in the importance of starting from the whole, then deriving the parts. In the Deming Institute Video series, he explains:

> *You design the system as a whole and derive the properties of the parts from the properties of the whole. As opposed to analytical design, where you start by taking the parts and extracting the properties of the whole from the characteristics of the parts.*

When it comes to writing a concept, starting with the "whole idea" means that, before we write the idea, we have an understanding of the idea as a whole. The idea exists in our minds as a three-dimensional entity.

Often you don't have that level of understanding. You might have a part—a customer, a problem you are solving, a benefit promise you are making, or even a product or service proof for how you will deliver on a promise that no one else can make. In these cases, we teach free writing as a means for thinking deeper about the idea before you begin writing the concept.

Free writing is a stream-of-consciousness writing process. You just put pen to paper or fingers to keyboard and start writing. You write everything that comes to mind about the idea:

- Who the innovation is for
- What problem it solves
- Why it's important
- What makes it newsworthy
- How it works

You keep writing and writing for 10 to 30 minutes. If you don't know what to write, you simply write: "I don't know what to write, I don't know what to write" over and over again until another thought comes to your mind.

After you've gotten it all out of your brain and onto paper, then you step back and think about it as a whole. From this, a new clarity will reveal itself. You will see the idea as a whole and now be in a position to write a concept. With Innovation Engineering, concepts are organized using a structure we call a Yellow Card.

A System for Clearly Defining Innovation Concepts

Over the past 35-plus years, I've tried literally hundreds of different formats for defining ideas.

- We once used images to define ideas. However, the visuals by themselves created confusion, as people often interpreted the ideas differently.

- We once defined it as simply a "headline" for what the news was. However, this was not complete enough.

- We once used three slide presentation decks to explain ideas and one-page narratives. However, this became impossible to eventually communicate to customers in the short amount of space or time we had in the real world to pitch our idea.

Target Audience	became	Customer & **PROBLEM**
Overt Benefit	became	Customer **PROMISE**
Real Reason to Believe	became	Product/Service/System **PROOF**
Dramatic Difference	became	**MEANINGFULLY UNIQUE**

In my earlier books, I talked about defining Target Audience, Overt Benefit, Real Reason to Believe, and Dramatic Difference. With Innovation Engineering, we simplified this to Customer, Problem, Promise, and Proof. Simplifying the language has made it easier to enable everyone, everywhere to communicate ideas persuasively.

THE YELLOW CARD:
A Framework for Clearly Communicating Innovations

The Innovation Engineering framework for communicating ideas is called the Yellow Card. It's a two-sided card that makes it easy for anyone to understand an idea. Here's a quick overview of each element of a Yellow Card.

1. NAME: An innovation needs a name. When it has a name, it becomes real. Ideally, it is a name that is suggestive of the Meaningful Uniqueness that your innovation promises to potential customers or stakeholders.

Names matter a lot more than you would think. We ran an experiment with an artificial intelligence "reading system." We trained the computer system by providing names of new products and data on how successful they were. We then tested the model with a separate set of names and asked it to predict success. Amazingly, with just the name, the computer model made statistically significant predictions of success. This finding was the basis for our development of some of the world's most advanced artificial intelligence concept evaluation tools—Idea Scan, Idea Coach, and Merwyn Truth Teller—each of which is built into IE Labs.

2. HEADLINE: This is a simple statement of the Meaningful Uniqueness that your innovation offers. It's the fundamental news. Meaningful Uniqueness correlates directly with marketplace sales. Specifically, at the 99% confidence level when an idea is Meaningfully Unique:

- It's more likely to survive in the marketplace.
- More customers are likely to purchase it in year one.
- It increases the amount of money a customer spends with a company in a year.
- It increases the percentage of customers who make repeat purchases.

(continued on page 126)

Yellow Card™
A framework for clearly communicating innovations.
Start from the front or back side of card. Fill in all that you can.

INNOVATION ENGINEERING®

Innovation Name: _____

NAME that is suggestive of the benefit the innovation delivers

NEWS HEADLINE: *In a sentence - what makes your innovation MEANINGFULLY UNIQUE.*

_____

_____

_____

_____

CUSTOMER / STAKEHOLDERS: *WHO, specifically, benefits from this innovation?*

_____

_____

Customer/Stakeholder PROBLEM: *WHAT problem, specifically, does this idea address?*

_____

_____

_____

Benefit PROMISE: *Make a SPECIFIC or numeric promise to SOLVE this problem.*

_____

_____

_____

_____

_____

WHAT the Innovation is and **HOW** it can deliver this promise is on the BACK of CARD...

PROOF: _WHAT is the Innovation & HOW does it work.._

_____

_____

_____

_____

Customer PRICE / Stakeholder's COST: _First estimate / goal for price or cost._

_____

Raw Math Game Plan: _Your choice: a) Sales Potential, b) Cost to Develop, c) Savings, d) Other_

DEATH THREATS: _Rather than compromise on the idea start the process of problem solving._

1. <u>Death Threat:</u> _____

   DO to learn more: _____

2. <u>Death Threat:</u> _____

   DO to learn more: _____

PASSION _This project is important because..._

_____

This Innovation addresses a: ___Very Important Opportunity ___Very Important System

This is best described as an: ___ IE CORE Innovation or ___IE LEAP Innovation

Inventor's Autograph: _____Date_____

(continued from page 123)

- It increases the number of times a customer purchases in a year.
- It increases customers' likelihood to tell others (word of mouth/social networking effect).

Meaningful and Unique are in tension with one another. Done right, Meaningful and Unique create customer excitement. Done wrong, failure is certain. Done right, it helps customers quickly understand how the new offering will make their life better. Ideally, the "better" is of sufficient unique value that they are willing to pay more money for it.

3. CUSTOMER OR STAKEHOLDERS: This is the "who" that the innovation serves. With new or improved products or services, it's the customer who is the final decision-maker for purchasing. With internal system innovations, it's the stakeholders who are engaged and involved with the innovation.

Clarity on your customer/stakeholder provides focus to development efforts. The more you can fully visualize your customer, the easier it is to find the right words. Insight Mining, as discussed in the previous chapter, can also help with this.

When thinking of the customer, it's helpful to be specific. Are you focused on new or current customers, technically experienced or rookie customers, innovation thought leaders or followers?

A question I often ask when coaching someone who is crafting a Yellow Card is: "What group of customers might be willing to pay the most for the solution your innovation offers?"

4. PROBLEM: All innovations solve a customer problem. The problem can be a complaint, a frustration, or a wish for a better way to accomplish something. When your innovation solves a problem, then you have a **Meaningful**

PROBLEMS that MATTER
PROBLEMS that are REAL
PROBLEMS that are SPECIFIC

Benefit Promise. When your innovation solves a problem, for which there is no good solution, you have a **Meaningfully Unique** Benefit Promise.

The Customer Problem your innovation solves is the purpose of your innovation. Problems create a tension that motivates change. Problems motivate you and your team to find solutions. Solutions to problems motivate customers to change their current behavior and purchase from you.

A common mistake is attempting to provide a solution to a nonexistent problem. For an innovation to have motivational power with customers, it must be meaningful.

Corporate marketing departments often call the problem an "insight." It's a statement of the purpose of the innovation. Ross Love originated the concept of "customer insight" when he was vice president of advertising at Procter & Gamble and chairman of the board of the Association of National Advertisers. He told me that he institutionalized insights to provide focus to marketing efforts.

When I showed Ross a set of insights from corporate clients, he laughed. *"These aren't insights. They're meaningless."* I then showed Ross data detailing that the percentage of corporate innovations that were meaningfully unique innovations had declined over 70% in the past 14 years. Ross responded, *"So the problem is they don't have a real innovation. They're trying to make something out of nothing."*

Here are examples of flawed customer insights: much ado about nothing, overstating a small problem, or stating a problem that is not a real problem. I've crafted revised problem statements along with potential promises to give you an idea of what "good" looks like.

Customer Insight that's Vague/Expected

Are you looking to treat yourself?

Customer Insight as a Problem with a Promise

Do you love chocolate but feel guilty when you eat it?

New XYZ is actually good for your heart when enjoyed in moderation. That's because it contains . . .

Customer Insight that's Vague/Expected

Do you dislike cleaning your bathtub?

Customer Insight as a Problem with a Promise

Are you frustrated with the odor in your bathroom?

New XYZ bathroom cleaner makes a bathroom smell great for a week. That's because it not only destroys odor-causing bacteria, but it also leaves a coating that prevents them from multiplying again for more than seven days.

Maggie Pfeifer, director of Innovation Engineering Education, explains how adding specifics transforms generic insights: *"In class we teach students how to move from writing generic to specific. Generic is vague and expected. But specific actually TEACHES you about the problem in a way you didn't know, or quantifies the issue, or causes real tension because you didn't know just how bad it was.*

Generic: Looking to swap out diet soda with a healthier option?

Specific: The artificial sweetener in diet sodas can trick your body into actually storing fat and sugar!

A good indication that you're on the right track is if the problem you are solving causes a healthy level of "tension" for customers. The greater the feeling of anxiety, fear, frustration, or concern that customers feel from the problem you are addressing, the greater the chances that they will notice and like your solution.

5. BENEFIT PROMISE: This is a clear and specific promise to solve a specific problem that a specific customer has. Customers get excited and take notice of your product or service offering when it promises to solve a problem they have. Benefit Promise answers the customer question: "Why should I care?"

Analysis of thousands of new product and service concepts finds that when a Meaningfully Unique Benefit Promise is made, the probability of business success—and the return on investment for the effort you expend—more than doubles. (See *Jump Start Your Business Brain.*)

	Probability of Success
High-Benefit PROMISE	62%
Medium-Benefit PROMISE	44%
Low-Benefit PROMISE	27%

This is good news! It means that by simply communicating how your product or service will uniquely help your customers solve a meaningful problem, you can increase your odds of marketplace success.

You don't need to be fancy, flowery, or clever with your words to win customers. Simply telling customers in a direct and easy-to-understand manner what you can do for them works.

In my work with businesses, I've seen as much as a 45% increase in sales as a result of simply communicating a Meaningfully Unique Benefit Promise. It's important to note, however, that I've also seen cases in which no amount of enhancement can help a business. In these cases, the core product or service is just not Meaningfully Unique enough. The only way to generate significantly improved results is by changing the product or service.

A classic error with Benefit Promise is to mistake features for benefits.

Benefits are what's in it for the customer. A benefit is what your customer receives, enjoys, and/or experiences in exchange for investing time, trouble, trust, or money.

Features are the facts, figures, technology, and details that make up the structure of your product or service. Features often enable Benefit Promises. However, without communication of the Benefit Promise, it is

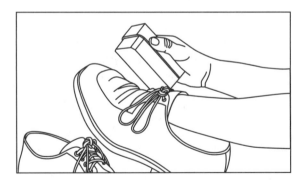

feature:
blend of three
waxes

benefit PROMISE:
shine that lasts two
times longer

left to the customer to figure out why the feature is important. And the more work required of customers, the less sales return you will realize.

Benefits are what customers pay for. They are the only profitable way to bring new customers to your business. The other option—deep discounts—is not a profitable choice. Customers acquired via low pricing usually are discount shoppers who just as quickly will leave for the next price deal that's offered.

The key to success with Benefit Promise is to be CLEAR. Research finds that writing a message that is easy to understand increases odds of success by 70%.

The key to success with Benefit Promise is to be FOCUSED. Research finds that by offering one or two benefits versus three or more benefits, your odds of success go up by almost 20%.

The key to success with Benefit Promise is to be SPECIFIC. Research finds that marketing messages with a numeric promise have a 52% greater chance of success in the marketplace. Ideally, it's a numeric promise such as "2X faster," "30% more effective," or "double the number of jobs created." Numbers really do matter. They make it very clear and very specific. Generic promises don't motivate.

6. PRODUCT OR SERVICE PROOF: This is a clear and easy-to-understand description of: 1) what the product/service innovation is and 2) how it makes the promise possible.

Benefit Promise gets customers excited. Proof helps you close the sale by providing the customer/stakeholder with the confidence that you will deliver on your Benefit Promise.

Customers are very cautious when it comes to making a commitment to purchase. Before they will act on their initial interest, they seek proof that the offering can/will deliver on the promise.

An analysis of thousands of new business concepts shows that providing Meaningfully Unique Product/Service Proof significantly increases your odds for success and, correspondingly, your return on effort expended.

	Probability of Success	
High PROOF	61%	
Medium PROOF	42%	
Low PROOF	28%	

Specific News

Numbers Matter!
Quantifying Benefit
Increases Odds of Success
by 52%

Proof is often simply explaining the product features that you avoid in the Promise. Proof is the innovation design features that make the Benefit Promise possible.

For example, the 2X longer shine from above—how can you promise that? Now it's time to talk about the features. That's because it has a blend of three waxes. The promise comes first, but the proof backs it up with the details of the "it." If it's a service, explain the steps in the process. If it's a new class, explain the curriculum. If it's a new type of chocolate, explain the ingredients that make the taste special.

Proof is becoming more and more important. Today, customer confidence in marketing promises is at an all-time low. The consumer research firm Yankelovich found that 93% of consumers do not have confidence in the advertising messages of major corporations. Customers' lack of confidence is not surprising, given the explosion of hype and lies they experience from marketing campaigns. The lies are extreme. From dot-com promises of great riches to politicians' campaign pledges, customers are subjected to lies and deceit. The trustworthiness deficit between customers and merchants has accumulated over time. The deficit has been built from hundreds of disappointing customer experiences.

Product/Service PROOF

The Product/Service PROOF
is **HOW** you will deliver
on your **PROMISE**

Problem ← PROMISE ← PROOF

Sadly, analysis finds that only 20% of concepts offer Product or Service Proof. That leaves 80% that don't. Is it a coincidence that just over 80% of all new products and services fail?

Telling the TRUTH is the primary and recommended way to communicate Product/Service Proof. There are also secondary ways to enhance credibility, such as pedigree, testimonials, test results, demonstrations, and guarantees. These are supplements, not replacements, for telling the truth about what you do that's different.

7. PRICE: This defines the cost the customer pays to receive the benefits promised. In the early stages of development, the price estimate will have high levels of variance. The fact that there is uncertainty is not a reason to not make a first estimate. The first estimate communicates your intentions for how Meaningfully Unique you anticipate your innovation to be. Guy Kawasaki, former Apple evangelist and best-selling author of books like *Selling the Dream* and *The Art of the Start,* told me:

> *Your selling price tells me what you think about your offering. If your price is higher than others, it tells me you think your offering is better. If it's priced the same, that means you think it's the same as others.*

8. PASSION: This is a statement of higher-order purpose. It gives clarity on why you care enough about this idea to dig into patents, do problem solving, and to address Death Threats, no matter how painful they appear to be. It is your intrinsic motivation for the journey. This is Deming's System of Profound Knowledge Point 3: Psychology.

Passion is what enables us to embrace the uncertainty that comes with ideas that are Meaningfully Unique. Argentinean chef Francis Mallmann defined the importance of embracing uncertainty:

> *My life has been a path at the edge of uncertainty. Today, I think we educate kids to be settled in a comfortable chair. You have your job, you have your little car, you have a place to sleep, and the dreams are dead. You don't grow on a secure path. All of us should conquer something in life. And it needs a lot of work. In order to grow and to improve, you have to be there at the edge of uncertainty.*

9. DEATH THREATS: This portion of the Yellow Card is about confronting the reality of the challenges that the innovation faces. Ideas that are Meaningfully Unique are by definition different from what has been done in the past.

The goal here is to acknowledge not resolve the challenges. Solutions will come through cycles of learning and adapting. What's most important is that we be honest with ourselves and with others about the challenges we see at this point in the process.

The Death Threats provide balance to the "customer pull" created by the customer-focused headline, problem, promise, and the "organizational pull" that the Math Game Plan sales forecast provides.

10. INVENTION SKETCH/MATH GAME PLAN: This is a space for creating the first drawing of the invention. It starts the process of defining the potential for patenting your innovation.

The Math Game Plan is a rough estimate of the benefit to the organization of the innovation. It can be an estimate of sales, profits, savings, efficiency improvement, etc. The estimate is a "back of the envelope" estimate that provides a starting point for "Plan, Do, Study, Act" cycles of learning.

Like all elements of the Yellow Card, the Math Game Plan estimate is a first hypothesis or theory of the Math Game Plan for the innovation.

Because of insecurity with math, many adults are scared of doing a Math Game Plan. In truth, these estimates are no more of a theory than the rest of the Yellow Card—customer, problem, promise, proof, and price.

Detailed principles, processes, and tools for doing first estimates and how to improve the estimates are outlined later in this chapter.

The Yellow Card: Your Idea Translated Into a Simple Story

The Yellow Card is a simple narrative that tells your story in simple language that hangs together. Here are some examples.

- **Customer:** Adults who love to eat fish when they go out for dinner

- **Problem:** Are you frustrated by the freshness of fish you buy at the grocery store?

- **Benefit Promise:** Now you can have restaurant-grade fresh fish at home.

- **Proof:** We can promise this because our fish is delivered daily to our stores, within 24 hours of coming out of the water.

- **Customer:** Conservation Advocates (this is an actual Yellow Card)

- **Problem:** Farmers are shooting cheetahs in Africa.

- **Benefit Promise:** Your donation of $500 will save the lives of five cheetahs over the next five years.

- **Proof:** Your donation will pay for an Anatolian Shepherd dog that will protect a farmer's cattle from cheetah attacks. Cheetahs don't attack cattle when there is a dog guarding them. And, when the cattle are safe, the farmers don't have to shoot the cheetahs. The estimate of five cheetahs is based on the average number of farm attacks and the reproduction cycle of cheetahs.

You Have Your First Yellow Card— Now the Improvement Journey Begins

With the first draft of the Yellow Card written, we now begin the process of improvement. Advertising legend David Ogilvy wrote: "I am a lousy copywriter, but I am a good editor. So I go to work on editing my own draft.

After four or five editing sessions, it looks good enough to show to the client." I feel the same about my book writing.

Originally we used an analytical editing approach of working on Problem separate from Promise and separate from Proof. This improved the clarity of each part, but most of the time it had little impact on the overall potential for the concept, as we missed the interactions of the parts.

Today, we look at our innovation concept as a "system." Recall our definition of a system: "Two or more parts that work together to accomplish a shared aim." This means that the success of the system is the product of the interaction of the parts.

To enable improvement of the concept as a "system," today we focus our energy on the interaction of the parts. We improve elements in the absolute and by looking at their interaction with other elements of the concept. In effect, we play Whack-A-Mole, trading off one element for another until we have the entire concept in balance.

The structure we use for looking at the interactions is called the "six tensions." The tensions provide a structural framework for editing our ideas and for giving feedback to others.

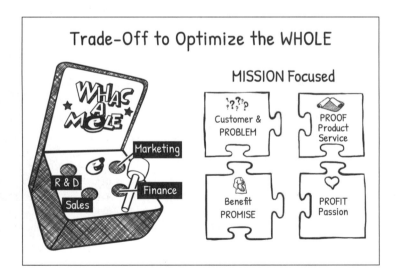

Look at the Concept as a System
Series of Six Tensions

Overall	Meaningfulness vs. Uniqueness
	───────────────────
	Problem vs. Promise
Fundamentals	Promise vs. Proof
	Problem vs. Proof
	───────────────────
Executional	Cost vs. Value
	Completeness vs. Simplicity

TENSION 1: MEANINGFULNESS VERSUS UNIQUENESS. This is the most fundamental of the tensions. The more unique your idea is, the more likely it is to be either a real "Wow" or really "Weird." It's a balancing act. We want to be different in a way that matters. In practice, organizations rarely pursue ideas that are Unique but not Meaningful. What is common is they pursue concepts that are Meaningful but not nearly as Unique as they think they are. No customer cares that you are pursuing an innovation that is "new to your organization." They only care about innovations that are "new to their world."

TENSION 2: PROBLEM VERSUS PROMISE. The more significant the Problem, the more significant the Promise needs to be. Problem and Promise must be in balance. For example, if the Problem is "you have a 60% chance of death," then a Promise that "you will cut your risk of death by 1%" is not significant. The Yellow Card format makes it easy to quickly review Problem versus Promise. Ask yourself the simple question: "If you had this Problem, would this Promise get you excited?"

TENSION 3: PROMISE VERSUS PROOF. This tension answers the customer question: "Why should I care?" The bigger the Promise, the bigger the Proof that is needed. The starting point of Proof is telling the truth about why you can deliver on a Promise when others can't. What are you doing that is different from others? When consumers do business with you for the first time, they perceive a risk. The risk they feel is even bigger if they are purchasing on behalf of a company. They perceive that a wrong decision could cause them to lose their job.

TENSION 4: PROBLEM VERSUS PROOF. Customers with a Problem have usually been disappointed by others in their quest for a solution. Each disappointment builds their distrust of those offering solutions to their Problem. The key question here is focused around clarity on what is being done differently? What is new? What is the WOW?

TENSION 5: COST VERSUS VALUE. This tension is the ratio of the difference in what the customer receives divided by the difference in what it costs. The key question is: "Will customers perceive the change we are offering, relative to cost, as a great deal?" They must get more for their money from you than they can get from others.

TENSION 6: COMPLETENESS VERSUS SIMPLICITY. We must be clear and complete with our Meaningful Uniqueness. However, our messages must also be simple enough to be easily understood. Resolving this tension often requires a fresh rewrite, using analogies to make the technical WOW of our offering easy to understand. Your goal is a reading level near the fifth-grade level. Most word processors have tools that measure the reading level of your writing.

The Truth and Nothing but the Truth

Your Yellow Card concept begins as a theory or hypothesis on what will both excite your customers and be profitably feasible for your organization to produce. Upon completing the cycles of learning, you have an outline for your marketing message. The most important advice I can give you at this point is to tell the truth and nothing but the truth about what your innovation delivers.

In today's world, customers are learning the truth behind marketing trickery faster than ever. With the internet and social media, the TRUTH—the WHOLE TRUTH about a new product, service, or even a new restaurant—travels faster than any marketing campaign.

To make it worse, internet price shopping and bidding systems make it easy for everyone to buy cheaper. And when there is no difference between offerings, the discounting systems become the true driver of sales volumes.

Great marketing communications tell the *truth* about what makes our innovation Meaningfully Unique. There are no lies, hype, smoke, or mirrors. In 1912, Harry McCann and four partners launched an advertising agency based on the philosophy of **"Truth Well Told."** I LOVE this slogan. If more businesspeople lived it, we would all be better off.

The problem with living "Truth Well Told" isn't the "well told" part. The problem for most business leaders is telling the truth. I don't mean the legal truth. Lawyers make sure of that. And if they don't, their competitors quickly do. I mean truth in the sense of telling customers exactly, precisely, what makes a product or service amazing.

When the "truth" is that your product or service is Meaningfully Unique, then telling the story well (well told) is easy. The reality is that **at least 95% of Marketing Problems are product/service problems.**

The greatest marketing guru in the world can't transform the "same old, same old" into something that is Meaningfully Unique. And, frankly, if a marketing person claims to be able to create magic with your commodity offering—fire them or don't hire them. The president of one of the world's most successful advertising agencies, after a few glasses of great red wine, confessed to me at dinner one night in New York City:

> *Give me a product that's really different in a way that matters [Meaningfully Unique] and I'll guarantee you great advertising that sells a lot of product. Give me a product that is the same as all the others and I'll give you expensive advertising that makes creative directors proud and wins competitions, but it probably won't work. Clients don't understand that advertising success comes from great products, not commercials.*

The most powerful means to build credibility is to tell customers the honest truth about what makes your offering innovative. The real truth has a natural vitality that customers can feel and sense like no amount of boasting, hype, or marketing speak can ever create. To quote Ben Franklin, "What you would seem to be, be really."

> *The most essential gift for a good writer is a built-in, shock-proof shit detector. This is the writer's radar and all great writers have had it.* —Ernest Hemingway

A clear test of an honest message is that you wouldn't hesitate to sign your name to it—or to tell your grandmother about it—or to tell your child about it. With real truth, there is no room for hedges of any kind. No "sort ofs," "mostlys," "in certain cases," or "kindas" are allowed. The message is just the truth and nothing but the truth.

This is good news. It means that marketing is not a magic art. It's simple. Just make a great offering and tell customers the honest truth about how it will make a meaningful difference in their lives.

Math Game Plan: The Gas Pedal for Change

Math Game Plan is a first math forecast of what impact the customer concept is estimated to have. It's what the organization will realize as a result of pursuing the Yellow Card. It can take many forms. Common Math Game Plans include estimates of sales growth, fund-raising revenue, or cost savings from a system innovation.

For a nonprofit, the number is often connected to their mission. Examples that Innovation Engineering pioneers have calculated for nonprofits include: the number of endangered birds saved; the number of youth graduating from college in science, technology, or engineering; and the number of inner-city youth getting jobs.

The greatest barrier to innovation at most companies is internal resistance to change. A primary reason for the resistance is that, while there is clarity on the costs and difficulties associated with an innovation, there is often little understanding of the value of the innovation. Math Game Plan estimates what the organization could realize as a result of pursuing the innovation.

Math Game Plan brings the Customer, Problem, Promise, and Proof to life. It's a first theory or a "game plan" on how the innovation will become real. This first estimate, just like Customer, Problem, Promise, Proof, has a high level of variation/error in it. We use it as a starting place for "Plan, Do, Study, Act" cycles of learning to reduce variation/error.

The problem with doing the math early in the development process is making estimates when there is high uncertainty. Fortunately, there are validated and proven systems for estimating math when you have little information.

The math section of the Innovation Engineering courses is one of the most important topic areas. It could fill a complete book by itself. However, my publisher says it would have a limited audience. Here's an

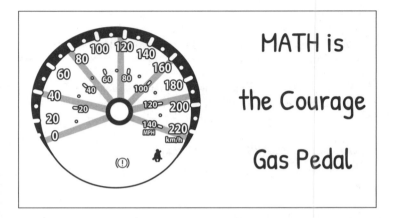

overview of some of the math methods we teach in Innovation Engineering courses on and off campus.

1. FERMI ESTIMATING: This is a method for estimating when there is high uncertainty. It's based on a methodology developed by Nobel Prize winner Enrico Fermi. In simple terms, it's a disciplined "back of the envelope" estimating approach that involves breaking your challenge into elements that you can easily estimate. For example, if you are estimating the sales for a new restaurant, you might deconstruct your estimate into the number of customers per night, the amount paid per customer for food, and the amount paid per customer for alcohol.

Fermi Estimates are first estimates. They have high variance and uncertainty but are invaluable in providing focus to commercialization efforts. As statistician George E. P. Box said:

> *"Essentially all models are wrong . . . some are useful."*

The elements that make up the first estimate with the highest variation/uncertainty become the focus of "Plan, Do, Study, Act" cycles of learning to reduce variation. Statistically, we teach students how to quantify uncertainty by taking the standard deviation of the estimate and dividing by the best estimate. If you're not a math person, don't stress. With IE Labs, we do all of the math and tell you with simple red, yellow, and green stoplight coloring where the greatest risk is. You then know where to focus your energy to get the greatest reduction in risk.

To Enable EVERYONE to Do Math, We Teach . . .
Fermi Estimating
Creating Estimates with Limited Information

Step 1: Deconstruct into a Few Factors You Can Estimate

Step 2: Estimate Factors and Give Reasons

Step 3: Do Simple Math to Answer Question

In Innovation Engineering courses, we teach and provide tools to reduce variation in estimates using: 1) Stimulus Mining, 2) Calibration versus known examples, and 3) Rapid Research Tests to measure values. Two very advanced tools that we teach, that are included in IE Labs, include:

- Trailblazer delphi is a systematic approach to estimating the unknown. Academic studies of delphi accuracy find that, by five to one, it beats both debating as a group to find an answer and averaging responses from experts.

- Risk-adjusted Monte Carlo simulation. It's a simple system on computers, where you enter the mean and uncertainty (standard deviation, best/worst case) for each measured and estimated input. Your innovation is then introduced into the market 10,000 times, resulting in 10,000 estimates of what will happen. This models the variance, allowing you to easily understand your probability of achieving various levels of sales, cost savings, or whatever your dependent variable is.

2. FOUR-WOODLOCK SALES FORECASTING: Fourt-Woodlock is the world's most validated method for forecasting sales for innovations that are Meaningfully Unique (ideas for new categories or that will grow existing categories). It's a trial-and-repeat model that builds your sales forecast from the ground up.

The equation for calculating Fourt-Woodlock is simple. The challenge with executing it is in gathering the inputs for the model. To do a Fourt-Woodlock forecast you need to estimate or gather from customer research:

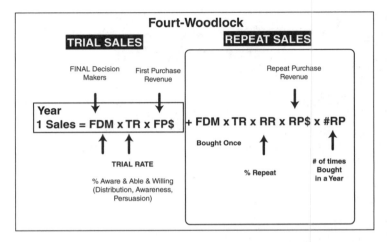

the Number of Possible Customers, Marketing Investment (customer awareness and distribution), Innovation Persuasion, Revenue per First Purchase, Percentage Repeat Rate, Revenue per Repeat Purchase, and number of additional Repeat Purchases per repeater.

3. COST AND PRICE ESTIMATING: A sales forecast is only half of your Math Game Plan. The other half is the cost to produce the product or service and the selling price for our innovation. Estimating of the cost of innovations and selling price for incremental CORE innovations involves benchmarking and adjusting for differences in your idea versus others that already exist.

With disruptive LEAP innovations, or innovations in new categories, it can be a challenge to develop estimates. To make the process easy, we teach how to use published data on percentages for Cost of Goods Sold, Overhead, and Profit to create a first estimate of costs or selling price. The first estimate is then adjusted based on the Meaningful Uniqueness of the innovation.

The percentages for all industries and sizes of companies can be found in government summaries of business tax returns. To enable you to do these estimates in just a few minutes, IE Labs includes a tool called New Market GPS, which includes key data for every industry in the world, categorized based on the size of the company. It makes it easy for everyone to do first estimates of cost and profits in minutes.

Great Thinkers Are Great Writers

Writing is hard because thinking is hard. With Innovation Engineering, writing is a thinking tool. Unlike tweets, conversations, or bullets on slides, concept writing is about communicating an idea that can make a difference in the world. It involves communicating your innovation with clarity.

> *Writing is something that you can never do as well as it can be done. It is a perpetual challenge and it is more difficult than anything else that I have ever done, so I do it. And it makes me happy when I do it well.* —Ernest Hemingway

The good news is that there are systems and processes that you can use to help you think deeper and write smarter. The ideas in this chapter are a start. Practice is required to turn the new methods into habits. As fellow University of Maine graduate Stephen King wrote:

> *If you want to be a writer, you must do two things above all others: read a lot and write a lot. I'm aware of NO SHORTCUT.*
> —Stephen King, *On Writing*

Communicating your innovation as a concept makes it clear to those inside and outside your organization what your idea is and why it is Meaningful to customers, to the organization, and to you. This Meaningfulness fuels the energy required to embark on the Commercialization journey— the subject of the next chapter.

What Did You Learn?

- Think of a time when you communicated well. What was the impact?
- Think of a time when you communicated poorly. What were the consequences?
- What format do you use to communicate your initial ideas?
- How is your format different from the Yellow Card format?
- Which of the six tensions do you most commonly do great on? Or do poorly on?
- Do you do the math? If not, why not?

8

LEARNING MINDSET:
Commercialize System

One of the things that really hurt Apple was after I left, John Sculley got a very serious disease. And that disease—I've seen other people get it too—it's the disease of thinking that a really great idea is 90 percent of the work.

And that if you just tell all these other people, "Here's this great idea," then of course they can go off and make it happen. The problem with that is that there's just a tremendous amount of craftsmanship in between a great idea and a great product.

And as you evolve that great idea, it changes and grows. It never comes out like it starts because you learn a lot more as you get into the subtleties of it.

And you also find there are tremendous tradeoffs that you have to make. There are just certain things you can't make electrons do. There are certain things you can't make plastic do. Or glass do. Or factories do. Or robots do.

And as you get into all these things, designing a product is keeping five thousand things in your brain, these concepts, and fitting them all together, and continuing to push them together in new and different ways to get what you want.

And every day you discover something new that is a new problem or a new opportunity to fit these things together a little differently. And, it's that process that is the magic.

—Steve Jobs
Steve Jobs: The Lost Interview

This interview with Steve Jobs, the legendary cofounder of Apple, aligns with my 40 years of experience with innovation. Ninety percent of the magic behind WOW products, services, or operational systems is the system used to move from idea to reality.

Does Your Innovation-Development System Increase or Decrease the Value of Ideas?

Sitting in the great room at the Eureka! Ranch are 10 top executives from one of the world's largest companies. They need help accelerating the discovery and development of disruptive LEAP innovations.

I start with a simple question: "What happens to the value of an innovation as it goes through your development system? Does the value (sales forecast for the project) go up, down, or stay the same?" There is an awkward silence. Then the chief technology officer speaks, "I know the answer. We did a study and found that when ideas come out of development they are worth a little less than half what they were worth when they went into development."

"So your system for innovation development," I responded with a smile, "is actually a system for managing the decline of ideas. The system is like hospice. It's palliative care. You are managing the decline of ideas."

There is a nervous laugh in the room as I set the vision for what is possible. "Now imagine if instead of declining by 50%, your system made them grow by 28%. That's what Innovation Engineering is delivering during commercialization."

The Secret to Growing 28% Versus Declining by 50%

To realize a growth in value of 28% instead of a decline of 50% requires a shift of mindset from "command and control" to one of never-ending innovation and learning.

The idea of "never-ending innovation and learning" is hard to argue with. However, the consequence of this is a need to embrace never-ending, continuous improvement in your ideas as they move from objective through development to reality. And at many companies, never-ending change is perceived to be uncontrolled chaos. Senior leaders at large companies prize consistency, as they don't have the time or mental bandwidth to keep up with continuous learning.

To ensure that the "never-ending innovation and learning" is productive, not destructive, employees are taught to leverage Dr. Deming's System of Profound Knowledge Point 4: Theory of Knowledge. It's known by many names: a) Plan, Do, Study, Act, b) PDSA, c) Deming Cycle, d) Shewhart cycle, or e) Scientific Method. The Innovation Engineering community has branded it irreverently as "Fail FAST, Fail CHEAP" (FFFC) cycles of learning. The all caps emphasis of FAST and CHEAP is on purpose. It puts the emphasis on being rapid and efficient versus failing.

The pursuit of cycles of learning requires that you are personally engaged in and excited about your innovation. As singer, songwriter, and Nobel Prize winner Bob Dylan said:

> *Everything worth doing takes time. You have to write a hundred bad songs before you write one good one. And you have to sacrifice a lot of things that you might not be prepared for. Like it or not, you are in this alone and have to follow your own star.*

A New Leadership Mindset

"Plan, Do, Study, Act" is a method for increasing innovation speed and decreasing risk. It is also a mindset for how to think, work, and lead in a world where change is accelerating. It provides a structure for learning, pivoting, and adapting to the changing world. It allows organizations to change faster than the marketplace is changing. **When a PDSA learning mindset is embraced, success is a certainty. The only thing we can't predict is how many PDSA learning cycles will be required.**

A learning mindset requires humbleness. It requires a willingness to admit "I don't know." This can be terrifying for adults who have mistakenly connected their sense of self worth with knowing all the answers. In days past, this might have been reasonable. Today, with the speed of technological and marketplace change, it's not possible to know everything.

The new world requires that leaders and organizational cultures embrace curiosity, and learning becomes the first priority for everyone, everywhere, every day.

Learning can't be random. It needs to be focused on one of the organization's strategic priorities to be meaningful. In the world of Innovation Engineering, these are called Blue Cards. They are explained in detail in the next chapter. Here's how the overall system works . . .

Leadership Sets Strategic Priorities (Blue Card)	Employees Create Ideas to Realize Strategy (Yellow Card)	PDSA Cycles of Learning by Project Teams	Organizational Success Metrics
			• Innovation Pipeline
			• Proactive Culture
			• Joy in Work

This system ensures that learning is strategically focused on the very important opportunities and challenges the organization faces. The business gains a competitive advantage, as it can learn and apply the learning faster than competition can.

"PLAN, DO, STUDY, ACT" Amplifies Learning Efficacy

"Plan, Do, Study, Act" reduces waste and randomness during the learning process.

PLAN starts the process with a clear definition of the goal. It defines what success looks like for the challenge we are addressing to develop the innovation defined on our Yellow Card. It could be a concept score with customers, a technical performance level, or a qualitative result, such as the approval of our organization's regulatory department to our new product design.

Challenges are called Death Threats. As in a Death Threat to the project succeeding. Tasks to be completed are clustered together as Milestones.

The name *Death Threat* provides emotional intensity that matches the feelings of fear that adults have when facing the unknowns that are inherent in Meaningfully Unique Innovations. The term also enables honest conversations about critical issues without igniting defensiveness. Instead of saying, "Your idea can't work," executives are taught to say, "There could be a Death Threat with this idea . . ." By defining the challenge as an "it" that is a Death Threat, we move it to the less confrontational third person instead of the more personal first person "I" or second person "you."

Defining Yellow Card development issues as Death Threats reduces defensiveness and makes for more productive conversations. A few years ago, during an Innovation Engineering project, an R&D director proposed a new product. The CEO, reverting to historical behavior, sniped, "That idea is ridiculous. Your math won't work."

The R&D director's enthusiasm deflated instantly.

I jumped in, speaking directly to the CEO, "Let's say that again the new way, 'There could be a Death Threat with making the math work for this Yellow Card.'"

A silence came over the room as everyone waited to see how the CEO would react. He smiled. "That's right, there could be a Death Threat with the math."

The room erupted in laughter and support for the CEO. He clearly wanted to learn the new way of working. He thanked me later: "I know there are unintended consequences from my behaviors that I don't even realize."

The R&D manager actually had thought through the math. And, in fact, that's why he was excited about the idea. However, in the old way of working, it would have been hard to get that message out.

The innovation ended up going to market with record speed. To his credit, at a meeting of the company's top executives, the CEO told the story of how this innovation had come to life. He admitted that he had been wrong and had reinforced the value of the new Innovation Engineering mindset.

DO is your theory of what action will help you achieve the success standard articulated in PLAN to make your Yellow Card innovation real. It can be a specific piece of work, an activity, or an experiment. To increase speed, we break achieving the PLAN into small, fast, and cheap learning cycles. By taking on achieving the PLAN "one bite at a time," we build momentum and maintain the ability to pivot based on new learning.

This can be a challenge for organizations, as they are "hardwired" on how their system accomplishes various tasks. For example, I was working with an industrial company on ideas that were in industrial markets that they didn't currently sell to. It was 5 p.m. The Death Threat was the unknown nature of the market. They explained that it would cost $50,000 and two months for an outside consultant to complete a study for them on the market.

"Hmmm," I said. "How could we do it faster and cheaper? How could we learn more?" No answer. So I turned it up a little. "How could we learn more by our next meeting tomorrow morning at 9 o'clock? I realize that it's 5 o'clock here. But it's morning in Asia."

They laughed. And when they realized I wasn't joking, they started to identify solutions. The next morning the meeting started 15 minutes late, as the team was on the phone with someone in Europe getting a briefing on the industry. From that call and other internet research and emails, they quickly learned that they had real advantages in the new market. They mitigated the Death Threat at this point and moved the project forward.

STUDY entails thinking deeply about what has been learned during the DO activities relative to the PLAN. Why did the activity not result in success? And, just as importantly, why did the activity achieve the desired outcome?

Note: In many Japanese-quality systems, the Deming Cycle is labeled PDCA (Plan, Do, Check, Act). Dr. Deming always called the third step STUDY. He always called it PDSA. Having lived through thousands of cycles of learning, I've come to realize that CHECK versus STUDY is a difference that matters.

CHECK IS TACTICAL. It's about ticking the box, as in "the activity worked" or "the activity failed." Check records task completion.

STUDY IS LEARNING. It's about THINKING DEEPLY. It is a theory of knowledge. It ignites new understanding and discoveries. Study creates hope for the future.

A recent project team I worked with had completed dozens of PDSA learning cycles. Each cycle was executed with discipline and documentation. We felt we were making progress. Then suddenly we hit a wall. What we predicted, based on our theory at the time, was not happening. The product suddenly got worse. We stopped and did a broader STUDY reflection across all of the cycles we had completed.

Our study session raised some questions we couldn't answer. We did Stimulus Mining of patent filings, academic articles, and commercial vendors. After about two hours, combining the learning from the PDSA cycles with the new Stimulus Mining, we discovered a new theory that could explain the bigger-picture factor that we had missed previously. We turned to our written documentation and, sure enough, in one of our early test runs there was a product that would confirm or disconfirm our new theory.

We ran to the lab and pulled the sample. Eureka! The sample confirmed our new theory. We had discovered a new and better way of making the product. When we had made that test sample, we had the wrong theory in our mind. As a result, we missed the discovery. It was only by stepping back and completing a deep STUDY that we discovered what turned out to be a major breakthrough.

When we reflected, as we often do, on what we had learned from the experience, my comment was: *"Dr. Deming was right—it's not enough to simply CHECK results versus the PLAN. We need to STUDY and THINK deeper. And frankly, in many cases real STUDY may require Stimulus Mining and diversity to reach real understanding."* The experience has made me fanatical in challenging teams to THINK deeply about what they really learned.

ACT is about deciding where the project should go next based on what has been learned. There are three common options:

1. Declare victory, as the PLAN has been achieved, thus the project's Death Threat or Milestone has been resolved.

2. Decide to archive the project because you conclude that the work required to achieve the PLAN is not worth the effort.

3. Repeat the cycle with a different activity and/or make changes to the Yellow Card based on what you've learned. For example, during early stages of PDSA cycles, it's not uncommon for new discoveries to identify an even more powerful Benefit Promise than what is currently on the Yellow Card. Or, to find that there is a different customer group that represents a bigger opportunity.

The most frequent option is number three because the challenge has been broken into a set of small steps.

In rare cases, the ACT step results in a recommendation to modify the success standard set in the PLAN. I would caution you to not do this unless you have learned something tangible and specific that makes it clear that the standard is no longer appropriate.

On a project for a company in Europe, we made a change in the PLAN standard, only instead of going down we took the standard up. This was done because, simultaneous with the weekly learning cycle, new research found that the success standard we had been using was not high enough to ignite word-of-mouth diffusion/awareness.

The impact of the higher PLAN standard was that the team had to be bolder with their changes to the concepts and products, which suddenly were not Meaningfully Unique enough. In this case, it was a positive change, as it inspired innovation. Within four weeks, two concepts and products achieved the new standard.

Most PDSA cycles involve one PLAN followed by multiple DO/STUDY iterations until the cycle is resolved. Others are more complex in scope, requiring simultaneous DO/STUDY efforts.

Mary Beard, a leader of the women's suffrage movement, captured the essence of the relationship between STUDY and ACT well when she wrote: "Action without study is fatal. Study without action is futile."

Four Keys to Success with "PLAN, DO, STUDY, ACT"

1. STUDY IS WHERE THE REAL LEARNING OCCURS: The most important of the four elements of PDSA is STUDY. It's where the real learning occurs. Importantly, this is not study as an independent entity. Rather, it's about STUDYING what happened as a result of the DO. It's about thinking deeply about why our theory worked or why it didn't. This is where the real learning occurs.

2. DOCUMENTATION: Documenting each step of the PDSA cycle creates accountability, alignment, and a sense of accomplishment for the team. Written "Plan, Do, Study, and Act" cycles enhance clarity. Documentation doesn't have to be complex; it can be one or two sentences. The world we live in is fast-paced, which is a good thing. However, when we stop to write precisely what our PLAN is, what we are going to DO, what we learned from our STUDY, and what our ACT is, we get smarter. Just as importantly, it is also possible for others, sometime in the future, to learn from our experiences as well.

Documentation is best done on a digital platform like IE Labs. When learnings are available in one place, instead of held in our heads or in dozens of individual digital files, we enable the exponential power of diversity. **Quick Rant:** At Procter & Gamble, when I took over a brand as brand manager, I would spend a weekend reading the brand filing cabinet. It contained hard copies of past business reviews and one-page memos. This quickly gave me an understanding of the brand history and the rationale for past decisions. Today, the digital cloud makes this a nearly impossible task. Last week it took 15 hours of searching on a company's server for a director of marketing to get details on just three new product introductions.

3. REGULAR RHYTHM: Innovation requires change, and most people don't like change. A regular rhythm of learning cycles builds momentum for change. The rhythm can be hourly, daily, or weekly. The best practice today appears to be two or three cycles a week. The longest recommended learning cycle is seven days.

The faster the cycles, the faster the learning. If a DO task requires more than seven days, it's recommended that you break it into subcomponents that can be worked in a week. This keeps the project at the top of the mind and builds momentum.

We've found it particularly helpful to use really fast cycles at the start of projects to ignite momentum toward change. Hourly cycles are built into four-day Innovation Engineering Accelerator projects.

4. SMALL STEPS BUILD COURAGE: A key component of PDSA is to embrace small steps with each learning cycle. It almost doesn't matter how big the steps are. What's most important is that they be completed with documentation and discipline. Personally, I prefer that teams execute 10 small learning cycles quickly versus three big ones slowly. That's because, with each PDSA cycle, learning, courage, and confidence grow. In Japan, this is a way of working and living called *Kaizen,* or improvement. As Robert Maurer, PhD, writes in *One Small Step Can Change Your Life: The Kaizen Way:*

> *All changes, even positive ones, are scary. Attempts to reach goals through radical or revolutionary means often fail because they heighten fear. But the small steps of Kaizen disarm the brain's fear response, stimulating rational thought.*

PDSA is not a justification for sloppy work. It's not about "throwing ideas against the wall to see what sticks." It's not a random walk of experimentation with low-cost activities. "Plan, Do, Study, Act" is a disciplined system of learning that enables great things. It is, as Dr. Deming defined it, a Theory of Knowledge. It's how real learning happens.

A common question is: How does PDSA work on long-term R&D projects at companies, universities, or government labs? In these cases, some learning cycles may be longer than seven days. However, weekly meetings, even if they are very short, are still important to maintain the learning mindset. The goal is always to try and learn something every week.

How to Organize the PDSA Cycles: The Phase Gate Model of Development

Phase Gate was created in the 1960s by the American Association of Cost Engineers and the NASA space program for managing high-risk and complex development projects. In the late 1980s, professor Robert Cooper created a version he branded as Stage-Gate.

The original purpose of Phase Gate was to control risk. In the old world, gates were used as decision points to inspect the product—or in our case, innovation—for flaws before making additional investments of time, energy, or money in the Innovation. This is how Detroit manufactured cars in the 50s and 60s. And this is also how most corporations manage their innovation development today.

The new world way of Phase Gate is to build quality into the system by enabling workers to create quality as they build the product or innovation. This is the way Toyota creates cars. This is the way Innovation Engineering companies manage their innovation pipeline.

The new world aim of Phase Gate systems is to Enable instead of Control. The Innovation Engineering community has developed systems for making the transition to a new world Phase Gate approach easy.

A Phase Gate System That Enables Increased Innovation Speed and Decreases Risk

Classic Phase Gate systems provide teams with checklists that tell them what standards they need to meet to get through the next gate. The Innovation Engineering system enables teams by telling them not only **what** needs to be done but also **why** it needs to be done and **how** to best accomplish it. The explanation of why and how enables employees to think more deeply.

WHAT defines clearly what success looks like for this Death Threat or Milestone. Sadly, most WHAT standards I've seen are soft, adaptable, and not always relevant for each project. The result is each project is treated as an individual event. Standards for success are set seemingly randomly on a case-by-case basis. The result is a world of chaos for those leading projects, as the rules for approval have massive variance.

WHY explains in simple language why this Death Threat/Milestone is very important for increasing innovation speed and decreasing risk. This understanding of the "bigger picture" creates greater engagement of project teams.

HOW provides a clear starting point for the organization's best practices for resolving this Death Threat or reaching this Milestone. Inside the IELabs.com portal it includes references to 100-plus short videos that teach how to do each best practice.

All of the Death Threats/Milestones are focused on reducing uncertainty and risk with the innovation. They are divided into three types of risks:

1. **Market Risks** involve the route to market and end user.
2. **Technology Risks** involve the development, production, and delivery of the innovation.
3. **Organizational Risks** involve financial, strategic, legal, regulatory, etc. issues.

THINK Before You Begin Development

To enable speed and success with innovation projects, we add DEFINE and DISCOVER phases before the classic DEVELOP and DELIVER phases. The aim of these disciplined front-end phases is to get clarity on the whole idea before entering the DEVELOP phase. We have found that adding these phases before development increases development success by up to 250%. Dr. Deming predicted this improvement in speed and effectiveness in his book *The New Economics:*

> *The secret to reduction in time of development is to put more effort into the early stages, and to study the interaction between stages. Each stage should have the benefit of more effort than the next stages.*
>
> *It is impossible to eliminate backtracking entirely, but under the scheme proposed here, backtracking will be reduced and will be more effective, the whole development speedier, with reduction of total cost.*

Phases vary by company and industry. The Innovation Engineering community uses simple names for the phases: DEFINE, DISCOVER, DEVELOP, and DELIVER. The time and money invested in each phase is not equal. As the following graphic indicates, the two big decision points are before DEVELOP and DELIVER, as these are where research finds the bulk of the investment (60% and 30%) is made. The purpose of the front-end phases, DEFINE and DISCOVER, is to reduce waste in these stages.

Step by Step:
DEFINE, DISCOVER, DEVELOP, DELIVER

In DEFINE, the entire idea is defined: Customer (stakeholder for system innovations), Problem, Promise, Proof, Price, Math Game Plan (sales, savings, improvement), and key Death Threats. Everything is defined at one time, as opposed to on a sequential basis of hand-offs from marketing to R&D to production and sales. This enables the innovation to be addressed as a system of interconnected parts.

In DEFINE, there is often a lot of uncertainty. Those areas with the greatest uncertainty are labeled as Death Threats and are often our first areas of focus during the DISCOVER Phase.

In DISCOVER, we run rapid cycles of "Plan, Do, Study, Act," learning to problem solve and reduce uncertainty in the project's Death Threats. As the project is not yet in development, the team is small and focused on optimizing the whole, as opposed to accomplishing departmental tasks.

In DISCOVER, teams focus on the biggest Death Threats first. We don't want the team working the small issues for six months, only to find out that, when they focus on the big Death Threats, the project is a no-go. Working on the biggest, most critical issues first is contrary to human nature. Procter & Gamble has found that it's important to start with the big issues. A. G. Lafley wrote:

> *Teams like to address easy issues first. At P&G we have flipped the sequence. Teams must identify so-called killer issues— problems that must be solved for the innovation to succeed.*

When the project is ready, a one-page Development Recommendation (sometimes called by companies: Basis for Interest, Business Case, or

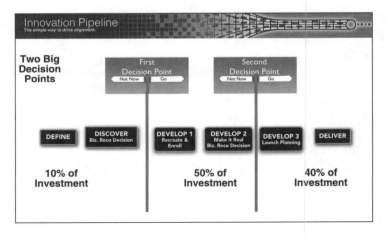

Business Opportunity Recommendation) based on the Procter & Gamble one-page memo format plus attachments is used to gain approval from leadership/investors to move into the DEVELOP phase, where the bulk of the work is done to make the innovation real. As the development has not yet been done, the Development Recommendation is very rough. It's a fact-supported "hypothesis" for what the innovation could become with the investment of time, energy, and money in development. It covers the strategic need (Blue Card), core idea (Yellow Card), preliminary customer research data, proof of concept/technology, rough economics, and ideas and advice from across the organization. Importantly, the Development Recommendation review process is used as a forum for gathering ideas and advice from leaders. We do this because leadership's wisdom is most valuable early in the process, when there is time to utilize it—before large amounts of time, energy, and money have been invested in the idea.

DEVELOP is where you make the idea real. It's where the bulk of time, energy, and money is invested. With small and midsize organizations, DEVELOP is often one phase. At large, complex organizations it is commonly divided into three phases. They are known as: DEVELOP One, DEVELOP Two, and DEVELOP Three—or as DEVELOP Alpha, DEVELOP Beta, and DEVELOP 1st Release.

When DEVELOP is divided into three phases, the first is one of "Re-create and Enroll." It's a phase dedicated to looking at the innovation as a whole. The purpose is to optimize the overall innovation to maximize speed to market and probability of success.

It's often done with a cross-functional team of managers from sales, finance, technology, regulatory, etc. Their mission is to think through the tactical consequences of the innovation. Their focus is on how to best optimize the idea to accomplish the overall strategic mission (Blue Card). This mindset of "optimizing the whole" to accomplish the project mission is maintained throughout the development process. This process of optimizing the whole is the same when developing innovations for upgrading internal systems of operations.

The focus of the second DEVELOP phase is to Make it Real. It's where the bulk of the work is done to make the innovation real. This is where lots of trade-offs occur, as the actual technology, the customer reaction to prototypes, and the costs don't come out exactly as expected. This phase concludes the presentation of a Go Live Recommendation to leadership. This is the time for leadership and project teams to confront the realities of the project with honest and critical thinking. The Go Live review is best done when the project is about 95% complete. This doesn't mean that the work is stopping at this point—rather that there are still final to-do tasks to be completed, be it final artwork design, marketing, product design details, etc.

The review is held at the 95% completion stage to provide time to work through the inevitable ideas and advice provided by leadership/investors on the business opportunity. From experience, we find that it is only when asked to make a real launch decision that leadership really, honestly focuses true critical thinking on business opportunities. By leaving some "space" to make changes, we reduce frustration, rework, and wasted effort prematurely going from 95% to 100%.

In our best-practice approach, approval to launch is contingent on a specific to-do list of tasks. These tasks are the focus of the third DEVELOP phase, known as Launch Planning. Here, the teams work through the to-do tasks, and they get operations, distribution, sales, marketing, PR, etc., organized to bring the innovation into reality.

DELIVER is when the product or service goes to market or the system change is implemented. It's about adapting quickly as customers/stakeholders and competition react to its introduction. The reality of life is that things will not happen as expected. I can guarantee you that you will be surprised. The customer and competition will react differently than expected. These changes do not mean that all your work during DEFINE, DISCOVER, and DEVELOP are wasted efforts. If you had not done them, the surprises you'd experience would be even greater. If your team has confidence in its ability to execute rapid cycles of learning, and to simultaneously engineer solutions, then they will simply continue the process of never-ending continuous improvement.

Organizing for Success: Innovation Roles

Positions on a sports team provide clarity of roles. The same is true with innovation teams. The Innovation Engineering movement has found four roles to be very important.

1. THE PROJECT LEADER: Without a doubt, this is the most fun role of the three roles. This is the primary driver of the project. He or she is the energy source that drives the idea forward. The role is modeled on the role of the Toyota Chief Engineer and the classic Procter & Gamble brand manager. The Project Leader leads the trade-offs of strategic mission, customer appeal/effectiveness with innovation feasibility and economic viability. Dr. Deming described what he called the program manager role this way:

> *The job of the program manager is to manage all the interfaces,*
> *to manage the system as a whole, not to optimize any stage.*

Like at P&G and Toyota, the Project Leader is responsible for accomplishing the project mission but has no authority over the various functional departments. Again, like at P&G and Toyota, the Project Leader structure creates a virtual matrix organization as they manage their project across departmental silos. The departmental silos provide checks and balances on the work of the Project Leader.

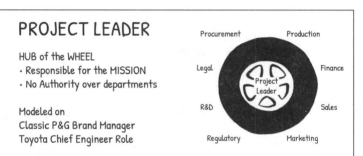

PROJECT LEADER

HUB of the WHEEL
· Responsible for the MISSION
· No Authority over departments

Modeled on
Classic P&G Brand Manager
Toyota Chief Engineer Role

Procurement   Production
Legal   Finance
Project Leader
R&D   Sales
Regulatory   Marketing

The idea of responsibility without authority works because four things shield the Project Leader from the negativity and reluctance to change that can come from departmental silos.

a. *The Strategic Importance of the Project* The fact that this project is a strategic priority that is VERY IMPORTANT to the leadership (of the company, division, department, etc.) helps the Project Leader gain engagement on the project.

b. *Quantitative Data and Math* 75%-plus of business managers have a logical and rational "Left Brain" thinking style. To speak their language, quantitative research on the offering, as well as risk-adjusted forecasts of sales, savings, or efficiency improvements, are used to create support for the innovation.

c. *PDSA Mindset and Optimizing the Whole* The Project Leader has a mindset that enables rapid cycles of testing. And, as the Project Leader is in the "middle" of the project and not loyal to any department, she or he is focused on optimizing the whole innovation for the accomplishment of the strategic mission.

d. *Management and Process Coaches* The Project Leader has the support of a Management Coach and Process Coach. They provide help with educating the Project Leader and working with the silos on the bigger-picture challenges and mission.

Project Leaders can come from any department and be of any level of experience. What's most important is that they have an intrinsic passion for the project and/or for innovating. Basically, they need to care and care deeply about the project.

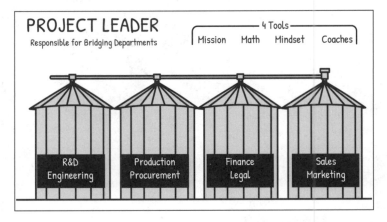

2. MANAGEMENT COACH: This is the most difficult of the three jobs. It is someone in the Project Leader's chain of command who has a big-picture view of the organization, its capabilities, and its resources. The Management Coach protects the Project Leader from the internal "political stuff" that results in wasted time and energy.

I once participated on a project with Paul Ferris, John Quench, and Jim Olver on how Product Leaders spend their time. Sadly, only about 7% was spent thinking. The bulk of their time was spent servicing "the system." Obviously, running a business has tasks that must be completed. However, 7% is insufficient. If the Management Coach can triple this from 7% to 21%, just think how much smarter and more effective innovations could be.

Dr. Deming felt strongly about the need for someone to help protect project teams. In *The New Economics* he wrote:

> *It will be necessary for top management to block the privilege of anybody in top management or in any other level to come along at the end of the line with a bright idea. A bright idea belongs in the "0th" stage, not in the last stage. The system of development must be managed. It will not manage itself.*

The Management Coach has two specific responsibilities: to be **Honest** and to be **Helpful.** This person must be absolutely Honest with regards to Death Threats, challenges, and issues. By knowing the challenges early, the Management Coach has the time and energy to find solutions. And this person must be Helpful by sharing industry and company wisdom, smoothing the way with inside and outside resources.

The Management Coach must be a hands-on participant. To use a flying analogy, Management Coaches are to be "on the plane" helping to fly the plane/project as copilot. If the plane goes down, they go down with it. Contrast this with various "mentor" and "sponsor" systems.

We are finding that Management Coaches are more effective if they have been educated in Innovation Engineering by attending Innovation College. Engagement of leadership is not a necessity of Innovation Engineering. However, tracking research on companies indicates that results decline by up to 85% when leadership is not fully engaged.

3. PROCESS COACH: This is the most rewarding of the three roles. They are often Innovation Engineering Black Belts. They provide coaching support for both the Management Coach and the Project Leader.

PDSA is part of their being. They have a natural curiosity for learning, balanced with a willingness to confront reality when needed. If the Project Leader and Management Coach are the pilots and copilots, the Process Coach is the navigator on projects. The Process Coach's job is to enable the system and to drive for never-ending continuous improvement, leading to higher levels of Meaningful Uniqueness. Just like the Management Coach, the Process Coach has a responsibility to be Honest and Helpful to the Project Leader.

In addition to supporting projects, the Process Coach/Innovation Engineering Black Belt also invests significant time in the never-ending innovation of the organization's system for innovation. They use the system to improve the system. This is covered in more detail in the next four chapters on subsystems. Dr. Deming and others estimate that in order to create a sustainable change, there should be Innovation Engineering Black Belts equal to the square root of the number of employees. Thus for a 100-person company, there should be 10. For a 500-person company, there should be 22. For a 10,000-person company, 100.

4. TEAM MEMBERS: These are people who help the Project Leader move the project forward. At the front end of projects (DEFINE and DISCOVER), they are volunteers who share a passion for the project or for innovating. Each team member brings diversity of experiences and skills to the project. When the project moves into DEVELOP, team members are full-time or at least half-time. Research indicates that to realize increased speed and success rates, it's better to have fewer people more fully dedicated than a lot of people spread thin over many projects.

A pet peeve that I have is that everyone on the team should do real work. I'm not a fan of people attending to comment, criticize, or try to control. If you're on the team, you're doing work.

How the Roles Work When the Organization Is Not Bought In

The four key roles described above are best done by separate people. Each brings a unique perspective and a different point of view that enables the exponential power of diversity.

If a pioneer or two are using the mindset on their own projects, without organizational buy-in, it's common to combine roles. The best split is for one person to be the Project Leader, and the other to combine the roles of Process Coach and Management Coach. This enables one person to stay fully engaged on the whole innovation and the other to deal with all the process and political stuff associated with working on a project.

In the case where there is only one pioneer, then he or she has no choice but to take on all the roles alone. In the case of Innovation Engineering, we suggest that a solo pioneer use the Collaboration Cafe in Innovation Engineering Labs to connect to other Innovation Engineering Black Belts for advice and support. The Innovation Engineering community is incredibly supportive of one another. It's not uncommon for people across countries and industries to invest hours helping out a fellow Innovation Engineering Pioneer.

Combining roles is not ideal, but it's still better than the old way of working.

Never, Ever Compromise on Your Mission

Meaningfully Unique innovations—the kinds of ideas that can transform an organization—have a high level of unknowns and uncertainty associated with them. The classic system of innovation development uses the "unknowns and uncertainties" as reasons for compromising on the innovation so as to make it more like the existing systems, services, or products.

As the story at the start of this chapter tells—and as independent research of executives confirms—at large companies, when ideas come out of development, they are on average worth less than half of what they were worth at the start. Lorenzo Delpani, president and CEO of Revlon, described the existing corporate system this way at a Eureka! session:

> *Ideas start as a sparkling star. Then one by one the sparkles and points are taken away until all you have left is an egg. And only chickens market eggs.*

The good news is that ideas don't have to decline in value. With never-ending PDSA learning cycles and the right mindset, your ideas can sparkle brighter as they go through development to market.

What Did You Learn?

On campus, most students consider Commercialization to be the most fun, and the most difficult, of the core Innovation Engineering courses. In large part, I think the reason is that this is the one place where you need to use your whole brain. You need to be able to both dream and do the details.

- From an emotional, right-brain perspective, what did you learn from this chapter?

- From a rational, logical, left-brain perspective, what did you learn from this chapter?

- Reflect on ideas you've developed that succeeded—what made them work?

- Reflect on ideas you've developed that failed—what caused them to fail?

- When did you use math to your advantage? When did you avoid the math?

- What methods in this chapter would make the biggest difference for your projects?

- Do you have clear roles during development?

- Do your innovations grow or decline in value during development?

9

Alignment Subsystem

Most corporate mission statements are worthless. They consist largely of pious platitudes such as: "We will hold ourselves to the highest standards of professionalism and ethical behavior." They often formulate necessities as objectives; for example, "to achieve sufficient profit." This is like a person saying his mission is to breathe sufficiently.

—Russell Ackoff

Enabling Organizational Alignment

Alignment means there is agreement first among the leadership and second between the leadership and the organization, from middle management to frontline employees.

Deming Master Walter Werner wrote of the importance of setting a clear vision. This applies to leaders of teams, departments, divisions, and organizations.

Leadership isn't about managing things and telling people what to do with those things. Leadership starts with a vision. Leadership creates a plan to accomplish the vision. Leadership then shares and explains the plan. Finally, leadership sets the entire organization on a path to fulfill the plan. The only thing you need to manage is matching resources to the plan, as they are required.

How many executives think their role is to manage the stock price, market share, customer satisfaction, the board, and the media. Do all that exceedingly well and your competitors will put you out of business in five years.

165

> *The statistics about how few people are engaged are depressing. Only leadership can change that. Everything we do must eventually persuade, educate, motivate, and kick start leadership. You can start at the bottom, the middle, or the top depending on which doors are open to you. In the end there is still only one goal: to change the way leadership is practiced.*

I believe, and conversations with Japanese company leaders confirm, that while the Japanese did a spectacular job implementing Deming's teachings in the factory, they didn't do so well with applying system thinking to strategy, innovation, and how the organization works together.

In the 1980s, this didn't matter—because to win market share, all they had to do was to create better quality versions of the products being made by Western companies.

When Japanese companies like Toyota went from following the Big Three to being the leader, they lost direction. They needed a bigger vision for the future. They needed to define how they were going to grow the market they were in and what new markets they would enter.

The Innovation Engineering Alignment system makes it easy to apply the system mindset of Dr. Deming to strategy, innovation, and how we work together.

Alignment Systems Enable You to Be the Leader You Dreamed You Would Be

When you dreamed of becoming the leader of your team, department, division, or company, you pledged you would be a different type of leader. You would be progressive, inspirational, supportive.

However, if you're like me, when you became the leader you found that there was so much "stuff" going on that it was hard to be the leader you dreamed you would be. I became reactionary instead of proactive, micromanaging instead of inspirational, and judging instead of supportive.

As I've aged, from my early years at Procter & Gamble through my time as CEO of various companies that I've founded, I've become more and more aware of when I am not acting the way I want to act.

My awareness is helped by Maggie Nichols, CEO of the Ranch and president of the Innovation Engineering Institute, when she pulls me aside and says, "What you just did in that meeting was not helpful to what I am trying to accomplish with the team."

Part of my problem is that I'm a Baby Boomer who grew up in a time when it was acceptable to lead with Command and Control methods. Today, the old approach is too slow, too dependent on the leader, and frankly not motivating to Millennials or anyone else.

Another flaw in my leadership is caused by my deep and detailed domain knowledge about our work. My experience with thousands of projects, quantitative research on innovation systems, and deep reading of thousands of academic articles can make me very impatient with those who are not keeping up. I am also blessed—or cursed—with incredible energy and passion for innovation. I really, really love helping accelerate WOW ideas. However, my knowledge and passion can make me impatient.

I am fortunate because, when I complain about someone or something being too slow, my wife of 40-plus years says, "Remember they aren't you. They don't know what you know. You need to slow down and teach them. They can't read your mind."

The alignment systems described in this chapter are an antidote to my leadership challenges. They enable me to be the leader I dreamed I would be. They also give me freedom of mind and spirit because I know that even when I'm off traveling the world, the Eureka! Ranch, Innovation Engineering Institute, and Brain Brew Scientific Spirits teams are doing the right things, for the right reasons, in the right ways.

Alignment: The Rational and Emotional Benefits

The importance of alignment is found in multiple studies of innovation results.

- Innovation Engineering Institute research finds that those companies in the top 20% of our Innovation Alignment survey versus those in the bottom 40% are 300% more likely to be successful with their innovations. That's 300%—not 10%, not 20%, not 30%.

- Research reported in *Research Technology Management* found that the three biggest drivers of innovation portfolio success are: 1.) Project aligned with business objective, 2.) Portfolio contains very high value projects, and 3.) Development spending reflects the business's strategy.

- Research of innovators attending the annual Innovation Engineering conference on their biggest innovation challenge found that most (62%)

felt lack of alignment was their top challenge. This was followed by a need to increase speed/decrease risk (27%) and a need for new ideas (11%).

- Research from Fast-Bridge in Europe found that strategic alignment had the highest correlation with positive business results (sales and profit growth). It was higher than even customer focus, co-creation, risk taking, creativity, and competitiveness.

The Two Most Important Alignments

The two most important alignments are:

1. VERTICAL ALIGNMENT: Connecting leadership's strategy for growth with employee projects.

2. HORIZONTAL ALIGNMENT: Connecting across departmental silos on innovation project management—WHAT to do, WHY to do, HOW to turn an idea into reality.

Improving Vertical Alignment between strategy and projects is the most impactful thing you can do as a leader of a company, division, department, or work group to improve your innovation success rates. When there is clarity on WHAT the mission is, WHY it is very important, and the BOUND-ARIES both strategically and tactically, then the employees are free to think, create, and activate your vision.

There are hundreds of ways to create and activate strategy. Most don't work. Here are some examples.

- Strategic alignment metrics don't work, as the focus is on inspecting individual department outputs as opposed to optimization of the inter-actions of departments. It is not uncommon for every department man-ager to achieve his or her metrics while the company is going out of business. That's because extrinsic metrics have replaced intrinsic focus on the broader mission. Remember, 94% is the system, 6% the worker.

- Inspirational talks on strategic vision don't work, as the pressures of the day-to-day make them fade from memory within hours. Inspiration without enablement of employees to take action is a waste of energy.

- Micromanaging to align to strategy doesn't work. The good employ-ees soon get frustrated and say something along the lines of: "Do you want to run this project or do you want me to run it?" By the way, what's worse is when they think it but don't say it. This creates "employee engagement cancer."

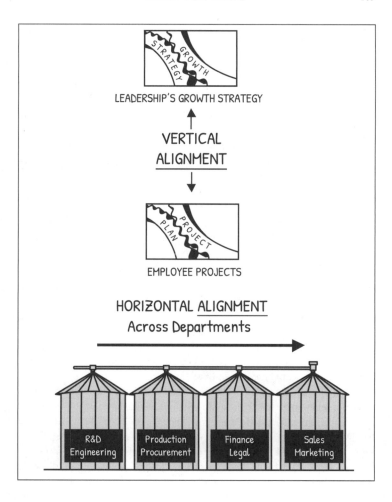

When ideas moved slowly, there was time to make lots of midcourse corrections to maintain alignment. However, as employees learn how to Create, Communicate, and Commercialize, ideas move much, much faster. The faster speed amplifies the problems caused by lack of strategic alignment. Reworks, starts, stops, and restarts create stress. Work is no longer fun. The more this happens the lower the return you realize from your human capital. Soon, once-energetic employees stop raising their hands to volunteer for innovation projects, as they see it as just not worth the effort.

I personally hit a crisis when I had to tell one of the Eureka! Ranch employees that the idea she was pursuing needed to be stopped because of some broader company issues. She asked, "How could I know that?" She went on: "I understand what you're saying. But what is our system for helping me not waste my time like I have. It's very frustrating to waste time."

At about the same time as this conversation, feedback from the Innovation Engineering community found similar challenges. As our methods for accelerating innovation speed improved, employee frustration with leadership decision cycles also amplified.

What we needed was a way for Leadership to define the strategic mission and boundaries so as to let the people work as fast as possible, without requiring approval each step of the way.

Strategy Activation: The Blue Card

When I asked the community of Innovation Engineering Black Belts on their private Collaboration Cafe online forum about their challenges with strategic focus, the outpouring was overwhelming. They spoke of working for months on an innovation, only to be told by management that the project was no longer a priority. They gave examples of getting stuck in mind-numbing rework loops between marketing, finance, and product development on the final design of an innovation.

This set off dozens of "Plan, Do, Study, Act" experiments to create, develop, and validate what has come to be known as the Blue Card.

The most common dysfunction we observed was that instead of being a mission with a clear strategic direction and boundaries, the strategy statement was just a set of metrics. Strategy-by-numbers results in each division, department, and employee focusing on their number (individual or department Key Performance Indicators or metrics). Achieving their number is more important to them than the success of the organization. This is because leadership makes it clear to them, either overtly or subconsciously, that their number defines their bonus, their ability to get promoted, their ability to keep their job. The consequence is that collaboration is only pursued when it will help each group hit their numbers.

The polar opposite of strategy-by-numbers was strategy-by-grand-vision. In these cases, leadership's vision was so "big picture" that no one understood what it meant and what their role was in making the vision happen.

Setting strategy is deciding where to focus organizational resources so as to best achieve the aim of the organization.

Strategy is selecting where to go.

Strategy is about making decisions.

Strategy is about focus, focus, focus.

Strategy is set by leadership, as only leadership has the breadth of view across the overall organization. The employees can't set the strategic direction—only leadership can.

Note: **Throughout this chapter, when I reference leadership, this ideally means the leadership of the organization. However, this can also mean leadership of a division, department, work team, or an individual's leadership of their own work.**

When leadership sets a clear and focused strategy, the result is a force multiplier of effectiveness. Employees and leadership are aligned on what the Very Important strategic missions are, why they are very important, and what the boundaries are to the scope. Strategic clarity creates a shared sense of mission that invites collaboration.

To develop the Blue Card, we ran lots of experiments and did lots of Stimulus Mining. During the process, we soon learned that we were reinventing something that the military of the USA, Canada, and all NATO countries had already created.

A United States Marine explained it to me this way: "Years ago, the military was focused on instant, willing obedience to orders. Today, we give the mission and explain why. When the troops know the mission and why it's important, we leverage their skills and knowledge."

Instant, willing obedience to orders is not fun. It's slavery. It turns employees into zombies. It creates disengagement between employees and the work.

Today, the military enables the troops to both think and do. They call it Commander's Intent.

COMMANDER'S INTENT: A clear and concise expression of the purpose of the operation and the desired end state that supports mission command, provides focus to the staff, and helps subordinate and supporting commanders act to achieve the commander's desired result without further order, even when the operation does not unfold as planned.

To distill Commander's Intent into a simple statement: "In the absence of further orders, you would know what to do."

A *Harvard Business Review* article in the November 2010 issue described Commander's Intent this way:

> *How does your team respond when a plan changes? Does everyone seem to know what to do or is there confusion, a lack of meaningful activity, or people standing around waiting to be told what to do next? Planning is difficult whether in business or the military.*
>
> *Military planners use Commander's Intent, a key element to help a plan maintain relevancy and applicability in a chaotic, dynamic, and resource-constrained environment. Commander's Intent is the description and definition of what a successful mission will look like.*
>
> *Employees must understand the plan and when they have to deviate to ensure the Commander's Intent is accomplished. Military personnel have to employ a "Spectrum of Improvisation" when they execute Commander's Intent and as they adapt the plan to meet Commander's Intent.*

When a mission was being defined, the leadership originally got one-third of the time available before deployment for developing their Commander's Intent. The troops were given two-thirds of the time available.

A lieutenant colonel in the Canadian Armed Forces told me that currently NATO countries have reduced the time available for leadership planning to 20% with 80% of available planning time going to the troops. He explained, "As a commander there is no way I have the specialized knowledge of the equipment and systems that the troops have. Given the complexity of today's equipment and systems, it makes sense that the troops will require more time for planning."

Contrast 20/80 with the classic strategic-planning process of many organizations. For many, leadership takes nine months to develop a strategy, leaving the employees with no time to plan or do before the strategic planning process begins again. This is no way for an organization to win in today's fast-paced, technology-enabled world.

BLUE CARD:
A System for Activating Vertical "Strategic" Alignment

We ran many experiments with different ways to communicate leadership's growth strategy. The result was given the name Blue Card. It was printed on blue paper, the color of the Innovation Engineering logo, in recognition of its importance. The purpose of the Blue Card is to maximize alignment between leadership's strategy and how employees invest available time and energy. Blue Cards provide a method for leaders to activate their strategy for where they want to take the organization. It helps them focus the time, energy, and money of the organization—no matter how large it is—on what is VERY important. The Blue Card activates strategy with a set of very simple elements:

1. SCOPE: The card starts with some simple yes/no questions to help you define the scale of your mission. Questions such as:

   a. Very Important Opportunity OR Very Important System? This defines if we are looking for new or improved offerings or internal systems for how we work.

   b. LEAP Innovations OR CORE Innovations? This defines if we are looking for high-risk and reward LEAP ideas or lower risk and reward CORE ideas.

   c. Long-Term Strategic Blue Card OR Project-Specific Blue Card? This defines if this is a longer-term initiative that will have many projects or if it's a more focused shorter-term project.

   d. Entire organization OR a specific division/department? This defines the scope of who is involved with this strategic mission.

2. NAME: Give this VERY Important Blue Card a name that is suggestive of the mission. The name gives clarity and focus to the strategic mission.

3. NARRATIVE: Tell the story of WHY it is VERY IMPORTANT that we focus energy on this Blue Card. The narrative should be so clear that if

(continued on page 176)

Blue Card™

Purpose: To maximize alignment between leadership's strategy and how employees invest available time & energy.

1. Very Important Opportunity *Innovations for current or new customers*	_____	**OR**	Very Important System *Innovations for how we work* _____
2. Looking for LEAP Innovations *Potential for High Impact & Risk*	_____	**OR**	CORE Innovations *Low Impact & Risk* _____
3. Long Term Strategic Blue Card	_____	**OR**	Project Specific Blue Card _____
4. This is for the Entire Organization	_____	**OR**	for Specific Division/Department _____

VIO/VIS Name: *Give this VERY Important Blue Card a name that is suggestive of the mission.*

_____

_____

Narrative: *Tell the story of WHY it is VERY IMPORTANT that we focus energy on this Blue Card. The Narrative should be so clear that if employees get no further direction they will be motivated to work on this Blue Card and will know exactly what the Leadership's intent is.*

_____

_____

_____

_____

_____

_____

_____

_____

_____

_____

_____

_____

_____

_____

Strategic Mission: *Finish the sentence with ONE mission, "We need ideas for _____"*

_____

_____

_____

Strategic Exclusions: *Ideas or types of ideas that we are NOT interested in.*

_____

_____

_____

_____

Tactical Constraints: *Design, time, resources, investment, regulations constraints.*

_____

_____

_____

_____

Project: **Exploration Areas**   **OR**   Long Term: **Innovation Road Map**

Areas to consider for stimulus mining when working on this project.

Estimate of the technologies / innovations we will pursue over the next 2 to 5 years in support of this strategy ideally with dates.

_____

_____

_____

_____

_____

(continued from page 173)

employees get no further direction they will be motivated to work on the Blue Card and will know exactly what the leadership's intent is.

Narrative describes in simple language WHY it is VERY IMPORTANT that employees focus energy on this mission. **Just as in the military, the narrative is written personally by the leader of the project, division, or company.** It cannot be outsourced to others. **Only the leader has the breadth of understanding to craft the precise words that define the project narrative.** The leader's narrative speaks precisely to the head and the heart of employees. It explains WHY this strategic mission is very important to the organization. It motivates employees and ignites intrinsic motivation. Writing a motivating narrative is not easy. It's hard. It's really hard. However, it's well worth the effort. Great Blue Cards inspire great Yellow Cards.

The narrative section takes up the most space on the physical Blue Card. It was first suggested by Joe Kanfer, chairman and CEO of GOJO Industries, as he explained, "People are motivated by narratives, not by metrics."

4. STRATEGIC MISSION: Finish the sentence with ONE mission. "We need ideas for _____."

The mission completes the simple statement, "We need ideas for . . ." Great mission statements make choices that give focus to employees. They provide direction but not a prescription. Missions that are vague result in wasted effort. Missions that are prescriptive waste the creative energy of employees. And, unless leadership is perfect with their prescription, there is a high chance of innovation failure.

We've found that it's very important that the mission be focused on ONE THING. If you need ideas for multiple things, think harder about it. Do you really need both, or are you simply not making a choice? FOCUS. FOCUS. FOCUS. What is the ONE THING you need? What is the ONE THING that when you accomplish it will set off a chain reaction of positives?

5. BOUNDARIES. These define the scope of the project. By clarifying your intentions, you reduce waste and rework. They provide "rules of engagement" to employees. Boundaries are both strategic and tactical.

Strategic Exclusions: *Ideas or types of ideas that we are NOT interested in.* Define what kind of ideas we are NOT looking for. They enable innovation by providing clear definition to where employees should focus and not focus their time and energy. The greater the clarity, the more efficient and effective the innovation effort is.

Tactical Constraints: *Design, time, resources, investment, regulations, constraints.* This provides specific clarity on tactical issues. It can include minimum sales goals, test standards, investment rules, and timing expectations.

I have found that it is often difficult for business leaders to be honest with boundaries. When they admit the "truth," they are often embarrassed by their reality—their lack of resources, their short-term thinking, their unreasonable timelines.

NOT defining the real boundaries at the start creates frustration later. When a go/no-go decision needs to be made, it is not the time for a team to learn about a strategic or tactical boundary.

6. EXPLORATION AREAS/INNOVATION ROAD MAPS: The final section of the card has two options, depending on if it's a short-term project versus a long-term Blue Card.

Project Specific—Exploration Areas: These are areas to consider when creating Yellow Cards to address this Blue Card mission. It is common to conduct Stimulus Mining on these areas, resulting in a Spark Deck that is used to ignite ideas as part of a Create session. To encourage in-depth, immersive mining versus skimming the surface when preparing for a session, it is recommended that a Project-Specific Blue Card have no more than three exploration areas. Importantly, these are "theories" on how to best address the Blue Card mission. As theories, they are suggestions, not orders. With the Innovation Engineering Mindset, leadership and employees embrace never-ending, continuous improvement. It is expected that exploration areas will change as leadership and employees learn more during their work on the mission.

Long-Term—Innovation Road Map: It is common for organizations to begin their Innovation Engineering journey with the acceleration of one or more individual innovation projects. This is valuable, as it builds sales and profits as well as cultural confidence and capability. The next phase of strategic development for leadership is to set a long-term innovation/technology road map. The road map defines an estimate of the technologies/innovations the organization will pursue over the next two to five years in support of this long-term strategy, with estimates of start dates. The road map makes it easy for everyone to understand how today's projects connect to the longer-term strategic plan. Again, as with exploration areas, they are "theories" based on what is known at the time—we expect them to evolve as we learn more and as market conditions change.

Innovation Pathway Tagging (advanced): The most advanced growth strategy subsystem is to set strategic areas for innovation investment. Where Road Maps most often set the strategic direction for this year, next year, etc., Innovation Pathways set the areas that will be explored by the organization today: Area 1, Area 2, Area 3. The Innovation Pathway approach goes by multiple names, including:

- Innovation Pathways
- Strategic Clusters
- Innovation Investment Areas
- They are even called Technology Road Maps by some companies.

Innovation Pathways are leadership's proactive declaration of where the leadership has decided to focus Research and Development investments. This includes both internal invention and outside licensing or purchasing of technologies and patents. They are structured longer-term versions of project exploration areas. Innovation Pathways create a concentration of energy in a strategic area that builds internal expertise as well as marketplace clarity on what sets your brand apart from others. They are especially helpful when you have a really big and bold mission.

Major strategic challenges are worthy missions. However, if we are not careful, they become vague statements that provide no direction. The result is massive waste, as it is left to employees to figure out where to focus their energy.

The Innovation Engineering Institute team learned this the hard way. Our simple mission is to develop systems that enable everyone to increase innovation speed and decrease risk. At first, this was fine, as we had a mission without specifics. However, as more and more creativity was applied, we were soon flooded with tools and systems for increasing speed and decreasing risk.

To bring order to the situation, Maggie Nichols (president and COO) and Scott Dunkle (VP of technology) and I met to bring order to the chaos. Our challenge was to put in a system that enabled and didn't control creativity.

Following a couple of PDSA learning cycles, we ended up with a set of simple Innovation Development Pathways that defined what method we would use to increase innovation speed and decrease risk. In our case, they were also the first-level menu items on our website: Innovation Project Pipeline, Collaboration Cafe, Merwyn Rapid Research, Patent ROI, Classroom, and Tools.

Within IELabs.com, Innovation Pathways is a company customizable option. They offer a way to easily sort and view the organization's pipeline of innovation projects on their metrics dashboard.

Blue Cards: Ideal Implementation

In the ideal implementation, the organization's Blue Cards lay out a clear, complete, and motivating vision for where the organization is going. The Blue Cards articulate the very important areas for new or improved services, products, and internal systems.

The organization's Blue Cards cascade through the organization's divisions and departments. Each of these subordinate Blue Cards defines how that division or department helps the organization achieve the overall Blue Cards.

There are often one or two additional Blue Cards that are specific to each division or department. These local cards often are designed to support future needs. They often focus on improving effectiveness or greater efficiency through enabling education, tools, or improved systems that the department needs today or will need in the future.

The Blue Cards are the organizational structure for activating the leadership's strategic vision. Each Blue Card has an innovation pipeline of projects—that is, a collection of Yellow Cards underneath it.

Blue Cards enable employees to contribute their ideas. Teresa Amabile, writing in the *Harvard Business Review,* explained it this way: "Creativity thrives when managers let people decide how to climb a mountain; they didn't, however, let employees choose which one."

A primary indication that the organization has activated a true strategic focus is when the agenda of company board meetings and leadership team meetings is two-thirds focused on reviewing where the company is going, as defined by Blue Cards, followed by one-third on short-term issues.

HORIZONTAL ALIGNMENT ACROSS DEPARTMENTS: Horizontal alignment across departments provides clarity on how innovations go from idea to reality. The process is accomplished through a set of checklists that document WHAT Death Threats/Milestones need to be accomplished, WHY they are important to be addressed, and HOW the organization will accomplish them.

As explained in the previous chapter, when an employee understands WHAT and WHY a Death Threat exists, they are empowered with knowledge. But when they also know HOW to address it, they are actually ENABLED to overcome it.

When employees are provided descriptions of HOW, there is increased speed and less waste, as they have standardized work plans to get them started. The HOW section of checklists provides details, including:

1. Clear instructions on tools and techniques for resolving the Death Threat/Milestone

2. Videos that educate when there is a specialized technique or an especially important organizational perspective

3. Links to internal and external organizational experts who can help

Frankly, the benefits of WHAT, WHY, HOW checklists are a no-brainer. When employees have clarity on WHY Milestones are important and HOW to resolve them, then innovation projects run smarter and faster. When there is no definition of WHY and HOW, then employees are left to guess the best way to resolve the Death Threat or Milestone. The result is chaos, randomness, wasted time, and epic frustration.

A checklist is needed because of the variance in innovation projects. The most obvious example is that incremental CORE innovations are different from disruptive LEAP innovations. With CORE innovations, the focus is on discipline and attention to details. With LEAP innovations, the focus is on learning, as these types of innovations by definition have more unknown dimensions.

A library of best-practices checklists is built into IE Labs, making it easy to customize a specialized list for your organization.

If your organization already has a Phase/Stage Gate checklist, it is easy to upgrade it by adding WHY and HOW. In time, you can add additional checklists for the different types of projects that your company executes repeatedly. Each checklist is customized based on the organization's unique requirements.

Checklists that define WHAT, WHY, HOW align how departments work together to accomplish organizational Blue Cards. For example,

OLD WORLD

ONE CHECKLIST
FOR ALL PROJECTS

ONE SIZE
FITS ALL

NEW WORLD

Digital Checklists
for the Common Types of Projects

CORE Maintenance Small Technical Changes We Have No Choice On	**CORE Customer Response** Customer-Driven Requests	**CORE Fast Track** Restricted to Using Existing Assests ONLY to be FAST and Profitable

CORE Projects Meaningful Upgrades to Existing Offerings that Meet Boundaries	**CORE Working Smarter Now** Small Projects by Frontline Employees
LEAP WOW Innovations High Risk & Reward Sales and Profits	**SYSTEM** Custom Projects to Improve Internal Systems

when someone has never done a sales forecast before, and a checklist requires it, it also directs them to talk to finance for help. And, because finance is aware of the requirement, they aren't surprised or alarmed when a Project Leader asks for some help with a sales forecast. This simple clarity on how we work together enables horizontal alignment.

The Other Two Alignments

Vertical and Horizontal Alignment are the two most important alignments. There are two other alignments that help increase speed and decrease risk.

PROJECT TEAM ALIGNMENT: This is how teams manage their projects. The alignment system for teams is simple—it's the "Plan, Do, Study, Act" method detailed in Chapter 8, Learning Mindset: Commercialize System. The PDSA process provides structure to the work. It creates a culture driven by learning, by facts, and discovery. In the absence of PDSA politics, debate and rework are epidemic.

CUSTOMER ALIGNMENT: This is how we get feedback on our innovations from potential customers—or, in the case of system innovations, from internal stakeholders. It's a process of never-ending learning. Customer Alignment is built into Innovation Engineering checklists at every phase—DEFINE, DISCOVER, DEVELOP, and DELIVER. It is about creating prototypes and reviewing them with potential customers or internal stakeholders in the case of system innovations.

Innovation Alignment: Putting It All Together

The following visual provides top-to-bottom clarity on how alignment is achieved using the Innovation Engineering approach:

A. STRATEGY STRUCTURE: Blue Cards define what is very important for the organization to focus its energy on. It makes it easy to communicate the strategic missions that leadership believes are the VERY important areas on which to focus innovation resources.

B. IDEA STRUCTURE: Yellow Cards define specific innovation projects that address the mission laid out on a Blue Card. They are written from the perspective of the ultimate customer or stakeholder in clear and easy-to-understand language.

Innovation Engineering System

HOW WE DEFINE OUR MISSION

<u>Blue Cards</u>: Our mission — WHERE we want to go, WHY it's important, and our BOUNDARIES and limitations.

HOW WE DEFINE OUR IDEAS

<u>Yellow Cards</u>: The structure we use to define ideas — Customer, Problem, Promise, Proof, Price.

HOW WE MAKE IDEAS HAPPEN

<u>Project Phases & Checklists:</u> Step by step how we make our ideas happen.

HOW WE WORK

<u>Plan, Do, Study, Act</u>: How we make sure we are working smart.

HOW WE THINK

<u>Our Basic Principles</u>: Learn More (Stimulus), Connect with Others (Diversity), and Fail FAST, Fail CHEAP (Drive Out Fear).

C. RISK MANAGEMENT PROCESS: This is the structure through which Yellow Card–defined innovations move across the organizational silos from idea to reality. It includes a set of phases—such as DEFINE, DIS-COVER, DEVELOP, and DELIVER—plus a checklist of key tasks to be done. As stated earlier, it documents: 1) WHAT tasks (Death Threats/Milestones) need to be resolved to move an innovation forward, 2) WHY the tasks are important, and 3) HOW to accomplish the tasks. The addition of WHY and HOW to the classic WHAT transforms innovation systems from a focus on CONTROL to one of ENABLING. When employees know WHY and HOW, they become more engaged and enabled. Most importantly, innovation checklists undergo never-ending innovation. Every month at system summits, they are refined and made smarter.

D. WORK PROCESS: This is how teams work their way through the risk management process to turn ideas into reality. It's focused on disciplined cycles of factual learning that follow the Deming Cycle—"Plan, Do, Study, Act" to address Death Threats or reach Milestones. PDSA maximizes alignment within the work team. Focused and fact-based learning replaces politics and opinions. As a result, leadership and employees find more joy in their work.

E. OPERATING PRINCIPLES: All of our work and interactions are guided by three simple principles: 1) Explore Stimulus (6 Minings to Spark Ideas), 2) Leverage Diversity (Internal and External Collaboration), and 3) Drive Out Fear (through Education, Alignment, Rapid Research, Patent ROI).

Frequently Asked Questions About Alignment

1. **We have too many projects already. How can we handle more?** It is nearly universal that work and projects expand to fill the time available for them. It's rare that managers and employees have nothing to do. When we define the organization's Blue Cards, and then define the Yellow Cards for the projects that are under way, we often find that over half of the projects are: 1) not aligned to strategy and/or 2) seriously flawed in design of Customer, Problem, Promise, Proof, or Math Game Plan. For example, when real math is applied to cost-saving projects, it is not uncommon to find that while they are all helpful, many are just not worth the effort. In one case, a company I worked with defined every

project on a Yellow Card along with the math for them. What they found was that if every project were 100% successful, they would achieve less than 25% of their growth objective. To use the physics definition, everyone was busy expending effort, but meaningful work wasn't being accomplished.

2. **What if, when we engage employees in innovation, we have too many projects? How do we handle that?** This is a GREAT problem to have. And the fix is really easy. You simply return to your Blue Cards and adjust your BOUNDARIES. If your Blue Card has a tactical BOUNDARY that all cost savings projects must have a minimum value of $1,000, move the BOUNDARY up to $5,000. If your Blue Card has a tactical BOUNDARY that all growth projects must generate at least $1 million in revenue, move the BOUNDARY up to $5 million.

3. **Don't BOUNDARIES reduce creativity?** Done wrong, they do. Especially if you are so prescriptive with your BOUNDARIES that there are no degrees of freedom for creating innovative solutions. Done right, the BOUNDARIES ignite deeper thinking. They reduce wasted effort. They also ignite employee motivation, as there is real clarity on what Commander's Intent is and isn't.

4. **How do we ensure we are working on the right projects (Yellow Cards)?** The key to Innovation Engineering is that employees get to pick which projects they want to volunteer their time on, in addition to their regular jobs during DEFINE and DISCOVER. This can cause some managers to get very nervous, as they want to control which projects are worked on. DON'T. The minute management becomes judge and jury for selecting projects, the motivation of employees dies.

In place of saying yes/no to innovations, the leadership has three tools that provide direction without destroying employee motivation. These include:

1. BOUNDARIES on the Blue Card
2. The specifications in the WHAT, WHY, HOW of the checklists
3. Setting the PLAN standards as Management Coach

If, as the leader, you have an idea you want to pursue and no one wants to volunteer for it, then you have three choices:

1. Provide an inspirational vision in the concept and/or math that ignites employee interest.

2. Archive the idea.

3. Become the Project Leader and run it yourself.

Classic Top Two Blue Cards

Grow Category
(Industry)

Work Smarter

5. **What is the right number of Blue Cards?** I don't worry much about the number of Blue Cards at the start. If an organization follows the process and has Strategy Summits every three months as part of management/board meetings, then the cards quickly get to the right number. For those looking for a more specific answer, an executive at a session in Northern Italy had a reasonable definition. He said we should have no more than we can count on one hand. Five is close to what we see at high-performance companies. These usually include two long-term cards, two short-term cards, and one card focused on operational improvements (cost, productivity, and/or quality).

I like to focus energy, even with large companies, on just two cards— one for how the organization will grow, and one for how the organization will work smarter—that is, improve its way of working. This level of clarity requires deep strategic thinking. It's rare that it occurs. However, when it does, it has a transformational impact on the organization.

Note: In all cases, the abovementioned numbers are overall organizational Blue Cards. It is expected that each division, department, or operating company underneath the overall company will have its own Blue Cards. Some of these will align with the overall Blue Cards, some will be unique for each group.

6. **It appears we have too many strategic priorities. Will this approach just not work for us?** This is very common because many leaders have not learned the definition of the words "Very Important." I've seen 15, 25, 50, and even 115 strategic priorities. There are three reasons for this: 1) The leadership confuses KPI's (key performance indicators) with strategy, 2) The leadership micromanages by defining strategy as projects, and 3) The leadership doesn't know where it wants the organization to go, so it starts covering every possible option. This last reason is the most difficult to resolve, as it requires the leadership to admit that "it doesn't know."

A disciplined Blue Card session leveraging stimulus and diversity from across the organization is invaluable to getting a clear direction. These Blue Cards are, to paraphrase George Box, **"Wrong but useful."** Over a year of quarterly Strategy Summits, the Blue Cards become even more useful as the organization and leadership evolves, adapts, and improves them.

7. **In your discussion about Blue Cards, you never spoke about leveraging our strengths.** I am not a big fan of focusing on company strengths. What I've observed is that when companies do that, they end up justifying the "same old, same old." Their innovation pipeline of 100% CORE innovations is justified based on their strengths. While they optimize their existing offering, the marketplace moves on to new technologies or options.

When an innovation is Meaningfully Unique, there is a good chance that the internal resources will not be able to support the design, development, manufacturing, packaging, or marketing of the idea. To reduce risk in these situations, we recommend that the organization collaborate with partners outside of the organization to make the idea a reality. As I write this, I'm reminded of a story my dad told me of a project he worked on at Nashua Corporation to increase the production capacity of a product they made at their factory in Merrimack, New Hampshire. When he looked outside the company, he found a vendor in Wisconsin that, because of a more efficient production system, could produce and deliver the product to Merrimack at a lower cost than that factory could manufacture the same product.

8. **We have an annual strategy system. How does this fit with it?** The simple way to integrate it is to separate strategy from budgeting. What the Innovation Engineering alignment process does is turn strategy from a "batch process" to one that approaches "continuous flow." This enables a longer-term strategic focus. Budgeting is handled separately from strategy. That's not to say that learnings identified in the business review and budgeting process don't impact Blue Cards. However, the primary focus of budget reviews moves to tactical Yellow Cards instead of strategic Blue Cards.

Alignment Is Easy When You Are Going Out of Business

Alignment is the primary reason that small business startups are 10 times more successful with innovations than large companies (50% versus 5% survive for at least three years). With a startup, there is alignment on the singular mission of staying in business. The CEO/owner has line of sight to all departments, and great small business owners reinforce the mission of survival to everyone, every day.

Alignment also occurs when a company is threatened with going out of business. Suddenly, old battles, prejudices, and misperceptions are vanquished, as survival is at stake. When this occurs, the organization suddenly becomes more productive, creative, and inventive.

I have been blessed—and yes I said blessed—with experiencing this level of alignment many times in my life. However, without a doubt, the most memorable time was when I was a very young assistant brand manager at

Procter & Gamble, working on an innovative toilet bowl cleaner called Brigade. It was Meaningfully Unique in that it was the only automatic toilet bowl cleaner that both cleaned and sanitized the toilet with a patented dispensing system. As a true innovation, the product was priced at a premium.

However, in test markets, the competition reacted fiercely with price discounts, causing P&G to respond with a wide range of promotions and coupons.

It was my job to develop the national expansion plan for the brand. I wrote the recommendation, and one Friday I learned it had made it to the desk of the CEO, John Smale. That weekend something was bugging me about the test market data. Over the weekend I did a pricing analysis using VisiTrend and a VisiCalc spreadsheet. To my shock, I discovered that, with a different set of assumptions of net consumer price, my national sales forecast dropped by as much as 50%.

While we could justify a higher price than the competition, the pricing premium we were projecting was simply too high for the sales volume we needed to pay out the cost of the marketing investment required to go national.

On Monday morning, I met with the project team to review my findings. It included representatives from manufacturing, R&D, sales, etc. It was not a positive meeting. The team questioned my data and analysis. Even my boss didn't support me. It didn't help that the company had already invested $50 million in building a plant to manufacture the product.

No one would listen to me. A couple days later, I got very frustrated because I had gone to P&G because I really "bought in" to the idea that the culture preached, that they do the right things in the right way.

In an amazing coincidence of timing, that week a recruiter called and offered me a very cool job working for Pizza Hut. Given my absolute love of pizza, as anyone who has attended Innovation College will attest, it was a natural fit for me.

I finally got so frustrated that I told my boss I was thinking of leaving the company because I just didn't believe in what I was doing. Within 30 minutes I was sitting with Ross Love, advertising manager for the division. He said, "We will talk about you leaving in a few minutes. First, I'm going to tie your feet to that chair and have you explain this data on Brigade that you've found. I need to understand it in detail."

I took Ross through the data, step by step. I explained my thinking—what I was confident of and what I wasn't confident of. He asked deep questions on each point.

Then he then did something that for the rest of my life I will never forget. Without hesitation, he picked up his phone and called the CEO's office and said, "John, you have a recommendation on your desk for the national expansion of Brigade. Take no action on it. I have just been shown new information that leads me to believe it might be a mistake to expand it. We will know more within a week."

He turned to me and said, "We need you here. I need you here. What is this about you leaving the company?"

It was a bold demonstration of leadership and character. My Pizza Hut dream job was quickly forgotten—this was someone I wanted to work for. This was someone I believed in. I was given a team of experts to help take my analysis to the next level. Within a week, the project was put on hold. However, given the investment, the team was given 30 days to see if they could reduce the cost of the product to hit the price point needed. And it was my job to help lead the effort.

While not everyone was happy with me, the P&G culture of doing the right thing in the right way accepted and supported me.

The stress of us "going out of business" created an amazing level of alignment. Within 30 days, the product was reinvented and the price reduced from $1.95 to $1.29. We changed the name and the packaging, created and filmed a new commercial, ran consumer research, and wrote a new expansion recommendation that detailed the benefits and the risks associated with the project.

At the final meeting to decide Brigade's fate, all but one voted to archive the project because the risks still outweighed the benefits. The one person who said yes did so because he didn't want it to be unanimous and didn't want to give up yet. The net conclusion was if we'd confronted this reality earlier it might have worked, but the costs of retooling were so great and at a lower net price that the profit return just wasn't there.

What Did I Learn from the Brigade Experience?

1. **Alignment Makes the Impossible Possible.** When a team has true alignment on what really matters, miracles can occur. In a month, the unthinkable was accomplished. Alignment is more

than a written mission statement. It's what the Project Leader says and does every day.

2. **Confront Reality and Do the Math Early and Frequently.** The Brigade experience is the key reason I am such a fanatic about doing math early and frequently during the innovation process. My rants are legendary on "no math, no project." And, importantly, the math can't be "outsourced." The project team—and in particular, the Project Leader—must be able to do the math. I believe that if you can't do the math (cost estimating and sales forecasting), then you can't successfully lead an innovation project. Project Leaders who don't "do" and "feel the math" can't make the right trade-off decisions.

3. **Great Leadership Matters.** Ross Love's action, without hesitation, going above his boss and boss's boss to the CEO, taught me what a great leader does. He had no problem admitting a possible mistake. He didn't play games, he didn't hedge it, he just said it. I would observe him exhibit inspiring honesty a number of times over the years. Sadly, Ross has passed away. However, his memory lives on these pages and in the soul of the Innovation Engineering movement.

Closing Thoughts on Alignment

Generating alignment when you are going out of business is easy. The real leadership challenge is generating alignment when you are not going out of business. It requires constant effort by the leadership. Aimee Dobrzeniecki, CFO of the Student Conservation Association and an early supporter of Innovation Engineering, described her vision of what it takes to gain alignment.

> *It starts by working with managers to help them understand that they must be the change they seek first. They themselves must change before they ask their staff to do something else. Their job is to think ahead and forecast where the organization needs to go and then chart the path for the company to take. The staff will rise to the challenge if a path is provided. Setting the strategy is management's job. Igniting hope for the future. That is leadership doing their job.*

What Did You Learn?

- Think of a time when you had very clear alignment with your leader's vision.
- Think of a time when you didn't have alignment with your leader.
- Think of when you were the leader and had alignment or didn't have it.
- How did you feel when you had alignment and didn't have it?
- On a very important project you are working on at this moment . . .

    —What is the "narrative"—the WHY behind the project?

    —What are the "boundaries," both strategic and tactical, that you've agreed to?

10

Collaboration Cafe Subsystem

Because they're doing the day-to-day work, frontline employees see many problems and opportunities their managers don't. But most organizations fail to realize this potentially extraordinary source of revenue-enhancing ideas.

—Alan Robinson and Dean Schroeder
Ideas are Free

Collaboration Leverages the Exponential Power of Diversity

Given a choice between hiring a creative guru or developing a network of internal collaborators, it's a no-brainer—the internal network is far more

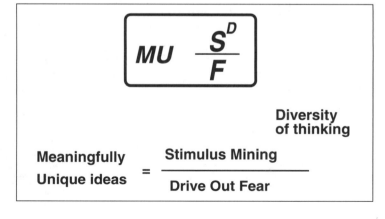

effective. The guru has but one mind—the internal collaborator can leverage the diversity of dozens, hundreds, thousands, or more to apply to challenges.

As detailed in Chapter 6, diversity of perspectives has an exponential impact on the ability of a person or team to discover Meaningfully Unique solutions to the challenge.

But the leveraging of diversity through collaboration doesn't naturally happen in most organizations. There are psychological and operational barriers that prevent most people from collaborating.

Alan Robinson and Dean Schroeder are among the world's leading researchers on the design and implementation of collaboration systems. And, yes, the Innovation Engineering Institute team collaborates with Dean on never-ending continuous improvement of our Collaboration Cafe system.

Collaboration Should Be Easy

In theory, collaboration should be easy. Cooperating with others is something we all learned in preschool. However, somewhere along the way to adulthood, especially in organizations, it becomes more difficult. Research we conducted with over 12,000 employees found that 95% didn't feel their organization collaborated very well. Poor collaboration prevents organizations from realizing the full value of employee brainpower. It also correlates with employees feeling disconnected, overworked, and isolated.

Compare times when you've been on work or sports teams in which everyone is in it for themselves, versus united to help one another. Think of how satisfied, confident, and engaged you felt in each case. A culture of collaboration increases the effectiveness of your entire organization. It creates a sense of belonging, teamwork, and trust that enables you to set strategic missions that are bolder and braver than your competition can.

Employees who are aligned to a common strategic mission (Blue Card) AND who trust their teammates realize joy from their work. They have the courage to tackle ideas and challenges that individually they would view as impossible. **"I can't" is replaced with "WE can."**

When leadership sets up employees to compete, then the organization realizes "less than the sum of the employees." When leadership sets up the organization to collaborate, then they realize more than the "sum of the employees." They realize the "product of the interactions of the employees."

IE Labs: Collaboration Cafe

The Innovation Engineering Institute invests significant time, energy, and money in never-ending continuous improvements of our digital collaboration subsystem. Collaboration Cafe is designed to address the 10 psychological and operational barriers and boosters to collaboration that are detailed later in this chapter.

I must openly admit, however, that while I believe we have the best sustainable collaboration system in the world, in my opinion we are not nearly as effective in the absolute as I believe we can be. We have a continuous project to improve, test, and rebuild our Collaboration Cafe approach. However, **the forces against collaboration are growing as fast or faster than we are with our improvements.** Employee willingness to collaborate with others declines every time there is a corporate downsizing that sparks fear, an internet hack of confidential information, or an embarrassing exposure of private conversations. However, as Ben Franklin said, **"As long as I have known the world I have observed that Wrong is always growing more Wrong, and that Right, however opposed, comes Right at last."**

The 10 Things We've Learned in Our Study and Implementation of Collaboration Systems

The Innovation Engineering Institute has built a Collaboration Cafe into the IE Labs portal. It includes a digital system for sharing and a human system for how to activate it. If you are building your own or evaluating commercial collaboration offerings, the following dimensions are what we suggest you look for in your digital and human collaboration system.

1. IDEA COMPETITIONS KILL COLLABORATION. Academic research and our field-testing finds, without a doubt, that idea competitions kill collaboration. When ideas are judged with prizes for "best idea," the intrinsic motivation to share ideas and advice is replaced with extrinsic rewards. This works once or twice, but soon no one makes suggestions. It doesn't matter if you evaluate using a team of experts or via crowdsourcing of the vote, the result is the same.

Think about it. If you have 1,000 entries in your "idea" beauty pageant, you end up with one winner and 999 losers. What do you think the odds are that the losers will submit the next time you ask for ideas? Now you understand a key reason old-fashioned or new digital "suggestion box" contests rarely go beyond two or three rounds.

To ignite collaboration, we must replace competition with cooperation. Collaboration is about the group winning. Done right, ideas are built from other ideas. Let's assume that there are "bad ideas"—here's the chain reaction. Bad Idea + Bad idea + Bad Idea = Decent Idea + Bad Idea + Bad Idea = Good Idea + Bad Idea = Great Idea. If you simply reward the end, you declare all of those who contributed along the way to be losers. AND you lose the ability to access the multiplier effect.

2. BRIBING PEOPLE TO COLLABORATE KILLS COLLABORATION.

Related to competing for the best idea is bribing people for ideas. Hundreds of academic studies validate that intrinsic rewards are far more powerful than extrinsic rewards. Intrinsic rewards mean a sense of meaningfulness, personal satisfaction, and pride in work. Extrinsic rewards are cash payments or prizes for contributions.

You can provide recognition for ideas. But recognition must be of the group because it is the group, not the individual, that ignites collaboration. For example, you can create a monthly breakfast or pizza party for those who collaborated (requesting or giving ideas) at least six times in the previous month. This nurtures a sense of belonging and provides an opportunity for group celebration. If you insist on giving out prizes (and frankly, some companies can't resist), randomly draw winners from a hat of those who collaborated six or more times that month.

3. LET PEOPLE KNOW SPECIFICALLY WHAT YOU NEED IDEAS FOR. As

you would expect, we did research among employees on collaboration. Surprisingly, the number one barrier was "lack of alignment on what is very important."

BIGGEST BARRIER TO COLLABORATION

- **Problem 1. Lack of alignment on what is very important** **45%**
- **Problem 2: Ego** **25%**
- **Problem 3: Don't know how to collaborate (who, where, how)** **16%**
- **Problem 4: Fear** **14%**

Problems and inefficiencies within organizations exceed the time available to work on them. Employees are aware of this. To generate momentum for collaboration, it's important to be clear about what you need help on and why you need that help.

When this research came in, we changed how requests for ideas and advice are executed in our Collaboration Cafe. We created a simple form that nudged those asking for help to fill in five boxes.

- **Request Name:** Suggestive of what you're requesting
- **Background Narrative:** Critical background you want responders to know. It's common for this to include the narrative from the Blue Card.
- **Request:** A specific description of what you need help with
- **Don't Request:** Things you are NOT interested in, if any
- **Expiration Date:** This aligns others on your sense of urgency.

Clarity of request creates alignment on what you need collaboration on. When I was a brand manager at Procter & Gamble, we needed a way to make it easy to build a display of our bar soap products in grocery stores. The only option appeared to be a multimillion-dollar investment in new equipment to create specialized displayable shipping cases. On a visit to one of our manufacturing plants, I gave technicians working the line a specific description of the challenge. After winning their trust and support, they started creating ideas. Soon we were cutting open cases, flipping around the product, and voilà—we had a case that could be created from existing cases. Versus the multimillion-dollar investment option, the employee idea required no capital investment and a running cost of just 5¢ per case, instead of $1.50.

4. USE THE PULL OF MISSION TO VAPORIZE THE EGO BARRIERS. I am amazed at how scared people are to ask for help.

- They see asking for help as a sign of professional weakness.
- They see asking for help as admitting they are stupid.
- Their sense of self-worth requires them to know all the answers.
- They view ideas as a zero-sum game. If someone else has an idea for them, they lose.
- "Not Invented Here" is culturally considered acceptable behavior.

The simplest way to vaporize ego challenges is to refocus thinking on something that is bigger and more important than the individual. When the Blue Card mission is bigger than any person or department, it's easier to sacrifice one's ego for the larger cause.

Another way to help overcome the ego challenges is to inspire intrinsic motivation instead of extrinsic. This is accomplished when we help one another as people instead of because of the level you have in the organization.

To enable people to help people, we have designed Collaboration Cafe to be a "many to many" idea system instead of a "many to one" system. Many to one collaboration systems bring ideas to a central command that screens ideas. Many to many systems bring ideas to the person closest to the work. This means that people are directly helping people, not an unidentified someone. The result? Instead of "showing off" for the boss, workers support someone in need of help.

The simplest "booster charge" we have found for encouraging collaboration is to say thank you to those who have contributed ideas. When a request is coming to an end in the Collaboration Cafe, the system nudges the requester to send out a thank-you note—using a simple click—to those who have requested. Nothing motivates more effectively than the overt, emotional, unconditional feedback of an honest thank-you. Whether it's a child, a friend, an employee, or a boss, an honest and direct thank-you works miracles.

5. DESIGN YOUR SYSTEM TO ADDRESS THE FEAR FACTOR. As you learned in the Create chapter, fear is crippling. When it comes to collaboration, employees may be afraid of looking stupid because they need help, exposing secrets inside or outside the organization, or being laughed at because their ideas aren't good enough. The simple way for an adult to avoid feeling fearful is to simply not ask for help or offer help to others. If you do nothing, you can't look stupid or make a mistake.

The first step in addressing fear is acknowledging that it is very real. Dissolving fear takes time. When employees perceive that the benefits of collaborating are greater than the perceived "costs" to them, they will collaborate.

One way to help build the courage to collaborate is to enable people to control their public exposure. We do this in the Collaboration Cafe by allowing them to create private networks for collaboration. Just as they have control over whom to friend on Facebook or LinkedIn, so, too, can they control whom they share ideas with. Another way to build courage is to make it possible for people to respond privately to the request post. This means only the person making the request can see responses, not everyone to whom the request was sent.

From a human system perspective, it's important that there be clarity from the leadership of the company, division, department, or work group on what can and can't be shared inside and outside of the company/

department. It doesn't have to be fancy—just a simple statement of what is confidential and what is not. It also helps to make it clear who an employee can talk with to get an answer if they are unsure on a confidentiality question.

One of the surest ways to kill collaboration is to raise fear, uncertainty, and doubt about information security. The most dramatic case of this I've seen was during a recent Innovation Engineering Accelerator project in Italy. Just prior to requesting help from a panel of outside experts, one of the company leaders raised the question of confidentiality. The executive leading the project explained that the outside Collaboration Cafe was private, and all on it had signed confidentiality agreements with the company. Sadly, despite this reassurance, when the participants had a choice, virtually none sent out requests to the outside Collaboration Cafe; they only used the internal Collaboration Cafe of people in the room. Just the hint from the boss that there might be an issue was enough to kill what would have been valuable collaboration.

6. OPERATIONALLY, MAKE IT EASY TO COLLABORATE. Make it simple and easy to collaborate. The more work it takes to share an idea, the less likely people will take the time to do it. In today's world, this means you must have a digital system that is really, really easy to use. The default standard is the Facebook timeline. It must be that simple.

Importantly, your system for collaboration must run on the "computer in employees' pockets"—that is, their smartphone and/or tablet. Make it painless for people to input their ideas, speak their ideas, send photos, and/or even a video in response to a request for ideas. We have found with Collaboration Care that it's helpful to have templates for different types of requests. Currently we use these four types of posts.

- **IDEA Post**: For sharing news, ideas, or insights
- **REQUEST FOR HELP Post**: For asking for ideas, insights, or advice
- **BLITZ CREATE Post**: For creating a REAL-TIME online chat session to create or problem solve
- **LEARNING REFLECTION Post**: For sharing and asking your team to share "What did you learn?"

We've also found that in larger organizations it can be hard for people to know whom to ask for help across the many departments and divisions. To make it easy to get to the right people, we set up collaboration groups of experts on special areas. Classic groups include:

- **Company Innovation Cafe**: For sharing with those who have been trained in Innovation Engineering
- **Writing Cafe**: For help with communicating ideas
- **Research Cafe**: For help with evaluating ideas and doing forecasting
- **Tech Mining Cafe**: For help finding technologies and vendors

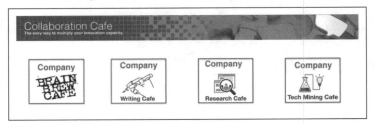

A simple human system for encouraging collaboration is morning stand-up meetings. Verne Harnish taught me about the power of these meetings. They are very quick meetings in which each person in your work group gives 1 minute on what they learned the day before and 1 minute on what they are working on that day, with specific requests for help they might need to get their work done.

7. LEAD FROM THE FRONT. A culture of collaboration starts with the leadership of the company/division or department asking for help. When you open yourself up to needing help, you make it socially acceptable for others to ask for help.

When, as the leader, you take the lead in asking for help, you start the transformation. When ideas come in, you need to be active in responding, being honest with your thoughts, and encouraging more ideas. You need to make it socially acceptable to have vigorous debate. As Edwin Land, inventor of the Polaroid camera system, said, "Politeness is the poison of collaboration."

When you, the leader, are open to new ideas and curious about others' opinions, and you embrace diversity of thought, then others will too. This means offering ideas to others as well as requesting ideas. Offer ideas—good ideas, foolish ideas, fun ideas, bold ideas. Be a part of the process.

When it comes to leading from the front, one of the best I've ever observed is Ken Grier, creative director of Macallan Scotch whiskey. No one is more open to new ideas and learning than Ken. He is a sponge for learning and ideas. He has crafted collaboration partnerships with one of the producers of the James Bond films, world-class photographers, and cutting-edge companies like Oakley. My personal take on what drives his openness to collaboration is his relentless passion for the Macallan brand. I've joked that, if he got a cut, he would bleed Macallan whiskey. His passion is addictive to anyone who connects with him.

8. INVEST THE TIME TO MAKE COLLABORATION A HABIT. The fear and ego issues that prevent collaboration are deep-seated. Simply turning on a digital portal will not change that. To make collaboration stick, it needs to become a cultural norm or habit. This requires collaboration becoming a proactive idea-discovery process, not just a reactive fire-fighting tool.

A collaboration culture will not happen without the involvement of leadership. This means, among other things, asking in every meeting, every day, a version of one of the following:

- From whom could we learn?
- Whom could we ask?
- Who might know another way of doing this?
- Who has done something like this before?
- Who has retired from the company that we could ask?
- What vendor of ours might know about this?
- What outside expert could help us?
- From whom could we get a second opinion?

We make collaboration among those in our company, division, department, or work group happen every week. This is done by creating a rotating responsibility to post a collaboration request each week. As part of regular department or team meetings, introduce the request and provide some stimuli to spark initial ideas. Post the ideas on the Collaboration Cafe digital platform to spark additional ideas from employees. To amplify participation, comment on posts. At the end of the week, sort and document ideas into "just do," "learn more," and "archive." And most important of all, write a thank-you to those who participated. I fully understand that it will take an investment of some time and energy to manage this system. However, given the exponential potential for diversity to enable Meaningfully Unique ideas, the payout on the investment of time and energy is a no-brainer. And, in the process, you will be creating a culture of collaboration.

9. ENABLE EXTERNAL COLLABORATION. Internal collaboration creates results. External collaboration transforms companies. Innovative companies like Apple, Google, Procter & Gamble, and GE are among the most aggressive collaborators with experts and innovators outside of their companies.

I can say with absolute certainty that somewhere in the world there is someone who can help you solve your work challenge faster and more creatively than you can by yourself.

At Procter & Gamble, the process of external collaboration is called "Connect and Develop." They have turned collaboration with outside experts into a fine art. One of P&G's top Connect and Develop experts in Europe told me they often use **inventions** to find **inventors**. When they are looking for outside expertise, they search for patents, academic articles, or entrepreneurial companies to contact. They ask the expert what they are working on now, if they can help with their challenges, or if they know someone who can help. The result is that they can quickly identify resources that can help them solve their challenges. Organizing vendors, suppliers, and partners into an external collaboration network turbocharges your employees' ability to DEFINE, DISCOVER, DEVELOP, and DELIVER Meaningfully Unique innovations.

The Innovation Engineering community calls external collaboration the creation of an Innovation Supply Chain. It's a set of one or more Collaboration Cafes established with outside experts, vendors, or even retirees of the company. It starts with sorting vendors into those who are willing and able to innovate versus those whose mission is simply to deliver low-cost production. It is not uncommon for vendors who are small players in your Product Supply Chain to become major Innovation Supply Chain vendors. Similarly, it's also common for vendors who are high-volume low-cost producers to not have the capability or interest in supporting new-to-the-world development projects.

The process of engagement requires leadership engagement because policies within procurement, R&D, legal, and finance will need to be adapted. Whereas before, vendors were simply reactionary to your organization's requests for quotes, now some are innovation partners. They invest their time, energy, and money into doing development for your organization and as such deserve to be compensated—especially if you desire to have their discoveries be exclusive to your organization. To amplify their capability, you create alignment on your needs and enable them with digital tools and education.

10. WORKING SMARTER NOW—ENABLING EVERY EMPLOYEE EVERY DAY. Dr. Dean Schroeder defines the minimum standard for effective collaboration systems as 12 ideas implemented per employee per year. The maximum he's seen is 100 ideas implemented per employee. This level of collaboration can't happen from a central command-and-control system.

A Working Smarter Now Blue Card is commonly set up by organizations to specifically ask for ideas by everyone in the organization. When they are fully implemented, a chain reaction of positives occurs. People believe. People become engaged. The company can adapt faster to market changes. The company's offerings are continuously improved. Work is fun again.

In simple terms, Working Smarter Now is about enabling bottom-up ideas. It's about enabling those who are "closest to the work," be it building maintenance, marketing, selling, production, finance, R&D, etc., to identify and address ways to work smarter right now.

Most of the frontline/bottom-up ideas have a low value. However, Dr. Schroeder finds that, collectively, these "bottom-up ideas" often offer four times greater quantitative impact than formal top-down projects led by continuous improvement experts. That means up to a 400% increase in ideas for goals like cost savings or efficiency, or for selling more. Enabling employees is the fastest, easiest way to increase the return on your investment.

> *Teamwork is the ability to work together toward a common vision. The ability to direct individual accomplishments toward organizational objectives. It is the fuel that allows common people to attain uncommon results.*
>
> —Andrew Carnegie

The commercial value of bottom-up employee ideas is just the start. As employees begin to trust in their ideas, and trust in the culture's willingness to listen to their ideas, they become more engaged in their work. They also become a valuable resource in problem solving transformational LEAP innovations as they are being developed.

Implementing ideas from employees is a key reason that Toyota's quality and efficiency is so far ahead of other car companies. They enable frontline employees to create, validate, and implement ideas for working smarter.

The key to making Working Smarter Now projects work is having a very clear Blue Card that defines the narrative behind the need for ideas and sets clear boundaries on which ideas can be implemented immediately versus kicked up to be larger-scale CORE or LEAP Innovation projects.

What Did You Learn?

- What did you learn about collaboration that confirms your preexisting beliefs?

- What did you learn about collaboration that challenged your beliefs?

- What holds you back from asking for help more often?

- What holds you back from responding to a request for help from others?

- Think of a time when you did collaborate—what did it feel like?

- Think of a time when you resisted collaboration—why did you?

- Of the 10 principles outlined, which do you use? Which do you not use?

- STOP. Right now. And go ask for help from three people on a challenge you are facing.

11

Merwyn Rapid Research Subsystem

Businesspeople who ignore research are as dangerous as generals who ignore decodes of enemy signals.

—David Ogilvy (paraphrased),
advertising legend

Before We Begin—An Explanation

I must admit that, as the founder of the Innovation Engineering movement, I have used my position to name the research subsystem after my father Merwyn Bradford Hall. I did this because without his insistence that I learn Dr. Deming's principles, there would be no Innovation Engineering movement. I also did it because of my appreciation for what he did for me. My appreciation for what he taught me about life and business grows as I age.

I chose research to honor my dad because research and enabling frontline employees to do the research themselves was very important to him. In a keynote speech he gave in 1981, he explained the importance of enabling workers.

All through our plant, we have eliminated quality control technicians. The operators do all of the testing and charting. By giving the tools to the workers, they get it right themselves instead of checking the product at the end of the process.

—Merwyn Bradford Hall

So that's where the name came from. You are welcome to use it in his memory—or simply call this subsystem Rapid Research. So with a toast to my dad, of 18-year Macallan whiskey, his favorite, we begin.

Why Is Rapid Research Important?

- Rapid Research builds our courage to innovate. Real feedback gives us courage to be bold.
- Rapid Research drives teamwork. Fact-based decisions create consensus and alignment.
- Rapid Research makes us smarter. Data enables smarter decisions that reduce risk.
- Rapid Research dissolves politics. Truth conquers ego-driven opinion.
- Rapid Research energizes. Confirmation that ideas are Meaningfully Unique ignites passion.
- Our ideas for innovations are theories of what might work. Rapid Research fuels the DO and the STUDY of our "Plan, Do, Study, Act" cycles of learning.

Rapid Research is usually conducted with the customer for the innovation. In the case of products or services, the customer is often one of the buyers of our offering. In the case of internal system innovations, the customer is also the stakeholders who are impacted by the new system.

As I was taught at Procter & Gamble, research is an aid to your judgment. It is not a replacement for judgment.

For example, as the Innovation Engineering Institute team was developing the 3.0 version of IELabs.com, our board of advisors asked us to explore where we could reduce our scope. They asked the simple question: "Which of the subsystems has the lowest customer interest?"

The answer was easy. The data indicated that patents had the lowest engagement and interest among executives. Despite negative feedback from customers, I felt we needed to pursue the development of Patent ROI (described in the next chapter). I explained, "It's good to be aware that executives don't see patents as important. However, I feel we need to lead in this area. It would be irresponsible for us to accelerate innovation and not provide systems to help turn the ideas into tangible capital assets through patenting."

There was a quiet in the room. The customer data said stop. However, despite the client data, I as the CEO was saying to go ahead anyway. I went on to explain, "I respect that this is not going to be easy. However, I feel it's still right to do, and in fact, in time it could well be our most important contribution to the field of innovation."

I waited for a response. The most experienced executive on the board, Dave Kilbury, then spoke: "You're right. Patents are the new world.

We need to lead on this. We have no choice. We are going to have to teach executives about patents—what they are and why they matter. And that is going to take time. We are just going to have to have patience."

Thus, in this case, it made sense to continue to work on Patent ROI, even though the customer saw it as not critically important today.

Conservative Companies Invest Time and Energy in Quantitative Research

Leaders and managers at conservative companies understand that innovation has risk. They also understand that with risk comes reward. Each point on the graph below represents a new product or service innovation. The more new and different an idea is, the greater the risk of failure as well as reward. Conversely, the less new and different the innovation, the greater the likelihood that you can't get a big wow with customers as well as a big failure.

Fortunately we can reduce risk dramatically before we have to make major investments. Conservative cultures understand this and as such are heavily invested in Rapid Research systems.

Conversely, companies that are "gamblers" rely on judgment instead of customer data to make decisions. As the chart below details, the goal

Drive Down Risk Before Making Investment

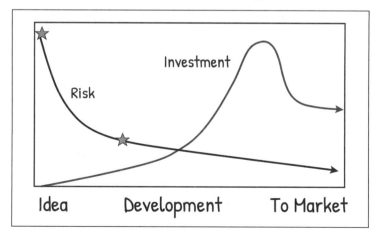

with Merwyn Rapid Research is to drive down risk before making major investments in the innovation.

Five Mind Shifts for Enabling the New Mindset Toward Rapid Research

In most organizations, customer research is used as a tool for controlling, not enabling, innovation. And, when it comes to internal system innovations, virtually no research is ever conducted, especially quantitative research.

SHIFT 1: LEARNING BECOMES THE PURPOSE OF RAPID RESEARCH. With the new mindset, research is a tool for enabling learning. Research is frequent and fast. There is no stress in a low test score, as it is a part of the learning process. Projects that have never had a failure in Rapid Research are suspect, as the team is "playing it safe." Decisions on projects are made through the combination of: 1) Strategic Alignment, 2) Forecast of impact (sales/profitability), and 3) Research data from customers/stakeholders.

SHIFT 2: THE PURPOSES OF QUALITATIVE AND QUANTITATIVE RESEARCH ARE NOT CONFUSED. The purpose of qualitative research is to gain understanding. From this come fresh insights and ideas. The purpose of quantitative research is to confirm that the theories are statistically reliable. One of the easiest ways to reduce innovation risk is to use more quantitative research to aid your decision-making.

SHIFT 3: MORE SMALL TESTS AND FEWER BIG TESTS. The new mindset involves lots of small yet still statistically significant tests as innovations go from idea to reality. This is in contrast to the old approach of months of work, primarily qualitative, leading to a big make-or-break test—the big test being either a quantitative test or simply a senior leader's judgment on the innovation. Jim Bangel, of Procter & Gamble's R&D department, taught me this. He said, "You learn more by running lots of small tests quickly—learning and adapting between each test—than you do by running big, slow, and expensive tests."

SHIFT 4: FAST, CHEAP, AND EASY. When research is fast, cheap, and easy, you can painlessly experiment with bolder, bigger ideas with less risk to your ego, budget, or reputation. Current quantitative research at companies is slow and expensive, with 72% of executives reporting that it takes a month or more to create and field research to get customer feedback on a new idea. The consequence of this slow "cycle time" is that we rely on opinions and judgment instead of factual learning.

Here's the math on the existing way and new way to do innovation research.

EXISTING WAY: 3 months to design materials, field a test, and analyze results means that you can do 4 cycles of learning a year!

NEW WAY: 4 hours to design materials, field test, and analyze results. This means you can run 2 cycles of learning a day, If we assume 250 weeks, that means 500 cycles of learning a year. And that's for the slowest of the Merwyn Rapid Research methodologies. The use of advanced artificial intelligence systems makes it possible to get data-guided feedback on ideas in microseconds.

SHIFT 5: QUANTIFY THE END RESULT, NOT SIMPLY THE IDEA. The old mindset evaluated ideas. The new mindset evaluates the impact of the idea within a broader framework. For new or improved products or services, this means a sales forecast. When we evaluate the whole, we take into account the chain reaction of changes that occurs for each distinct idea. For example, research finds that ideas with a higher level of Meaningful Uniqueness amplify the impact of an equal marketing investment on awareness, distribution, and repeat rate. In the past, turning ideas into sales forecasts was painful. In today's digital world, it's painless to do sales forecasts for every idea.

What Customers Can and Can't Tell You in Research

Customers cannot tell you what innovation to create for them. As Dr. Deming said:

> *A customer can seldom say today what new product or new service would be desirable to him three years from now, or a decade from now. New products and new types of services are generated, not by asking the consumer, but by knowledge, imagination, innovation, risk, and trial and error on the part of the producer, backed by enough capital to develop the product or service and to stay in business during the Lean months of introduction.*
>
> *Did customers ask for the electric light? No. They never asked for it, the producer produced it. No one asked for a car,*

> *nor a telephone. No one asked for a copy machine or a fax machine. Innovation does not come from the customers. Innovation comes from the producer, from people who are responsible for themselves and have only themselves to satisfy.*

What customers can do is react to ideas that you present to them. They can react to stimuli that is shown to them. They can score their likelihood to purchase and how new and different they perceive your idea to be.

When reviewing customer feedback, it's important to remember that all customer results in research are overstated or understated. In a tracking study that involved 4,707 customer reactions to new products, among those who say they definitely will buy, only 50% to 60% will actually end up buying. And, among those who say they definitely won't buy, 15% to 25% may actually buy. Therefore, it's important that you use a system, such as the Merwyn Rapid Research tools, that adjusts for overstatements and understatement.

Designing for Faster Speed and Lower Cost

Most market research systems were created in an era of paper-and-pencil questionnaires and manual data analysis. When the digital world arrived, the old systems were translated to the digital world. Merwyn Rapid Research is a rethink of how we do research. It's designed to enable speed of design, fielding, and analysis. Just a few of the things that we leverage in our IE Labs tool set and that you should consider in your research system:

DESIGN QUESTIONS TO REDUCE SAMPLING ERROR BY A FACTOR OF FOUR. The most common customer survey format uses a five-box response system asking customers if they:

- DEFINITELY WOULD BUY
- Probably Would Buy
- Might or Might Not Buy
- Probably Not Buy
- DEFINITELY WOULD NOT BUY

Analysis is done based on a population proportion approach in which you review the percentage of customers who say they definitely would buy (top box) or definitely plus probably would buy (top two boxes).

With Merwyn Rapid Research, we recommend using the average value on a 0 to 10 scale in which 0 = Definitely Would *Not* Buy and 10 = Definitely *Would* Buy.

DEFINITELY NOT BUY							**DEFINITELY WOULD BUY**			
0	1	2	3	4	5	6	7	8	9	10

We do this because it allows us to use a smaller sample size to get the same level of sampling error. Specifically, if you do the math on sampling error on a population proportion versus an average (or mean), you find it takes about four times more respondents with a population proportion to get the same sampling error.

I recognize that this may not sound right to those who don't have a love of statistics. To validate it for yourself, pull out your college statistics book and look up sampling error for a population proportion (percentage rating above a certain level) and the sampling error for an average (mean value). Then solve the equations for sample size at the same sampling error. Eureka, as we say. It takes four times more people with % top box to get the same reliability. Of course, in both cases you need a high-quality, random sample.

BUILD AUTOMATED SYSTEMS FOR CROSS TAB CORRELATIONS AND DATA ANALYSIS. Yesterday it took days and weeks to do statistical analysis. Today, we've built into IELabs.com automated analysis of results. The result is instant statistical significance and one-click exploration of responses by various groups of respondents.

LEVERAGE ARTIFICIAL INTELLIGENCE SYSTEMS TO PROVIDE SMARTER FEEDBACK. The technology exists today to read ideas and give feedback on them.

MODEL THE UNCERTAINTY OF DATA. All research data has uncertainty. The classic approach to reducing uncertainty is to use very large base sizes. This results in high cost and slows development time. The alternative is to use the same risk-adjusted modeling that is done in the financial world. It's called Monte Carlo simulation. As detailed previously, it's a simple system in which you enter the mean and uncertainty (standard deviation, best/worst case) for each measured and estimated input. Your innovation is then introduced through the simulation into the "virtual" market 10,000 times, resulting in 10,000 estimates of what will happen.

This analytical technique enables you to find the collective impact of the various data points you've gathered through your Rapid Research.

KEEP IT SIMPLE. If you want to understand customer perceptions of problems, ask questions using simple language. For a series of possible problems customers might have with your product or service, ask "how big" and "how frequent" each problem is. If you want to know how Meaningfully Unique they perceive your offering, ask purchase intent on a 0–10 scale and uniqueness on a 0–10 scale. Then multiply the average purchase score by 60% and the average uniqueness score by 40%. Then add them together to get the best overall rating. We call this the overall rating or 60/40 score.

How to Calculate Meaningful Uniqueness

Purchase Intent	**New & Different**	**Meaningfully Unique**
0 to 10 Scale Average	0 to 10 Scale Average	
Times 60% +	Times 40% =	**60/40 Score** Or **Overall Rating**

Research Is Our Friend

Sometimes managers are scared to do research on their innovation for fear that they will fail. A number of years ago I was asked by a senior leader at a Fortune 50 company to meet with an innovation team to figure out why they were struggling with development. The company had invested in a couple of years in R&D, and management was getting frustrated with the lack of results.

The technology involved a new type of water filter that "made tap water taste better than bottled water." It was a simple promise. The team had lots of technical data that showed how much purer their water was. They had charts showing how much money a person would save using this filter instead of buying bottled water. They also had an impressive presentation on how much better for the environment it was.

There was one thing missing. They had no data to show that the filtered water tasted better than bottled water. I asked, "How much better does it taste?" They had no answers.

"How long would it take to find out?" I asked.

"A taste test would take three weeks," the market research person explained.

"THREE WEEKS? How about 30 minutes?" I asked.

The researcher responded, "That's impossible."

"What if we changed our approach?" I explained, "I'm guessing 500, if not 1,000, people work in this multibuilding office complex. And in about an hour and a half, they will all be going for lunch. What if we set up a table outside the cafeteria? We could have people test our filtered water and one of the best-selling bottled waters. Within 30 minutes I'm guessing we could have a decent feeling for how we stack up."

The response from the team was nearly violent. They didn't want to run the test. They couldn't. They wouldn't. Their spin was worthy of the worst of politicians. Their whining matched the worst of a terrible 2-year-old.

It was clear that there was a problem they weren't mentioning. I sensed that each of them instinctively felt that the technology was not as good as promised. They knew that the technical test results, while impressive, did not result in better-tasting water. And, frankly, it might actually result in water that actually tasted worse!

Sadly, the conversation that day was about a year too late. The company management was out of patience. The team was out of time, energy, and money to adapt. The project was soon canceled.

However, it didn't have to be that way. If early in the process they had run lots of small taste tests, they could have found out where they stood. They could have used this feedback to continuously improve their filtering process to optimize taste. The project might have been saved.

By knowing where you are strong and weak, you can problem solve. Not knowing where you stand can cause you to fiddle and tamper with your innovation based on guesses and hunches.

A Need for Faster and Cheaper Research Led Us to Building Advanced Research Tools

The Innovation Engineering Institute team didn't intend to build advanced research tools. In fact, we avoided it for some time because of the investment required. However, we quickly discovered that, given the design of commercially available research tools, it was almost impossible for our students on and off campus to run rapid cycles of "Plan, Do, Study, Act" learning that were cost efficient, disciplined, and statistically reliable. Online do-it-yourself survey tools were fast; however, they lacked the "intelligence" to guide the students in smart test design and statistical analysis.

Without Rapid Research, employees can't make smart innovation decisions. This is not a new problem. Lloyd Dobyns reported in the Deming Library video series, "In one group of 300 Ford Company workers [in the early 1980s], only six of them could identify their customer." Dr. Deming then explains, "How can you do your work if you don't know how the customer is going to use it? The simplest task is not defined by procedures; it's defined by the use that's going to be made of your work."

The Merwyn Rapid Research tool suite enables all employees to get qualitative and quantitative feedback on their idea. The world record for Rapid Research was a four-day Innovation Engineering Accelerator project in which some 407 research tests were conducted. They were spilt about 50/50 between qualitative and quantitative. Most important, 100% were disciplined and documented. The result of was the highest sales forecasts—fueled by the highest concept tests—ever achieved.

Here's a quick list of the Merwyn Rapid Research tools for doing research faster and at lower cost:

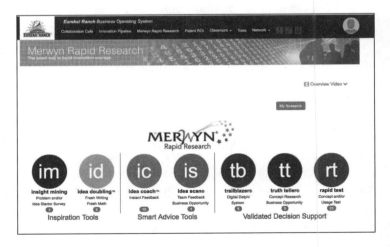

1. INSIGHT MINING: This tool is used to ignite the creation of smarter innovations. It is a simple test that allows the testing of up to 12 "customer problems" and/or "idea starters." The output from the test includes graphic display of results, statistical testing, demographic, and psychographic correlations to identify who relates to each problem/idea starter. Best of all, it's all done automatically—the test can be set up in 5 minutes—and all statistical testing and report generation is done through intelligent software systems. A Video Cross Tab module allows for easy capture of customer perceptions using a smartphone or tablet. This is perfect for use at trade shows or by frontline field staff.

2. IDEA COACH: This is the fastest way to improve your Yellow Card. The system is an artificial intelligence engine that "reads" the idea and benchmarks it on standards that are predictive of success. The system provides ideas and advice in a low-stress, nonconfrontational basis. The inventor of the idea can run the idea through Idea Coach repeatedly to get advice for improving it. Participants say that Idea Coach improved their ideas by an average of 40%.

3. IDEA DOUBLING: When employees get "stuck" on what to do with their innovation concept or math, idea doubling opens them up to fresh ideas. The system allows them to send their Yellow Card concept and/or Math Game Plan to pre-established panels inside or outside the company (secure panels of people who have signed confidentiality agreements) for ideas and advice. In minutes, there are fresh ideas and options for Name, Headline, Customer, Problem, Promise, Proof, Pricing, or each element of the Math Game Plan to spark fresh ideas.

4. TRAILBLAZER DELPHI: This is a simple-to-execute system for effectively accessing the collective intelligence of a work team, department, or group of experts. It enables employees to explore bold ideas by reducing uncertainty and increasing confidence. Classic uses include quantifying the potential for disruptive LEAP innovations; forecasting future trends; and estimating development timing, technical challenges, and competitive reactions.

5. IDEA SCAN: This is a calibrated system for idea evaluation that provides feedback from innovation team members or management against validated standards. It's a simple-to-execute system that involves sending the Yellow Card for feedback and gathering calibrated scoring on the idea plus ideas and advice for improvement. Idea Scan is very addictive. It enables rapid cycles of concept improvement. When run before a management review meeting, it drives out waste by reducing rework and focusing the conversation.

6. TRUTH TELLER: This is the smartest concept and sales forecasting system in the world. It's based on a patented artificial intelligence system. It involves scoring your idea by five calibrated concept raters on 50-plus market-validated factors. It's not an easy test. It predicts, as happens in reality, that most innovations fail. That said, it is the single most truthful test I have ever experienced. One study found it to be seven times smarter than executives at picking winning innovations. It directly inputs into the risk-adjusted Monte Carlo sales forecasting system.

7. RAPID TEST: More important than reaction to the written innovation concept is customer reaction after having used or tried your new or improved product, service, or system. Rapid Test makes it easy to gather customer reaction to both your idea and the actual offering or prototype. Testing can be done on a single product or paired comparison basis, depending on your goals. You get a graphic display of results, statistical testing, correlations versus demographics, and psychographics plus video cross tabs. With preestablished email panels or onsite testing, you can generate a statistically significant test sample in as little as 90 minutes.

8. DIFFUSION OF INNOVATIONS POWERED 5-YEAR SALES FORE-CAST: In today's digital-driven marketplace, word-of-mouth diffusion is often more important than marketing spending. When an innovation has high scores on Meaningfully Unique, it has the potential to ignite a chain reaction of growth. This proprietary model blends a Four-Woodlock trial-and-repeat model with a Bass Diffusion modeling of word-of-mouth. An integrated Monte Carlo simulation provides you with graphical reporting on the probability of various levels of sales, profits, and unit sales. The result is that frontline employees can conduct unlimited "Plan, Do, Study, Act" forecasting cycles to optimize their ideas and business opportunities.

All of the tools listed above are invaluable when working on new or improved products and services. They are equally, if not more, valuable when pursuing system innovations inside your organization. Asking for feedback from employees makes you smarter AND also tells them you care about their opinions.

What I Have Learned About Rapid Research

I've been involved in the testing of tens of thousands of innovation concepts. The four most important things I've learned fielding innovation research are:

1. DISCIPLINE IN RESEARCH DESIGN, FIELDING, AND ANALYSIS:
Sweating the details of a research test is critical if you are to get data that is reliable. This is not hard; however, it does require some education. With Innovation Engineering, we have engineered intelligence into our systems to make it easy to do the right things. If you are doing it yourself, PLEASE, get with someone who understands statistics to help you design, implement, and analyze the research.

I caution you on the use of online market research panels. There are published studies that show they are highly variable based on factors that are rarely controlled. I use them at an early stage to give direction, so long as they are fast and cheap. However, as projects move forward and the decisions are more important, it's my belief that face-to-face quantitative interviews or systems like Truth Teller are much more reliable. And, today, we often find it's actually cheaper to do face-to-face interviews, if you have a system, than it is to do online research.

2. FEEL THE RESEARCH: If discipline is the "logical left brain" aspect of research, feeling the data is the "right brain visualization." I strongly believe that you can't do research analysis or reviews remotely. The more you see, feel, and touch the data, the deeper your understanding becomes. I recognize that this is not for everyone. Classically, it has required understanding how to run statistical analysis programs or at least a spreadsheet for sorting and resorting data. To make it easier, we have incorporated some point-and-click cross tab analysis and forecasting capabilities so that anyone who is willing can get a "feel" for the numbers and their interaction.

Multiple times over the past 35 years, after I've done statistical analysis, I have visualized an answer to a very important challenge. My subconscious mind has sorted through the data and provided me the structure of a solution. The process consists of three steps: 1) immerse in the data, 2) visualize hypotheses, and 3) validate hypothesis through additional analysis or experimentation. The statistical models behind the Truth Teller and Idea Scan tools were invented this way.

If feeling the data is too painful for you, then feel the qualitative inputs. Watch videos repeatedly of those who like and dislike your idea. Feel the pain of your customers by experiencing how your offering and competitive offerings perform. Observe and listen to what customers feel. Over the years, I've spent hours watching butter being purchased in grocery stores, working at a funeral home, following pork from farm to plate, experiencing technical products in action, and feeling the pain of service people working without the proper tools. In each case, visualization was useful in helping me make sense of the thousands of qualitative inputs I'd gathered.

This concept of visualization of ideas is also something that Steve Jobs practiced.

> *If you just sit and observe, you will see how restless your mind is. If you try to calm it, it only makes things worse, but over time it does calm, and when it does, there's room to hear more subtle things—that's when your intuition starts to blossom and you start to see things more clearly and be in the present mind. Your mind just slows down, and you see a tremendous expanse in the movement. You see so much more than you could see before. It's a discipline; you have practice it.*

—Steve Jobs
biography by Walter Isaacson

3. TRUTH BEYOND A REASONABLE DOUBT: As I mentioned earlier, research is an aid to judgment, not a replacement for judgment. In the case of qualitative and quantitative research, we must continually challenge ourselves on the validity of our conclusions. We need to remember that qualitative data has high variance. We need to remember that 95% significance does not mean 100%. If you have 100 factors that you analyze—random dice rolls will result in about five that show up as significant as a result of chance. The challenge is to know which are meaningful and which are not. The same is true with cause and effect. Statistics just indicate that the variables are related—it is up to the researcher to determine if it's actionable cause and effect.

When evaluating Rapid Research results, I ask myself, "Is this research design, execution, and analysis of such a convincing character that I would be willing to rely and act upon it without hesitation in the most important of my own affairs?" In effect, I combine "discipline" with my gut "feel" for a whole-brain decision on taking action.

Note that much has been made about Steve Jobs's disdain for classic market research. However, while he didn't do quantitative tests, we learn in Isaacson's biography of him that he had well over 100 people whom he would bounce new ideas off of. With that number of people, there is a discipline and a feeling that he achieved that provides the same "truth beyond a reasonable doubt" of the largest of quantitative research studies.

4. MOST COMPANIES' SUCCESS STANDARDS FOR INNOVATIONS ARE WAY TOO LOW: This is arguably the most important insight over the past 10 years. When evaluating innovations, it is common to compare test results versus "success norms." These norms are developed based on the minimum level needed to achieve success in the marketplace.

For many years, these norms have stayed stable. However, the world has changed; innovation success rates have gone down. Thinking about this, we developed the hypothesis that in today's world, to break through the clutter and to generate word-of-mouth diffusion, decision standards needed to be increased.

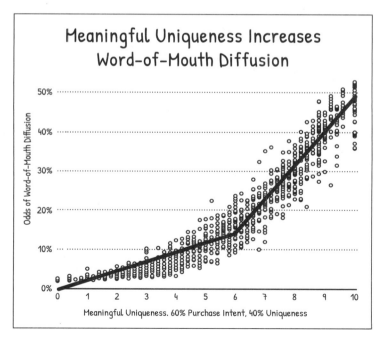

We ran a test of a wide range of innovations that were new to the marketplace. We asked people how Meaningful (purchase intent) and Unique (new and different) they perceived each innovation. A few weeks later, we contacted them again to see if they had purchased and if they had told others about each of the ideas. The research found that there was a threshold where word-of-mouth diffusion grew dramatically. When the "news" value of your idea is above 6.0 (weighting Purchase intent 60% and Uniqueness 40%), the odds of customers telling others about your innovation (word-of-mouth diffusion) goes up dramatically. As the graphic on the previous page shows, the research found that if we took the success standard from 6.0 to 7.5, we could more than double our odds of word-of-mouth diffusion.

The hypothesis was confirmed. What was "good enough" is not anymore. **To win in today's marketplace, research test standards need to be increased.** The good news is that when you do, you have a greater chance of setting off the all-important word-of-mouth chain reaction that generates massive awareness, sales, and profits.

What Did You Learn?

- What surprised you about the new mindset on Rapid Research?
- What confirmed what you already knew?
- Think of a time when research aided your judgment.
- Think of a time when you avoided conducting quantitative research and it cost you.
- How many times does your average innovation get quantitatively tested on its way to market?
- Do you have a conservative organization that is committed to data-based decisions?
- Does your organization approach innovation as a gamble—making decisions on judgment?
- Are your test methods state-of-the-art? What would it take to upgrade them?

12

Patent ROI Subsystem

If you didn't have patents, no one would bother to spend money on research and development. But with patents, if someone has a good idea and a competitor can't copy it, then that competitor will have to think of their own way of doing it. So then, instead of just one innovator, you have two or three people trying to do something in a new way.

—James Dyson
inventor of Dyson Vacuum, Fan, and Heaters

What Is a Patent?

Ideas that are patentable are Meaningfully Unique innovations. Conversely, when an idea isn't patentable, then by the strictest definition it is not a Meaningfully Unique innovation. That's because an invention can be patented if:

- It has never been done before.
- It is not an obvious leap to someone with ordinary skill in the industry.
- It is novel and useful.
- It fits a category of patents.

Patents are legal property. On a balance sheet, they are capital assets. Factories and land are physical capital assets. Patents are intellectual capital assets. As a capital asset, patents can be bought, sold, borrowed against, or loaned. When they are loaned, it's called licensing. Paying a royalty for the right to license a patent is no different from paying someone rent to stay in their house.

Patents enable you to make money on your imagination. When you are paid royalties for the right to use your patent, this is often called Mailbox Money. The profit margin on Mailbox Money is generally 100%. At

Procter & Gamble, the external licensing of their patents, trade secrets, and trademarks generates profits equal to a billion-dollar brand as a result of Mailbox Money.

Why Do Patents Matter?

Patents are the way to wealth in the new world. In the old world of business, physical capital, and assets, the defining measure of wealth was land, buildings, machines, and inventory.

In the new world, intellectual capital—patents, trademarks, copyrights, and trade secrets—are the defining measure of wealth. Estimates of the value of these nontangible assets range from 70% to 80% of the valuation of the average company.

Every product, service, or individual exists on a continuum from Total Commodity to Total Monopoly.

Total Commodity. . . . . .Total Monopoly

The mere word *monopoly* brings with it visions of illegal activity. A monopoly can wield its incredible power improperly. It can flex its power unfairly to destroy potential competitors through artificially low pricing or other strong-arm tactics. For that reason, governments monitor the actions of monopolies very closely.

A patent is a legal monopoly that is supported by governments. Governments around the world support patents because innovation has proven to be the most effective way to build jobs and wealth. And patents are the best way—even if imperfect—to ensure that courageous inventors are able to receive financial benefit from their inventions.

When you have a monopoly on a Meaningfully Unique invention, you realize increased sales and profitability. Patents are also an "insurance policy" for realizing a financial return on your investment in research and development. Without a patent, it's perfectly legal for others to reverse engineer your trade secrets and, in the process, cash in on your inventiveness.

To give you a sense of the importance of patents, Google has over 20,000 patents and applications in progress.

An academic study by Andries and Faems, published in the *Journal of Product Innovation Management,* found that, over a three-year period, 17% of small companies and 43% of large companies filed for at least one patent. The study also found that, for both small and large companies, those that filed more patents realized a higher profit margin.

A separate study by the Innovation Engineering Institute team found that one of the best indicators of a proactive culture within small and mid-size companies was if they had filed two or more patents. The conclusion is simple—patents matter.

To the Patent Owner Goes the Reward

The importance of technology ownership is significant. For example, the original iPod from Apple was designed in the USA and manufactured in China. However, a study by Portelligent, Inc., found that Japanese companies realized the bulk of the manufacturing value from the iPod. Specifically, 83% of the manufactured cost went to Japanese companies for the hard drive, display, and display driver, as they owned the patents; 11% to USA companies for the Player CPU and video processor; 3% to China for assembly; and 2% to Korea for the SDRAM.

To accelerate their profitability, China's published innovation strategy is to reduce dependence on foreign technology below 30%. They intend to do this by graduating 2.9 times more engineers per year than the USA, and to make major investments in wind and solar energy technologies, information technology and telecommunications, and battery and manufacturing technologies for automobiles.

The History of Intellectual Property in the USA

Patent law in the United States is authorized by Article One, Section 8, Clause 8 of the US Constitution, which states: "The Congress shall have the power . . . To promote the progress of science and useful arts, by securing for limited times to authors and inventors the exclusive rights to their respective writings and discoveries."

Exclusive rights means that, in exchange for having the courage, creativity, and commitment to create something that is genuinely original, the inventor is granted a monopoly on the production and sales of their invention. As stated above, basic economic theory finds that when you are the one and only, the sole source, the exclusive provider of a Meaningfully Unique invention, then you are able to charge more and make more money.

Patent Literacy Exam Overview

Before I go any deeper into patents and how to build an effective Patent ROI system, I need to get your attention. To do this I'd like to assess your patent literacy.

The Innovation Engineering Patent Literacy Exam is a collection of 16 true/false questions. The questions are based on the US patent system at the time of this writing. I apologize in advance to my friends outside the USA. In general, the rules are similar in most countries. I needed a base to work from, and given the size of the US Patent Office and the importance of the US marketplace, I felt it reasonable to do the exam and chapter based on the USA. In no way am I diminishing the value of patents in my native Canada or any other country.

Patent Literacy Exam

1. A filed provisional patent application can be seen or searched by your competition.

    True   or   **False**

2. Patent trolls have usually stolen or illegally acquired the rights to patents.

    True   or   **False**

3. In general, businesspeople around the world have become more convinced about the value of patents and are filing significantly more patents.

    True   or   **False**

4. If you find an innovation in another country and file a patent application for it in your country, you can own it.

    True   or   **False**

5. A laboratory or invention notebook, signed and dated, is a first and important protection for your invention.

    True   or   **False**

6. Ideas are not patentable.

    True   or   **False**

7. A new benefit for an industry is usually patentable if the specific benefit is properly documented and explained in the patent.

True or **False**

8. A provisional patent application filed in the USA reserves your right for most of Planet Earth for the term of the application.

True or **False**

9. It usually costs $20,000 or more to prepare and file a patent application in the USA.

True or **False**

10. If you have done an intensive search of the patent databases around the world and find no other patent filings that infringe, you are clear to file and are virtually certain to be granted a patent.

True or **False**

11. A patent in the USA is a great way to stop products being made in the USA, even if they are going to be sold and marketed in another country.

True or **False**

12. With technology changing as fast as it is, patents have no real value in today's business world.

True or **False**

13. Business methods are patentable if you are the first to put conventional steps together as a process used by your organization.

True or **False**

14. When technology is changing fast, the easiest way to get a patent is to make the next logical leap in a technology.

True or **False**

15. A provisional patent application lasts only 12 months and cannot be extended.

True or **False**

16. A registered patent attorney or patent agent must be the author of provisional applications.

True or **False**

Answers to the Patent Literacy Exam

1. A filed provisional patent application can be seen or searched by your competition. **FALSE**. Provisional patent applications are kept secret and only made public if there is litigation associated with a filing date. This is important, as it reduces your risk when filing them. If you file a provisional application and later decide to keep the invention as a trade secret, you can. In addition, if you keep the innovation a trade secret, it protects you from others legally filing a patent on your innovation and thus preventing you from using your trade secret.

2. Patent trolls have usually stolen or illegally acquired the rights to patents. **FALSE**. Patent trolls have almost always acquired the patents by simply buying them. The negative views on patent trolls, as they are sometimes called, are usually associated with their harassment tactics. They will ask for royalties from those who don't have the money to fight them or who find it easier to simply pay them off. In truth, there is nothing illegal about owning a patent. And there is nothing wrong with asking those who are violating a patent you own to either stop infringing and/or pay a royalty for the right to use the patent.

3. In general, businesspeople around the world have become more convinced about the value of patents and are filing significantly more patents. **TRUE**. As the chart in Chapter 1 shows, patent filings in the USA have grown at exponential levels. This is especially true among companies located outside of the USA.

4. If you find an innovation in another country and file a patent application for it in your country, you can own it. **FALSE**. An invention must be new to the world. If it's been done in another country, then you cannot own it. Note that if a year has gone by and the person who owns the patent in another country has not filed in the country you live in, then you are free to use the patent in your country at no cost, as it has become public domain knowledge in that country. However, you can't file a patent on it.

5. A laboratory or invention notebook, signed and dated, is a first and important protection for your invention. **FALSE**. Prior to March 16, 2013, the date of invention was determined by

documentation in things like signed notebooks. Today, the date the invention was filed at the patent office is the date that matters. That means the first to file wins today. This is why it's important to have a system in place to go from idea to provisional patent application filing as quickly as possible.

6. Ideas are not patentable. **TRUE**. What is patentable is the method of accomplishing the idea. For example, the idea of "walking on water" is not patentable. However, the method for accomplishing it, assuming you can, is patentable. This is a common point of confusion—businesspeople think in terms of ideas, not "enabling methods." To use the language of the Yellow Card, benefits are not patentable—what is patentable is the method or the proof of how you do it. Importantly, the "how" must be a nonobvious leap from what has been done before.

7. A new benefit for an industry is usually patentable if the specific benefit is properly documented and explained in the patent. **FALSE**. Benefits are not patentable. Only the method of construction, design, composition, etc. is patentable if it's a nonobvious leap from what has been done before. Patents are about the "how" of what you are doing. This is another reason why building prototypes, and getting your hands dirty, is so critical to innovation.

8. A provisional patent application filed in the USA reserves your right for most of Planet Earth for the term of the application. **TRUE**. A provisional patent application filed in the USA establishes your rights on Planet Earth. At the end of the term—one year— you must then file full patent applications wherever you desire to own the invention.

9. It usually costs $20,000 or more to prepare and file a patent application in the USA. **FALSE**. The cost for filing a provisional patent application is $130 to $260, depending on the size of your company. Legal fees are usually less than $1,000 for a provisional. For most full patent applications, if the inventor is engaged in the process, the total cost for fees and legal fees should be about $5,000, plus or minus. Very complex inventions can cost more. Even these costs can be reduced dramatically through the use of the Ideas to Patent application found on IELabs.com. The cost for patents goes

up dramatically when you file in lots of countries and/or get into long litigation. Note: Most patent fights never go to court. Most of the time a "cross licensing" of patents is worked out between the lawyers of the two parties.

10. If you have done an intensive search of the patent databases around the world and find no other patent filings that infringe, you are clear to file and are virtually certain to be granted a patent. **FALSE**. Someone doesn't have to have filed a patent to block your patent. If someone has been publicly practicing your invention or disclosed it in the public domain previously, then their work will block your patent.

11. A patent in the USA is a great way to stop products being made in the USA, even if they are going to be sold and marketed in another country. **TRUE**. Patents cover the practice of producing, distributing, or marketing of an invention in that country. The great challenge many Western companies will face is when China achieves its mission of Chinese companies filing millions of patents. This could block the manufacturing of Western products that are covered by Chinese patents.

12. With technology changing as fast as it is, patents have no real value in today's business world. **FALSE**. In practice, many patents build on one another. This is called patent stacking. As new versions of products are developed, companies build on what they had filed earlier. When your organization can innovate faster than the competition, it also makes it possible to have both patents and trade secrets. When you file a patent, you have to tell all that you know. However, what you learn after you file you can keep as a trade secret. This is commonly done by filing a patent on the "article of manufacture," then keeping the manufacturing process as a trade secret.

13. Business methods are patentable if you are the first to put conventional steps together as a process used by your organization. **FALSE**. While business methods are patentable in the USA, they must be nonobvious. If your invention is a collection of conventional steps that are assembled such that someone with ordinary skill in your area of invention might think of it, it is not patentable.

With method patents, it's especially important to identify not only what you are doing, but also what you are excluding from the invention.

14. When technology is changing fast, the easiest way to get a patent is to make the next logical leap in a technology. **FALSE**. Logical leaps are not patentable. Smart and intelligent steps forward are deemed obvious by patent law. To be granted a patent, you need to be nonobvious. This means being surprising or even a rebel with your invention.

15. A provisional patent application lasts only 12 months and cannot be extended. **TRUE**. Provisional Patent Applications define your rights around the world for 12 months. To extend your rights, you need to make a formal filing of a full patent application before 12 months from the filing of the provisional application.

16. A registered patent attorney or patent agent must be the author of provisional patent applications. **FALSE**. Provisionals, like all patents, can be written and filed by anyone. However, it is not advised to do this, as you could make mistakes without knowing it. That said, you can save significant money by doing much of the writing of the first draft of your patent applications yourself.

The Barrier to Patents Is Ignorance

Add up the number of questions you answered correctly from the quiz, then divide by 16 to get your percent correct. If your score is low, don't be surprised. Look upon it as an opportunity for learning. A small-scale test among business executives found that they got an average of 62% correct. Recall, as a true/false test, 50% would be right by pure guessing!

There is a need for a massive education effort on patents and intellectual property among business leaders to teach them how to lead their companies' efforts at building value and competitive advantage through patents. There is also a need to teach employees the fundamentals because, every day, they are inventing new machines, methods, and tools that have the potential to add value to their organizations' intellectual capital.

That's why we've developed Patent Workshops taught by Innovation Engineering Black Belts. They make it easy for everyone to understand and utilize patents.

Patent Growth Is Uneven

Some industries are embracing patents—others, ignoring them. Not surprisingly, profitability is higher in industries in which companies have more patents and thus offerings that are Meaningfully Unique.

Leading or working at a company that is focused on patents has a tangible benefit to you—you can make more money! **The US Patent Office found that, on average, wages are 42% higher for those employees who work in intellectual property–intensive industries versus nonintellectual property–intensive industries.** The reason is simple. At these companies leaders and employees are paid more because they use their brains more!

What Is Patentable?

At its most basic, a patent is an invention that is Meaningfully Unique. In the language of the patent office, this means it's useful, novel, and nonobvious. (Technically, it also has to fit a statutory class, as well, such as a process, machine, article of manufacture, composition of matter, plant, or design.)

By far the toughest of these standards is the need to be a nonobvious leap, even for someone who has ordinary skill in your area of invention. This takes some time to think through. A few questions that I ask myself when trying to understand if I have an invention include:

- Is the invention nonobvious, based on what others have done before?
- If I were challenged to create this invention, could I get to it with some simple thinking?
- Am I doing something that shouldn't be done and getting an unexpected result?
- When I explain how it works to someone who knows the area, does it surprise them?
- Does the invention "break the rules" of conventional wisdom?
- Would someone who is knowledgeable argue feasibility with me, if they heard about the idea but didn't see it demonstrated?

The Old World and New World of Patents

The global and digital marketplace, plus major changes in patent law, have created tremendous opportunities for how company leadership thinks about and manages their patent portfolio. To realize these opportunities, a new mindset and system is needed.

Gone are the days when patents were something done by just a few "invention" experts.

Today, everyone who is responsible for finding ways to work smarter needs to be educated on patents. This is done so as to not lose opportunities for building the company's intellectual capital valuation. It is also done because public domain or free patents are quite simply one of the most powerful forms of stimulus for inventing innovations that are Meaningfully Unique.

Gone are patent review committees that decide on what is patented and what is not.

Today, filing of provisional patents is a no-brainer that should take hours, not weeks. AND the organization's innovation development system needs to be fast so that the organization has real knowledge about the potential business value of the invention when they have to make the bigger decision about filling a full patent application a year after filing the provisional patent application.

Gone are the high legal bills for searching and writing patents.

Today, artificial intelligence writing and search systems can enable everyone to write a provisional patent application in about an hour.

Gone are the days when buying or licensing a patent is a long and painful process.

Today, tools like Business Opportunity Forecasts create transparency and common ground for coming to an agreement. Specialized search systems like Patent Flea Market make it easy to find and buy distressed patents for a few thousand dollars.

Gone are the days when patents are an expense.

Today, licensing patents and other intellectual property turns the patent group into a profit center. Tools and systems are available to make it easy to value technologies and to translate them so that other organizations can easily assess and license them.

What Is Patent ROI?

The Patent ROI is a set of tools built into IE Labs. Their purpose is to increase the Return on Investment realized from the patent process. It does this by enabling everyone to use patents for inspiration and to write

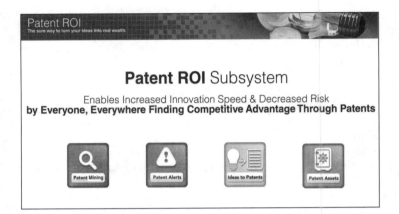

and file a patent on their invention. Patent ROI makes the patent process inclusive. An organization's patent department moves from being judge and jury to an enabler of education and engagement by employees.

Enabling employees to use, define, and file patents is critical for success. That's because only employees can file patents. The patent office does not recognize companies as inventors. Only people invent. The inventor can then assign the rights to an organization.

There are four major parts to the Patent ROI Subsystem:

1. PATENT WORKSHOPS: The foundation of Patent ROI is education in the world of patents. The curriculum covers the what, why, and how of patents. It's taught using the same patent-pending Cycles to Mastery system that is used to teach Innovation Engineering on and off campus. It consists of a collection of digital classes plus hands-on lab classes in which the learning is made real. At the end of the workshops, participants know: 1) What patents are and why they are important, 2) How to use patents to spark new ideas, 3) How to search for patents and set up alerts, 4) What is and isn't patentable, 5) How to write a patent in about an hour, and 6) How to quantify the business potential for a patent.

2. PATENT BLUEPRINTS AND ALERTS: Patents are step-by-step plans or blueprints for building new products or systems. The Patent ROI subsystem on IELabs.com contains an up-to-date version of the US patent database. It divides patents into three sets:

a. FREE Patent Blueprints: These patents are great stimuli for inventing new ideas. They are free for anyone to use, as they are in the public domain for various reasons.

b. FLEA MARKET Patent Blueprints: These patents are a great buying opportunity. They are patents for which the owner has not paid maintenance fees—and thus they have "given up" on them. There is a six-month grace period during which they can often be bought from the owner at a good price and reinstated with the payment of maintenance fees and a small penalty.

c. IN FORCE Patent Blueprints: These are patents that are current and valid. They can help you identify opportunities for licensing. They can also help you identify companies that might be interested in buying your invention, as they are active in patents in your area.

The Invention Blueprints database has three other very cool features:

a. SUB CLASS QUICK SEARCH: This feature allows you to quickly find the 40 to 60 most relevant patents for searching. It does this by helping you quickly find and review the right set of the 150,000+ sub classes that patents are divided into.

b. CAROUSEL QUICK REVIEW: This allows you to review the key info on a patent—name, abstract, and first drawing—in seconds. A click of a button allows you to peruse hundreds of patents quickly and mark them for deeper consideration later.

c. PATENT ALERTS: This feature alerts you each week to your choice of patents—new Flea Market or Free Blueprints, as well as filings by your competition or in a specific sub class that is important to you.

3. IDEAS TO PATENTS: This is a seriously cool system that enables anyone to define, search, and write a decent provisional patent application in about an hour. The process starts from a well-written Yellow Card and a drawing. It's powered by an artificial intelligence engine that takes the inventor through three "Plan, Do, Study, Act" cycles. The output is a report that can be taken to a patent professional for reviewing, editing, and filing.

4. PATENT ASSETS: A simple system for translating patents into business opportunities that anyone can understand in two minutes or less. The system involves translating the patent into a Yellow Card, then doing the math to estimate the sales potential. Tools like Fair Market Royalty calculator, created with funding support from the Kauffman Foundation, provide transparency and common ground for valuing an innovation. They also make it easier to negotiate a fair market licensing agreement.

What I Have Learned About Patents

I have always loved the idea of patents. The concept of turning ideas into capital assets is exciting. I was always frustrated by how hard it was to understand them. Innovation Engineering has given me the opportunity to learn how to use them and how to make the system easy for anyone.

My educational mentors on patents include David Lafkas, a registered patent lawyer on the full-time staff at the Eureka! Ranch, and my oldest daughter, Kristyn, who is a patent examiner at the US Patent Office in Washington, D.C. The three biggest things I've learned about patents are:

1. PATENTS ARE WORTH THE LEARNING CURVE. I will admit it— patents are often hard to find, read, and understand. However, I have found that it's well worth the effort. And it's not nearly as hard as it seems when you are taught a few simple lessons.

Nothing—and I mean nothing—is more valuable for inspiring ideas than the FREE Patent Blueprints. I often challenge senior leaders to a competition. I will take five of their lowest-level employees plus the Patent Blueprint database. They get their five most brilliantly innovative employees. We both get 24 hours to invent solutions to a significant innovation challenge. The best invention wins. Sadly, no one has taken me up on the challenge. I've even offered to compete for a bottle of 18-year-old Macallan whiskey.

In addition, nothing gets leadership more excited than when you build their capital assets by filing a patent. Patents increase the value of the corporations. And they provide the potential for a legal monopoly.

2. FILE FAST AND OFTEN. Changes in patent laws mean that the first to file wins. What this means is—if in doubt, file. And, as you make improvements on your invention, file again to "stack" your provisional patent application with layers of richness. Once you have filed your provisional patent application, you have 12 months to file a full patent application. Use this time wisely by quickly completing "Plan, Do, Study, Act" cycles to determine if the invention documented in the patent has commercial viability. Sadly, many companies are still treating patent filings as "precious."

The truth is, there should be 100X more provisionals being filed than are being filed today. They are critical to protect your rights to own your invention. They are also important to protect your ability to practice your invention. In today's world, if a competitor files a patent on an invention that you discovered but didn't file for or disclose publicly, then they can stop you from being able to use the invention in your product or processes.

3. PATENTS IGNITE EMPLOYEE INNOVATION. Nothing will build an employee's pride and energy for innovation more than getting his or her name on a patent. This is because those who "have a patent" are considered "geniuses" by most of society. In a world of false creative gurus, patents stand out as a validated declaration of true innovation. They document that the person named as inventor has created something that is a nonobvious leap, even for someone with skill in the area of the invention. This is a big deal!

Quantifying Patents

The value of a patent is quantified by translating your patents into business opportunities.

To give you some perspective on the number of patents that an average company receives, in the USA about one patent is issued each year for every 1,400 employees. In states with high numbers of innovative companies like Washington State and California, one patent is issued each year for every 600 employees. This is the average—the best of the best are much higher.

On innovation projects, I use a simple perspective—no patent, no project. I feel this way because if we're going through all the trouble to make a new idea happen, we might as well own it.

What Did You Learn?

- What surprised you about the new mindset on patents?
- Look back at the questions you got wrong on the Patent Literacy exam—what are the costs/consequences of not understanding the new reality of patents?
- Think of people you know who have patents—what is your perception of them? Would you like others to perceive you the same way?
- What confirmed what you already knew?
- What changes in how you think and take action on patents would provide the greatest benefit to your organization?
- What impact would it have on your organization to require that all innovations be patentable?

I know from readers of draft versions of this book that this chapter creates lots of engagement and conversation. My wish is that this engagement be turned into action. I think NOW is a good time. Please stop reading this book and do an internet search for Patent Searching in your country, or simply go to google.com/patents. If you are at a company with IE Labs accounts, go to Patent ROI, where you can use the fast flip carousel, search by sub class, and sort by Free, Flea Market Patents, etc. Then invest a half-hour searching to get a feel for what patents are like. Focus your energy on: 1) Patent Name, 2) Abstract, and 3) Drawings/Images. I think you will quickly find that patents are not as scary as you thought—and they are an invaluable source for new ideas.

13

How to Create an Innovation Culture

*Never say no to adventures. Always say yes. Otherwise you
will lead a very dull life.* —Ian Fleming
author, James Bond novels

*Tis easy to form a good, bold resolution, but hard is the task
concerning execution.* —Ben Franklin

They say I'm extreme.
I say I'm a realist.
They say, "Sure we need 'Change.'"
I say we need "REVOLUTION NOW."
They say, "Conglomerate & Imitate!"
I say, "Create & Innovate!"
They say, "Globalization is a bumpy road."
*I say, "India and China and Asia in general are within two de-
cades of running the show: Get ready or get trounced."*
They say, "Install cost controls with teeth."
I say, "Grow the Top Line."
*They say "Wait your turn, honor those who have marched
these corridors before you."*
They say this is just a Rant.
I say this is just Reality.
They say, "The man is not nice."
I say, "The times are not forgiving."

—Tom Peters, email to the author

Four-Step Quick Start

Whenever we teach Innovation Engineering, it is not long before someone says, "OK, I get it. How do I create an innovation culture in my _____ (team, division, company, community)?" The starting place is always with yourself. You need to believe in your ability to innovate before you can engage others. The fastest way to do this is to begin with creating ways to work smarter in your daily work. Kevin Cahill, grandson of Dr. Deming and executive director of the Deming Institute, taught me the concept of focusing your efforts first on your "sphere of influence." To paraphrase from the interview with Kevin in the appendix:

> *I know my grandfather said quality starts in the boardroom, and I've heard so many people say, "Well, unless you're at the top, it's not worth doing." I disagree. I believe that every single person in every single organization has some sphere of influence; they can impact something. If they have some understanding of these ideas, some understanding of what the limitations of the system that they're currently operating in are, then they can make a difference in what they're doing.*

So the best way to get started is to just begin. Here's a four-step quick start.

STEP 1: WORKING SMARTER BLUE CARD. Craft a Blue Card defining a Working Smarter challenge. The process of writing the Blue Card will bring clarity to what your challenge is and why it's important to create new solutions for it. Need inspiration to get started? Here are some stimulus prompts.

- In your daily work, what frustrates you?
- What is harder than it should be?
- What problems have become habit?
- What needs to be done but is being ignored?
- What would improve effectiveness or efficiency?

STEP 2: STIMULUS MINING. With your project mission defined, the next step is to do some Stimulus Mining to fill your mind with fresh ideas and insights about your challenge. This involves asking questions, listening to answers, and leveraging the knowledge power of the internet.

STEP 3: CREATE SESSION. Leveraging the perspectives of others has an exponential impact on the quantity and quality of ideas created. It can be done in person or virtually via text, email, or by using the IE Labs Rapid Research tools. Alternatively, you can simply "walk around" and talk to others about your challenge, sharing some of your stimulus findings. The output of this is a collection of Yellow Cards that define the Customer, Problem, Promise, and Proof of your fresh ideas.

STEP 4: PDSA CYCLES OF LEARNING. Make one or more of your Yellow Card ideas real through rapid cycles of "Plan, Do, Study, Act" to resolve Death Threats. You run "Fail FAST, Fail CHEAP" experiments to develop and validate your new idea. Voilà! You've done it! You've Innovated. There is still much to learn; however, you've taken the most important step. The first step.

10 Lessons for Changing a Culture

Getting started is easy on an individual or even a work team level. Changing a department, division, or an organization is more challenging. Obviously, every organization is different. The concept of "variation" is fundamental to the Deming System of Profound Knowledge. That said, there are some simple lessons that can provide guidance on the process. With help from Bill Conway, here are 10 lessons for how to create an innovation culture.

Lesson 1: Understand and Respect Diffusion of Innovations

To create a culture of innovation or to introduce an amazing new product or service, you must, Must, MUST respect Diffusion of Innovations.

Dr. Everett Rogers was a research pioneer on how human beings communicate and adopt ideas. In 1962, he published his *Diffusion of Innovations* theory. It defines how new ideas, methods, and technologies spread through cultures. His *Diffusion of Innovations* book is now in its fifth edition. It is well worth reading.

URGENT: Let me stop the narrative of this book for a minute for emphasis. PLEASE, if you want to be a great leader, buy and read *Diffusion of Innovations*. While you are at it, also buy a copy of *Out of the Crisis* by Dr. Deming, as well as *The Leadership Challenge* by Jim Kouzes and Barry Posner, also in its fifth edition. Collectively, these three books will teach you everything you need to know about leadership.

Overly simplified, Rogers found that within any population of adults there is a distribution of mindsets toward change. This distribution follows a bell curve that is commonly labeled as follows:

INNOVATORS "VENTURESOME": These pioneers are obsessed with innovation. They are the first to try new things. They love change. They have a high tolerance for new ideas that aren't perfect. They see past the flaws and embrace the good of the new.

EARLY ADOPTERS "RESPECTED": Early Adopters like to lead change, but they also know that their opinions are respected, so they are very judicious in their support. They don't accept the flaws that innovators accept. When they feel that the innovation is fully right, they pass the word to the Early Majority that it's time to embrace the new way.

EARLY MAJORITY "DELIBERATE": The Early Majority adopts new ideas before the average member of a culture. However, they rarely lead. They listen to the ideas and advice of Early Adopters. However, they still take a while before they commit. They don't want to be the first or the last when it comes to innovations.

LATE MAJORITY "SKEPTICAL": The Late Majority is very reluctant to change. They usually change only when they are forced to change. The

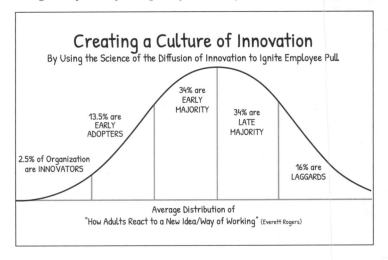

Creating a Culture of Innovation
By Using the Science of the Diffusion of Innovation to Ignite Employee Pull

34% are EARLY MAJORITY

13.5% are EARLY ADOPTERS

34% are LATE MAJORITY

2.5% of Organization are INNOVATORS

16% are LAGGARDS

Average Distribution of
"How Adults React to a New Idea/Way of Working" (Everett Rogers)

pressure of the majority of the culture is necessary before they will take action. They need to feel that it is very safe to change.

LAGGARDS "TRADITIONAL": Laggards live in the past. They are very suspicious of change. In their minds, it is totally reasonable and rational to not change—now or ever. When the organization has made the shift but they themselves haven't, they will organize together to reinforce their belief that change is not necessary.

What I've learned is that the Diffusion of Innovations theory and the distributions are real. You need to respect that the change of a culture—the sustained change of a culture—takes time. To this end, when I attend quarterly meetings with the leadership of companies that are embarking on creating a culture of innovation, a key question I ask them is, "Are we going too fast or too slow with culture change?" When you go too slow, you lose momentum. When you go too fast, you lose people in the process.

Deming Master Walter Werner described the Diffusion of Innovations phenomena to me in a more colorful way. I've reprinted it here in its entirety, as it brings to life the fact that you can't force change. His percents are a little different, but the idea is the same.

> *One thing you will always fight is resistance to change. It occurs at every level. Draw a normal distribution. Now draw two vertical lines equally spaced so they contain about 60% of the population. Draw two more lines on either side so each cuts off about another 15%. Draw two more that cut off about 3% each. The final tails each contain about 2%.*
>
> *Label the horizontal axis RESISTANCE TO CHANGE increasing from left to right.*
>
> *The LEFTHAND tail are EXPLORERS. They are very antisocial people and will always try any new idea. When it works they come back to civilization and they say: "There's land in Kentucky. You have to fight the Indians but there is land in Kentucky!"*
>
> *The next group are labeled PIONEERS. They hate civilization too, but they are a little more cautious. All they need to hear is that the explorer came back alive and over the hill they go. Sooner or later they come back for supplies and they say: "There's land in Kentucky. Oh you have to fight the Indians but there is land in Kentucky!"*

The large central group are labeled SETTLERS. They are patient types but they will move. Once they hear about Kentucky often enough they move too.

They bring schools, churches, doctors, lawyers, and children. They bring civilization. When they move you have won.

The next group are nice people. Call them STRAGGLERS. They are always a day late and a dollar short. They just bought their first VCR and want to tell you about it. Don't worry about them.

The final group are called RESISTERS. "Good enough for Grand Mom is good enough for me!" You will never move them so don't try.

I like to sketch this and use a large anchor for the last group. They hold our culture to its roots, which can be both good and bad. Not every change is good, but some changes have to occur.

Every generation has all five groups. You must find the first two in the left tail for your initial trial activities. You must publish every success so the settlers know about them.

Now keep the same horizontal scale but add a new vertical scale called leadership. Make this sketch a large rectangle. There are people all through the organization that have leadership skills. You hope this includes the executives. Look for the person everyone in a department turns to for advice or the one they always listen to even in group discussions. It is very helpful to get some of them in your early projects.

There are two ways to leverage Diffusion of Innovations to transform a culture.

The "Deming approach" is top-down, leadership driven. Top management leads the transformation, starting with one business unit, then leverages Diffusion of Innovations till the entire organization is innovating.

The other approach is a bottom-up "Instant ROI" approach. A few volunteer "Pioneers" are educated in the new mindset and then set loose on an innovation challenge that a senior or middle manager faces right now. It could be for restarting growth or profitability, new or improved offerings, or ideas for improving an internal system. The pioneers create and accelerate an abundance of ideas, file patents, and fill the metrics dashboard with results. They achieve a tangible return on investment for the project.

The success of the pioneers creates a PULL for innovation within the organization. Other managers soon ask for help solving their challenges and accelerating tangible results. More people volunteer. A chain reaction of positives is experienced as ideas spark new ideas. "I can't" is replaced with "we can."

Instead of going outside the organization's existing work systems, the pioneers work within them. This reduces stress and disruption. For example, instead of removing a company's phase gate product or service development system, the existing system is upgraded to be more effective. This approach to "upgrading not destroying," "improving not starting over," and "collaboration not confrontation" is critical if broad-based cultural support is to be realized.

Eventually, the Diffusion of Innovation also includes the organizational leadership.

Both approaches, top-down or bottom-up, can be successful.

Lesson 2: Educate Everyone

Lesson number two for getting started is education. Dr. Deming understood that leadership had never been taught how to approach business as a system. Famously he would give a bit of a rant when asked if managers were doing enough to change their mindsets. *"Managers don't know about it. How could they know? How could they know there was anything to learn? How could they? How could they? How could they know there was any other way to manage?"*

The creation of a culture of innovation requires education of employees, managers, and leadership. Over the years, we've learned that we are most effective when we teach mixed classes of different levels of employees and across departments. Basically, diversity of student life experiences and responsibilities is very valuable.

Lesson 3: UNSHAKABLE Belief Among Just 10% of Employees Ignites Cultural Change

Over the years we have observed that focusing energy on developing deep belief among a few people is the best way to create a culture of innovation. Research by scientists at Rensselaer Polytechnic Institute confirms this. They reported: "When just 10% of an organization holds an UNSHAKABLE belief, their belief will always be adopted by the majority." UNSHAKABLE belief was defined as "True Believers. People who are completely set in their views and unflappable in modifying those beliefs."

Basically, culture change follows the Bass Diffusion model. Efforts to change "the whole" at one time rarely sustain. Rather, you need to start with a small highly committed group. When the group with UNSHAKABLE belief reaches 10% of the organization, then the new mindset spreads.

Without UNSHAKABLE belief you have virtually no chance of creating a culture of innovation. The professors found "When the number of committed opinion holders is below 10%, there is no visible progress in the spread of ideas. It would literally take the amount of time comparable to the age of the universe for this size group to reach the majority."

From thousands of experiences we've learned that reading a book (sadly, even this book) is unlikely to create UNSHAKABLE belief. Watching a video or even attending a class won't do it. Books, videos, and classes provide foundational understanding but not belief.

UNSHAKABLE belief only comes from hands-on application. To quote US Founding Father Benjamin Franklin, "Tell me and I forget. Teach me and I remember. Involve me and I learn."

To develop UNSHAKABLE belief employees are educated through IE Blue and Black Belt courses. As part of the course requirements, they apply the new mindset and methods on a wave of projects that are within their "sphere of influence." With each success their confidence builds.

The next step is the application of their new confidence on a wave of bigger projects. The innovation zealots are hands-on involved in creating ideas and turning them into realty. They confront and resolve the multitudes of Death Threats that are inevitable with meaningfully unique innovations.

Ideally, upon completion of the second wave, they achieve Innovation Engineering Black Belt certification. Certification is more than a credential to add to a resume. We have specifically designed the Innovation Engineering Black Belt certification process to align with what it takes to build UNSHAKABLE belief. A US Department of Commerce study found that it works. On average, those who complete IE Black Belt certification go on to lead an innovation pipeline that has a valuation that is 28X higher than those who simply attend training but don't achieve certification.

The new Innovation Engineering Black Belts are now ready to teach, coach, and lead others in the new mindset. With coaching support from a veteran IE Black Belt, they then lead others through the journey they have just completed. As they teach others, their UNSHAKABLE belief continues to grow.

Company executives say what they like best about this application-focused learning approach is that while they are investing in their people and culture, they are simultaneously receiving tangible business benefit from the innovation projects that are being accelerated. It's not uncommon for 10 to 50 projects to be accelerated in a year. Note: it's often a blend of many CORE innovations with a few LEAP innovations.

This process of learning with direct application works. The biggest challenge we've observed is the need for what Dr. Deming called "constancy of purpose." It can't be a start and stop. It needs to be focused and continuous to be successful.

Lessons 4 to 9

Before he passed away, I had the honor of spending time with Bill Conway, the former CEO of Nashua Corporation, who was instrumental in igniting and creating the Quality movement with Dr. W. Edwards Deming in the early 1980s.

I met with Bill and his daughter Mary Jane King, CEO of Conway Management. My purpose was to learn his perspective on how the quality revolution started—what worked and what didn't. My hopes were to use that learning to help accelerate the Innovation Engineering movement.

Bill met Dr. Deming when he was in Japan for a meeting with Ricoh. Bill brought Dr. Deming back to the USA to work with his company. This developed into a long alliance. Bill's boardroom was the scene of the first meeting between Dr. Deming and the Big Three US automakers. Nashua Corporation was featured in the NBC White Paper production "If Japan Can, Why Can't We?" When Bill retired as CEO, he created a company called Conway Management, teaching the Deming system to hundreds of thousands around the world.

Lesson 4: Absolute Conviction

The first impression from Bill is an aura of ABSOLUTE CONVICTION. Even at age 84, his absolute belief was still clear and persuasive. He made it clear to me that absolute belief in the power of system thinking was critical for success.

He told me, **"You can't dip your toe"** into the new mindset. You have to jump all in. You must believe that there has to be a better way and that you are not going to stop until you find it and make it work.

Talking with Bill, I got the impression that quality is not a task or a job—it's a religion, and he believes in that religion with his heart and soul. Nothing is more important. Bill told me the story that on one of Dr. Deming's visits he told him he would miss a morning meeting because of a previously booked appointment. Dr. Deming scolded him, "You don't have anything more important to do." Bill canceled his appointment.

Lesson 5: Work on the Right Things

Bill explained that the first role of leadership is to make sure everyone is working on the right things. I explained that many companies are currently focused on cutting costs because customers perceived their offerings as commodities.

Bill's response was clear and direct, **"Then they are not working on the right things. They have to stop working on reducing cost and start working on innovation."** I explained that it was hard to convince them of this. His response was clear, firm, and direct: **"then they're stupid."**

Hearing an 84-year-old man say "then they're stupid" in a loud and firm voice was a bit shocking—even if it was a true statement. I gently challenged him on his directness. He then went on to explain that Dr. Deming was very **impatient** and **sorrowful.**

Sorrowful that he was unable to save every company.

Sorrowful that he could not get through to every leader.

Impatient to get to those whom he could convert, as companies in the early 1980s were dying very fast. Bill explained that they would explain the importance of focusing on quality/continuous improvement twice and if the leader didn't get it, and I quote Bill directly, "then to hell with them." Many CEOs felt insulted by his and Dr. Deming's directness; however, given their absolute conviction, they moved on, without regrets, to those who were willing to learn and apply.

In the case of Innovation Engineering, working on the right things means setting the Blue Cards. I have come to believe that the single most impactful thing that leadership of a company, division, department, or work group can do is to set clear Blue Cards. Then let the enabled minds of employees (enabled with education and tools) discover and develop innovative solutions to address the Blue Cards.

Lesson 6: Leaders Getting Close to the Work

Bill was very clear that one of the big problems with most companies today is that the leadership has become separated from the real work of the company. They don't fully understand the reality of the challenges that workers face. He advocates leaders spending time on the frontlines, learning the work.

To quote Bill directly, **"The bosses need to get close to the work. The work of Sales. The work of Manufacturing. The work of R&D. They need to fully understand the root causes of the workers' challenges."** They can only do this when the SEE, FEEL, TOUCH, and EXPERIENCE the REAL WORK. You cannot get it from meetings, reports, or PowerPoint presentations.

Lesson 7: Offer Amnesty and Admit Failure

When the leadership adopts and applies the new Innovation Engineering mindset, it's common for flaws in past decisions to be revealed. Bill found that it was effective to offer amnesty and forgiveness for all past mistakes. He also encouraged the CEO to take responsibility for the past failures. CEOs were advised to say, "I am the problem because I am responsible for the company's systems and I am working to change."

Lesson 8: Don't Waste Time on "Dippers" and "Oxygen Eaters"

"The world is filled with people who waste your time," Bill said. "You need to work with the willing." The urgency of getting to those who are ready and willing to take action caused Dr. Deming and Bill to be relentless in avoiding two types of "time wasters." He defined "dippers" as those who come to education programs so that they can say, "I've been dipped." They talk a lot and never take action. He defined "oxygen eaters" as those who want to hold long conversations about the virtues of the program—asking for details, references, case studies, etc., as methods of delay from taking action. They seem like they're interested, but in truth they are not.

When educating executives on the system thinking, Bill and Dr. Deming found that people either "got it" or didn't. Given Dr. Deming's age at the time, the sense of urgency drove them to move on to those who got it. As referenced earlier, when people didn't get it, they were sorrowful but took an attitude of "to hell with them."

Lesson 9: The One Big Mistake They Made

I asked Bill what was the biggest mistake they made. **"Given how obvious and common sense our message was, we thought that the change would be**

easy. Looking back, it's clear that we didn't comprehend how difficult change was going to be. The leaders needed much more training and support than they thought they did and that we thought they did." Bill explained. "It is such a change they can't absorb it in the multiday training—they need more help." He went on to explain that if he were to do it all again he would have put in place more teaching of the tools, application of the tools, support systems, and coaching.

The Innovation Engineering movement has confirmed Bill's insight on the need for much more education and support the hard way. The old-world mindset is deeply ingrained in people, cultures, and company systems. And, no matter how hard you try, you can't beat the Diffusion of Innovations curve. It takes time to realize sustainable change—to reach the tipping point of the Late Majority. What is important is that every week, month, and year, you get smarter than you were.

Sustained change takes time. My father wrote that in applying system thinking to manufacturing, "It is not a quick fix. It is a way of life, and according to Dr. Deming, it will take at least five years to fully implement the program."

Today, with the support of engaged and involved leadership, advanced software, and hands-on mentoring systems, tangible results can be seen in 6 months and meaningful transformation in 18–36 months. However, as my father observed, sustained change in a culture still takes three to five years.

The president of a company engaged in Innovation Engineering, when asked how long it will take, said irreverently, "It will take us three to five years. You don't go to bed an alcoholic and wake up cured."

Lesson 10: Enable Everyone, Everywhere Every Day

We started Innovation Engineering on college campuses so as to tap into the rigor, discipline, and wisdom of the academic community. A side benefit was that they also taught us invaluable lessons in how to motivate, ignite, and lead the new generation of Millennial managers and employees.

I can report from firsthand experience living on campus and teaching undergraduates and graduate students for full semesters that Millennials are different from Baby Boomers. I can also report that with system-driven leadership, Millennials are the most effective, dedicated, and technically skilled workers ever!

As a Baby Boomer who was taught that management was about "command and control" driven by objective and inspection, I found the campus experience to be transformational. I personally experienced a new way of leading from the heart, as leadership expert Jim Kouzes teaches. Leading from the heart is about igniting intrinsic motivation by focusing on what matters and what's meaningful.

I learned about believing in the potential for every student. On campus, I've observed liberal arts students who were self-proclaimed "not math people" learn how to do high-quality Fourt-Woodlock Sales Forecasts for innovations in just 15 minutes that 95% of senior business executives could never do.

I'll never forget the student who came to a homework session and submitted his first sales forecast into Innovation Engineering Labs, then came to my desk to watch me as I reviewed it. He waited in anticipation as I reviewed his math and assumptions.

"Well?" he asked.

I looked up and smiled. "It's perfect. You got it."

His eyes misted up as he said, "Since elementary school, I've never been able to do math. You don't know what this means to me."

I have also observed engineering students embrace flights of imagination that are awe-inspiring. They are transformed when the classes connect them to their imaginative right brain, as well as their logical left-brain.

I've worked with top leaders at Disney, Nike, and American Express; starred on network television shows; and written best-selling books, but never in my life have I experienced anything that matches the feeling of satisfaction that comes from enabling students on and off campus to innovate.

When I went on the first of my sabbaticals from the Eureka! Ranch to campus (I've now done it twice) I was getting ready to retire to a world of writing, speaking, and sailing my beloved Winnijean sailboat. At the end of the semester I found myself making a 25-year commitment to teaching Innovation Engineering both on and off campus.

You can also experience the same satisfaction if you believe in your heart of hearts that people are fundamentally good. And, that 94% of the innovation problem is the system; only 6% is the worker.

On a whim I funded one of the singer Donnalou Stevens's Kickstarter campaigns to support the production of a music video. In exchange she agreed to write a song for the Innovation Engineering movement. After many cycles of collaboration it came to life. To hear it or download it, go to innovationengineering.org/wings. Here are the lyrics.

Everybody's Got Wings

A voice unspoken is a voice unheard
A song not sung deserves your words.
A vision unseen might pass you by.
and Wings won't grow till you choose to fly.

CHORUS

Everybody's Got Wings. Everybody can fly.
Everybody's got a song to sing inside.
Everybody can dance, if given a chance.
Everybody's got a gift to bring.
Everybody's got wings.
A past forgotten is freedom's friend
Can you let your self be born again
and can you give your dreams your new found wings
and let the world hear your voice ring

CHORUS

lada die die die, spread your wings and fly
lada die die die, and fly
Together we'll fly across the sky
bringing light to the darkest night
We'll fly to the moon and then beyond
and the dreams we've dreamed will carry on.

CHORUS

Igniting Employee Engagement

When you flip to this new mindset of enabling innovation by everyone, everywhere, every day, you unleash amazing potential.

As reported in the introduction, Gallup research quantifies the employee engagement challenge. It finds that only 38% of managers are engaged in their work, and only 29% of workers are engaged. This is arguably the greatest of wastes at our companies, governments, and universities. But you don't need data to prove it—just ask on social media, ask at your kids' daycare center, ask at the local pub, "Who loves their job and is passionate about what they do for a living?"

The solution to this epidemic of apathy toward work is a new form of leadership. Gallup data gives us some clues. When they analyzed their data to find what could be done to ignite engagement, they found some simple things:

- The mission or purpose of my company makes me feel my job is important.
- This last year, I have had opportunities at work to learn and grow.

As another of my mentors, Barry Bruns, retired USAF colonel, taught me, what is needed is leadership that enables workers to be "Willing and Able."

Being Willing comes from doing what is meaningful. Being Able comes from providing education, growth, and the tools to make meaningful ideas happen.

Closing Thoughts

When my time with Bill Conway was over, I asked him what advice he had for me as I embarked on the journey to create an innovation revolution. He put his hand on my shoulder, looked me straight in the eye, and said:

You have to do it. America needs it now. The country is failing because bosses are not doing the right things. Do it now. Do it faster. Have no tolerance for excuses.

Bill said "America," but frankly my friends in Canada, Mexico, Europe, Asia, and South America are feeling the same urgency. Now is the time to reinvent our community, our company, our country, and the world.

The process starts with you taking personal responsibility. You won't do it right, you won't be perfect, but you will get smarter and smarter with each cycle of learning—and that's how you can and will change your world. When he feels I'm discouraged, my mentor, Walter Werner, often quotes what Dr. Nelson taught him long time ago:

"You are the best we have. Now go do it."

So, too, it's time for you to just go do it. And by doing I mean applying what you've learned AND, even more important, making a personal commitment to never-ending, continuous learning. When this book was finished, I sent an email to Walter and Barry thanking them for their ideas and advice during the writing process. True to form, Walter responded with a challenge to me to continue my learning journey.

Thank you for letting me help. Each of us grows as we go through life. Dr. Deming used to tell us in the most humble voice: "Please help me. I just want to learn." He was never being false or coy. He lived to learn and to grow. We are building a cathedral of ideas one block at a time. Each idea has to be shaped and placed only when its time has come. We each need to learn and to grow so we can teach and share. I can't share what I don't understand.

Fisher gave us statistics. Shewhart gave us control charts. Deming gave us a system of thought that allowed us to put these tools and many others to work in modern organizations. Innovation Engineering defines, refines, and expands the purpose of Deming's system.

There is no end to PDSA. No one can truly say they have done Deming and then wipe their hands as if they completed anything. There is no end to Deming. There is no end therefore to Innovation Engineering. What we understand and document today is only the foundation for tomorrow. There will be another generation after this one and another after that.

PDSA never ends. Knowledge is never complete. Wisdom is only gained a tiny bit at a time. There is so much left to do. Be safe my friends.

So what are you waiting for? Get up, get out, get going! As Ben Franklin said over 200 years ago:

"Up sluggard and waste not life, in the grave will be sleeping enough."

One last time. Stop and step back and THINK.

Backstory: Who is Dr. W. Edwards Deming?

It's so easy to do nothing. It's a challenge to do something. Learning is not compulsory; it's voluntary. Improvement is not compulsory; it's voluntary. But to survive, we must learn. The penalty for ignorance is that you get beat up. There is no substitute for knowledge. Yet time is of the essence.

—Dr. W. Edwards Deming

The Innovation Engineering movement is focused on changing the world by enabling innovation by everyone, everywhere, every day, resulting in increased innovation speed and decreased risk. This is not marketing puffery but rather a clear statement of intent that is grounded in the success that Dr. W. Edwards Deming had in helping rebuild and restart the country of Japan in 1950 and the Western world in 1980.

The Transformation of Japan

After World War II, the country of Japan had a negative net worth. It owned no natural resources. All oil, steel, wood, etc. had to be purchased off the island and shipped in. Its infrastructure was in shambles. There were no factories, no communications, or transportation system.

Further, its reputation was clearly defined worldwide as a maker of very poor- quality products. And the reputation was a truth, not a perception. I remember growing up seeing "Made in Japan" on something and, even as a child, knowing that it would be poor quality. Nowhere in the world today is there anything that even approaches the reality of how bad Japanese quality was.

It has been said that the poor quality of goods made in Japan, to support their troops, was a key contributing factor to their defeat in World War II.

At the end of World War II, General Douglas MacArthur was charged by US President Harry Truman with leading the process of postwar reconstruction of Japan. One of his immediate problems was that he could not communicate with the Japanese people. There were no newspapers, telephone systems, radio broadcast systems, or even radios of sufficient quality for the people to hear broadcasts.

Homer Sarasohn, an American radio engineer working in the American Army's Civil Communications Section, was assigned to help rebuild the Japanese electronics industry. It soon became clear to Sarasohn that rebuilding the companies in the way they existed previously was not a viable option. A total transformation was required.

Sarasohn, who is often forgotten by history, is the one who ignited the start of the transformation of Japan. With the approval of General MacArthur, Sarasohn and Charles Protzman developed an eight-week training program based on the work of Walter Shewhart of Bell Labs. The course taught the basics of how to build quality goods through the application of basic system thinking and statistical quality control. It also taught a somewhat idealistic view for the time of the importance of management and workers collaborating for a common purpose.

The new leadership of Mitsubishi, Fujitsu, Hitachi, N.E.C., Toshiba, and others attended the course. I say "new leadership," as MacArthur had fired the 2,000 top leaders of Japanese electronics companies due to concerns about their involvement in the war effort. In some cases a person from the factory was suddenly and sometimes randomly selected to be a company leader.

The new leaders did as they were told. Of course, what choice did they have? The occupying army had told them they had no choice and had already removed their bosses.

The replacing of all leadership and the rebuilding of companies from the ground up made for a once-in-a-lifetime experiment in the power of implementing a new method of leadership thinking. The result was a far greater cultural transformation than would later occur in the USA, Canada, and other parts of the world where companies adopted incremental components of the mindset, as opposed to embracing a total transformation.

When you understand the situation in Japan, it's easier to understand the words of Dr. Deming from the opening of his book *Out of the Crises* on the need for a total transformation of mindset.

> *The aim of this book is transformation of the style of management. Transformation of management is not a job of reconstruction, nor is it revision. It requires a whole new structure, from the foundation upward. Mutation might be the word,*

except that mutation implies unordered spontaneity. Transfor-
mation must take place with directed effort. The aim of this
book is to supply the direction.

Dr. Deming Arrives in Japan

In 1950 Sarasohn and Protzman returned to the USA. To keep the quality movement going, Sarasohn and others suggested that Dr. Deming should lead a series of training programs to help take the Japanese companies to a new level of quality and success.

Dr. Deming was an early student and longtime collaborator with Shewhart. His work with the War Production Board helped America produce the goods needed during World War II. He was also familiar with Japan, as he had taught there in 1947 and 1948 on behalf of the US Department of Defense.

At the Hotel De Yama, on July 13, 1950, Dr. Deming designed a course on "Elementary Principles of the Statistical Control of Quality." In the audience were industrial leaders representing around 80% of the capital of Japan. On the black board he drew a drawing of manufacturing as a system as opposed to as a set of parts and pieces.

To view a video of background information on Dr. Deming and his delivery of the "Deming Drawing" from the Deming Library courtesy of Clare Crawford and Bob Mason, go to innovationengineering.org/drawing.

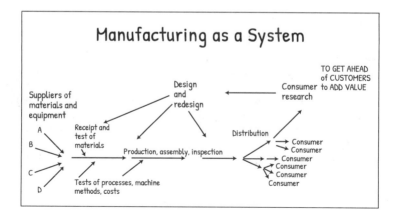

In my mind there are two very important concepts in the drawing. Both of these concepts have never been well understood by leadership of companies outside of Japan.

Deming Drawing Key Concept 1: Collaboration

Fundamental to the drawing is the interconnected nature of the entire system. All functions are interdependent. All departments are part of a system whose aim is to help the end customer/consumer. Success, as Dr. Ackoff teaches, is the product of the interaction of the parts. The value of a department lies in its ability to aid the rest of the departments in the delivery of value to the end customer/consumer.

Contrast this mindset with the current reward structure in most organizations that primarily rewards individual, then departmental excellence, then to a minor extent, if at all, the value of collaboration. **By design, groups compete with each other for rewards and resources. The result is victory for the few and defeat for the organization.**

For example, an automobile plant makes cars with low initial defects by investing in intensive inspection and rework to remove obvious defects. However, because quality is inspected in and not built into the vehicles, defects that can't be seen still exist. These defects result in warranty claims that for many manufacturers end up costing twice what Japanese car companies pay. In the end, the automaker claims their cars are high quality as a result of low initial defects—but still goes bankrupt because of warranty claims.

Deming Drawing Key Concept 2: Innovation

The other concept embedded in the Deming drawing is the use of innovation to spark never-ending continuous improvement. The drawing indicates the need for consumer research. I've added the words "To Get Ahead of Customers," as this is the primary driver of the Deming Cycle. In the video, Dr. Deming outlines the need for proactive innovation as the key driver of change in his manufacturing system: **"Products are distributed. There is consumer research. Not just to find out what went wrong. But it ought to be to learn what will help the customer in the future. What will get ahead of the customer, to entice him to buy it."**

Lean and 6 Sigma programs usually misunderstand this continuous improvement loop. They interpret its primary purpose as being the reduction of cost. For Dr. Deming its primary purpose was what he called Constancy of Purpose—this meant changes in what products and services are offered so as to assure the longtime success of the organization.

He wrote about it this way in *Out of the Crises*.

> *Establishment of Constancy of Purpose means accepting obligations like the following:*

a. **Innovate.** Allocate resources for long-term planning. Plans for the future call for consideration of new service and new product that may help people to live better materially, and that will have a market. One requirement for innovation is faith that there will be a future. Innovation, the foundation of the future, cannot thrive unless the top management have declared unshakable commitment.

b. **Put resources into research and education.**

c. **Constantly improve design of product and service.** This obligation never ceases. The consumer is the most important part of the production line. It is a mistake to suppose that efficient production of product or service can with certainty keep an organization solvent and ahead of competition. It is possible and in fact fairly easy for an organization to go downhill and out of business, making the wrong product or offering the wrong type of service, even though everyone in the organization performs with devolution.

Deming Is a Hero in Japan and Ignored in the USA

Over the next 30 years Deming's fame grew in Japan. They were so impressed with him that they named the national award for quality the Deming Prize. In the USA he was ignored. His daughter Linda Deming Haupt said, "Whether he would admit it, I don't know. He's a very proud man. But I think he hurt. It's hard to have your mission and not have anyone listen."

While it was Sarasohn who started the transformation in Japan, it was Dr. Deming who took Japanese industry to a world-class level. As Sarasohn wrote of Dr. Deming in Frank Voehl's book *Deming The Way We Knew Him:*

> *What he actually accomplished, using the quality process as a tool, was a breakthrough in the conscience of hidebound, status-quo-oriented industrial leaders. He looked beyond mere*

statistics and saw the process of controlling quality of perfor-
mance as the mechanism by which the functions of manage-
ment could be continuously improved. He recognized the es-
sential nature of a total system. A manufacturing operation, for
example, was not a succession of individual events, as was the
common conception. It properly must be regarded and treated
as a continuous interrelated stream of activities.

Why the USA Ignored Dr. Deming after WWII

After World War II, North American factories were still standing while those in Europe and Japan were destroyed. There was an immense pent-up demand for goods because during the war all resources had been focused on supporting the war effort.

In response to the huge demand, USA and Canadian manufacturing focused on producing quantity not quality. In effect, short-term greed prevented company leadership from focusing on building quality. The focus was on making as much as possible as fast as possible. Friction between labor and management grew during this time period. Managers were taught that their job was to manage by numeric production objectives.

The mindset is understandable, to a degree. When demand is high and you are the only one who can supply the demand, you make more money if you make more products. To be honest, the demand for products was so great even an idiot could have been successful leading a manufacturing company in the 1950s and '60s.

A new focus was placed on the "management of the finances" instead of on the creation of WOW products and technologies. To be specific, the National Center for Education Statistics reports that from 1970 to 2008 the percentage of bachelor's degrees in the USA doubled for business majors and declined by 50% for engineers. Interestingly, despite the proportional decline in engineers, it remains the number-one field of study for Fortune 500 CEOs. You can't manage your way to profitability. Profitability comes from products and services that offer WOW value enabled by technology that is Meaningfully Unique versus what your competition offers.

The real damage caused by post-wartime was that a generation of management came to believe in a set of values and operational principles that were not sustainable or healthy. As a result, some very bad management habits have become cultural norms.

The Problem in the Western World in the Late 1970s

In the late 1970s, the US automobile industry was in a panic as the market share of the Big Three (Ford, GM, and Chrysler) had dropped from 82% to 78% in just three years. The damage was so bad to Chrysler that in the fall of 1979 they had to apply to the US government for a financial bailout.

From 1980 to 1982, the perfect storm hit and the US economy went into recession due in part to the Iranian oil embargo. Other beliefs for the recession included:

- 90% of industry executives felt that excessive regulation was the reason for the decline in US productivity. For example, in the auto industry automakers were required to include airbags and other safety elements.

- Lazy workers were thought to be the problem. In particular, union workers. Ronald Reagan brought this issue into the public consciousness when he dramatically and decisively fired the air traffic controllers who had gone on strike.

However, the real root cause of the problem was that the quality of American cars and electronics was no longer viable in the face of higher-quality products from Japan. And, as Dr. Deming had taught, when you improve quality using a system approach, the cost of production also goes down.

The other root case of the automotive problem was that the Japanese had anticipated the future. They had invested in cars that were smaller and that got higher gas mileage. When you think about it, given the tension in the Middle East, it didn't exactly take a rocket scientist in the 1970s to imagine a scenario in which oil prices might go up, causing disruption to the auto industry.

The CEO Who Brought Deming to US Industry

While most executives were giving excuses to Wall Street, one CEO confronted the reality and took a different path. Bill Conway was the CEO of Nashua Corporation, a Fortune 500 company at the time, located in

Nashua, New Hampshire, that made carbonless paper, computer disks, tape, and copy machine toner.

During a trip to Japan in 1979 to work with Ricoh on toner for their copiers, his meeting was delayed because they were preparing their application for the Deming quality prize. The idea that top leadership would be involved in quality was not something Bill was familiar with. He would later tell me that no Fortune 500 CEO thought that quality was their responsibility. They had in effect outsourced the company's quality to a department that measured and managed it.

In a meeting with Dr. Deming during March of 1979, Bill learned that quality had to become part of his job. He had to be personally involved if the Nashua Corporation culture was to make the transformation from being a maker of quantity to a maker of quality.

If you think back to the Deming Drawing, it's obvious that if quality comes from the interaction of the departments, only the leadership, who are above all departments, can provide the Constancy of Purpose that true quality requires.

A TV Producer Introduces Dr. Deming to American Companies

During late 1979, Clare Crawford-Mason, a top producer and correspondent for NBC News, was working on an NBC documentary with the working title, "Whatever Happened to Good Old Yankee Ingenuity?" During her background research she found Dr. Deming.

Mary Walton, in her book *The Deming Management Method,* describes what happened.

> *One day, she heard from a faculty member at American University. "There's this guy named Deming who lives out in American University Park." Deming, she was told, had done a lot of work in Japan. Crawford-Mason contacted Dr. Deming, who invited her out to talk. He spoke of his work in Japan and showed her yellowed clippings of stories the Japanese had written. Crawford-Mason didn't know what to think. He was nice, if eccentric: he reminded her of her father; but what he said, if true, was astonishing.*

"He kept going on and on and on that nobody would listen to him." Not for nothing had Crawford-Mason put in all those years as a reporter. "I thought, 'Here's a good story.'"

Their first conversation led to five interviews, consuming twenty-five hours. The more they talked, the more impressed she was, and the more suspicious she got. It was simply incredible. "Here is a man who has the answer, and he's five miles from the White House and nobody will speak to him." She contacted a high-ranking economics official from the Carter Administration and asked if he knew W. Edwards Deming. He didn't.

Crawford-Mason wanted to know if anybody was using his techniques. As it happened, Dr. Deming had just recently acquired a major client, Nashua Corporation.

On June 24, 1980, at 9:30 p.m. with Lloyd Dobyns as narrator, the newly named documentary *If Japan Can, Why Can't We?* aired. After setting up the challenge, Dr. Deming was presented as a solution. Nashua President Bill Conway reported that Nashua was saving millions as they improved the quality of their carbonless paper. This was the project my father, M. Bradford Hall, worked on.

The next day, the phone rang endlessly. Procter & Gamble, Xerox, GM, Ford, and Chrysler called Dr. Deming's basement office. Mary Walton describes the situation:

"We were bombarded with calls," recalled Cecelia Kilian [his assistant]. "It was a nightmare. Many of the callers sounded desperate. They have to see him tomorrow, or yesterday, or their whole company will collapse."

Deming, who was 80 at the time, instantly became a global celebrity. He gave four-day seminars as many as 40 times a year for up to 400 people.

Constancy of Purpose and Innovation

When I asked Bill Conway what was the most important thing that Dr. Deming taught him, his reply was instant: Constancy of Purpose. He went on to explain that without Constancy of Purpose there is no future.

To paraphrase Dr. Deming from this book *Out of the Crises.*

> *Establishment of Constancy of Purpose means acceptance of the obligation to innovate. It means to allocate resources for long-term planning of new products and services that may help people to live better materially, and that will have a market.*
>
> *One requirement for innovation is faith that there will be a future. Innovation, the foundation of the future, cannot thrive unless the top management have declared unshakable commitment to staying in business long term.*
>
> *Your customers, your suppliers, your employees need your statement of Constancy of Purpose—your intention to stay in business by providing product and service that will help many to live better and which will have a market.*

It is the CEO's job to ensure Constancy of Purpose. Great leaders anticipate the future by focusing the organization on the very important opportunities and systems required to keep the company alive and to provide jobs for employees.

When the CEO has Constancy of Purpose, short-term sacrifices are made to maximize long-term success. Sadly, when the CEO is a "hired mercenary" brought on for a short-term task—be it to fix the stock price, take the company public, or clean the company up so it can be sold—then there will be no Constancy of Purpose.

When the CEO is the founder of the organization and committed to being a part of it for the long term, there is Constancy of Purpose. Family owned and operated companies are more likely to have Constancy of Purpose. Nonprofit organizations are more likely to have Constancy of Purpose, as the mission of the organization, not short-term returns, is the driver.

Special Cause Versus Common Cause Errors

To repeat because it really matters: Core to understanding the Deming mindset is understanding the difference between special cause and common cause errors. The worker causes special cause errors. Examples include if a worker didn't show up on time, fell asleep on the job, or didn't follow the process. Common cause errors are a result of the system. For example, if raw materials are highly variable and cause issues or if the tools, training, or technique given to the worker results in unreliable results.

Special cause errors have a relatively clear and assignable cause. Common cause errors are more complex, as they are usually a result of a multitude of system interactions.

The differences between common cause and special cause errors can be easily identified using control charting of standard deviation. As Sarasohn wrote, what Dr. Deming did was connect the statistics to management.

He taught that 94% of the problem was the system; 6% was special causes (due to the worker). And if management is the only one that can improve the system by investing in new training, tools, or techniques to reduce variation in the system, then 94% of the problem is management; 6% is the worker.

In a paper for the Instrument Society of America, in 1982 my father, M. Bradford Hall, wrote:

> *No improvement of the system will take place unless management attacks common causes with as much science and vigor as the production workers and engineers attack special causes.*

I've come to believe that Dr. Deming was about right with his estimate that 94% of problems are caused by the system.

I've also come to believe that he was wrong in stating that 94% of the problem is management. While only management can lead the transformation, they can't do it by themselves. In today's world of rapid change and increasing technical complexity, management can't fix the system by themselves. The workers need to also take responsibility for improving the system. Yes, management must provide the workers with training, resources, and most importantly of all, clear strategic direction. But the workers—those close to the work—must also take responsibility for the long-term success of the organization.

Deming's Relevance and Business Descendants

In today's service and digital-focused economy Dr. Deming's system mindset is even more important. The Deming drawing principle of collaboration is still fundamental for success. The principle of using innovation to get ahead of the customers is a basic survival skill in today's marketplace.

A genuine challenge with applying Dr. Deming's teachings to today's world lies in drawing control charts of human work systems to separate common cause from special cause variation.

Gathering the data to draw control charts is very challenging with human systems because of human insecurity. A machine doesn't worry about what you will think of it when it gives you data. However, a human becomes defensive and quickly starts to "game" the data, making it meaningless.

When you do get the data on human systems, you quickly find that most human work processes have massive variance. They are, in Dr. Deming's words, "out of control." The variance in technique, raw inputs, tools, materials, and worker training results in slow speed due to rework and high risk due to variability.

Sadly, instead of focusing on fixing the system, managers are instructed to manage by objectives, to "get the right people on the bus," to provide more aggressive reward structures. All these things do is make the situation worse in the long term, as they prioritize individual achievement over Constancy of Purpose.

A case could be made that Dr. Deming's teachings are more relevant today than they were in 1980. Realizing the benefits of the teaching is hard. It's very hard. Old beliefs must be replaced with new ones. A massive investment must be made in the education of how we think, create, and lead.

The Deming seminars identified a huge market opportunity for experts, gurus, authors, and consultants. In time, Deming's message of how he had helped turn Japan into the world's second-biggest economic power would be repackaged in a multitude of ways. Descendants of Dr. Deming's work include: 6 Sigma, Lean, Toyota Production System, Continuous Improvement, Baldrige Award, ISO Certification, and others.

Deming Today

Today, advocates of Dr. Deming's teachings are still learning, studying, and applying his teachings. Peter Senge at MIT has taken systems thinking to new places with his book *The Fifth Discipline*. Russell Ackoff transformed management thinking around the world through his work at the Wharton school and books.

The Deming Institute runs annual conferences, where experts take Dr. Deming's work forward. Sadly, Kevin Cahill, Dr. Deming's Grandson, told me, "In the Far East there is a strong interest in my grandfather's work. In North America and Europe it's more challenging to get leaders to adopt the mindset."

A recent Deming success story is Pixar, the company that transformed how animated movies are created with such successes as *Toy Story, Cars, Monsters Inc., Finding Nemo, A Bug's Life,* and others. Ed Catmull, co-founder of Pixar with Steve Jobs and John Lasseter, credits Dr. Deming as a guiding force behind their success: "Deming's work would make a huge impression on me and help frame my approach to managing Pixar."

A Toyota Leader Predicts the Future

In 2002 I gave a keynote address to 1,000-plus Toyota executives. For dinner I was seated with one of the very senior Toyota leaders. I asked him, "What automaker are you most concerned about . . . Detroit, Germany?"

He shook his head. "No. Korea."

"But Korea makes crappy cars; the quality is horrible."

He smiled. "So did we for many years. But your Dr. Deming taught us a system for making them better." He then went on to say. "Korea has studied how we did it. They are hungry to learn. We have lost that hunger."

The Rest of The Story

The decline of market share in the automobile market by USA companies has continued. In 1980 the panic was about a decline from 82% to 78% in just three years. Today the market share of the Big Three has dropped from 78% in 1980 to under 43% in 2009.

Dr. Deming's mindset was embraced by the Big Three US automakers, to varying degrees. The Ford Motor Company, the only one of the three with founding family involvement, made the greatest commitment to the Deming mindset. Bill Conway speculated to me that it was probably the reason that Ford was able to avoid the bankruptcies that occurred with Chrysler and GM.

The prediction of the Toyota leader I had dinner with also came true, as Korean car manufacturers have gone from a low single-digit market share to nearly 10% of the US market.

Perspective on Japan

The challenges that the Japanese economy has faced in recent years does not diminish the miracle of what they have and are accomplishing. They are the 61st largest country in the world in land mass, and the 10th in terms of population, yet today they are third in the world for gross domestic product, after the USA and China.

Sony has lost its way since the retirement of founder and Deming follower Akio Morita. Akio anticipated the music revolution and led them to great success with Walkman products. The company totally missed the shift to digital music players. Actually, they designed and built two different digital players that were not easy to use or even compatible with each other.

Toyota is a global success. They anticipated the world of hybrid vehicles long before others did, and as a result they own many patented technologies in the area. In the recent short term, they have experienced some quality challenges. With the return of the family to leadership, with Akio Toyoda becoming CEO, there are indications that the leadership are confronting reality and returning to following the Deming way of anticipating the future.

Innovation Engineering Is Just a Small Part of Deming's Teachings

Innovation Engineering applies the system thinking of Dr. Deming to innovation. It also applies his teachings on: alignment of the organization behind a common aim; "Plan, Do, Study, Act" cycles of learning; focus on the end customer to determine true value; the need to get ahead of customers; theory of variation; collaboration with suppliers, customers, and between employees; Constancy of Purpose; responsibility of leadership; and common versus special cause errors.

However, there is much, much more to learn from Dr. Deming. His System of Profound Knowledge outlines 14 points for management and 7 deadly diseases. To learn more about Dr. Deming's teaching, the best place to start are his two books: *Out of the Crises* and *The New Economics*. To learn even more attend one of the Deming Institute Seminars. For information on them go to deming.org. I hope to see you there.

FINAL REFLECTION: The words on these pages are not the answer. Rather, they are the start of a conversation that needs to begin around the world on how we enable everyone to dream, create, and think. Everybody's got wings . . . as the song lyrics state.

This book is imperfect but it's a start. As Dr. Deming would say at the conclusion of his seminars, "I have done my best." And with that, I close the file on this book and send it off to my publisher. Tomorrow, work begins on the next edition. There are more cycles of learning to complete.

Interview with Kevin Cahill

President and Executive Director of the Deming Institute, Grandson of Dr. W. Edwards Deming

Doug Hall: What is the Deming Institute's primary mission?

Kevin Cahill: The institute's primary mission is to carry on my grandfather's [Dr. W. Edwards Deming's] work and teachings. **To inspire people to learn, and as he always said, to seek new knowledge, and transform their businesses, schools, and communities so they're better prepared for the future** and not the past.

Doug: What are the methods you use to accomplish that?

Kevin: We start by promoting a greater understanding, and an awareness, and application of Deming's System of Profound Knowledge. System of Profound Knowledge is the transformative philosophy that he developed at the end of his life.

We do this through an ever-expanding series of learning programs, initiatives, events, outreach programs, and partnerships with different like-minded organizations.

Note: **To learn more, visit deming.org.**

Doug: What its the history of the Deming Institute's creation?

Kevin: He decided when he was in his 90s, at the end of his life, that he really didn't want to focus on building a consulting practice to carry on his work. What he decided to do was to create a nonprofit organization whose primary mission we just discussed.

He decided to create the organization as a nonprofit, with the belief that doing it that way would open up interesting doors and unique opportunities that might not necessarily happen as a for-profit consulting business. He started it right before he passed away. It was literally months before he passed away, and then it was up to those who were initially on the board to create the initial aim of the organization and method by which to carry out that aim.

Doug: What would you say is his most important contribution to the business community in the world?

Kevin: There are two parts to my answer. I think one naturally leads to the other.

The first contribution was viewing an organization as a system. From what I've read, and seen, and looking through his journals and everything, it began when he went into Japan in the 50s. At the start of every single lecture or seminar that he did, he drew the organization as a system. Then he went on to define that your organization isn't an organizational chart; your organization is a system. He defined that system as a network of interdependent components that work together to accomplish the aim of that system. He was saying that the aim of any of those systems should be that everybody gains, not just one part of the system at the expense of the other.

And, I think that that contribution became part of the second part of my answer, which would be the larger contribution, which I think was truly the culmination of his life long work, and that's what I mentioned before, which is the **Deming System of Profound Knowledge.** I think that, in terms of being an important contribution, it's an incredibly effective theory of management that provides that framework of thought and action for any leader wishing to transform, and create, any kind of a thriving organization, and using that to improve the quality of people's lives.

Doug: I agree on both points. And, I have to thank you for pointing me to the System of Profound Knowledge. And your being relentless in emphasizing it's importance. I had missed it, as my dad didn't teach it to me. Recall, my dad worked with your grandfather in 1979 at Nashua Corporation when it was not yet formed in Dr. Deming's mind—the four principles were there but not organized as elegantly as would be in later years.

In working with it, we have found that if you change the order a little it becomes an amazingly powerful and very simple step-by-step method for improving systems. Recall, we swap the order of Psychology and Theory of Knowledge (PDSA). It then reads . . .

Step 1. Appreciation for a System: Make the system visible—Aim, Stakeholders, Flowchart, etc.

Step 2. Knowledge about Variation: Identify areas of high common cause variation (training, tools, resources, etc.).

Step 3. Psychology: Identify areas of negative psychology.

Step 4. Theory of Knowledge (PDSA): Run experiments to improve the system.

Kevin: Exactly, and that PDSA is your theory to improve it.

Doug: By flipping numbers three and four it became easier to understand as a whole. We have seen very positive reaction from executives. It has an elegance to it. And it's so easy to get started with it—you can review it on a piece of paper in just minutes.

Kevin: What's interesting, Doug, and I'd be interested in your opinion, I don't think that flipping the order makes that much difference. I think it's whatever works best, don't you?

Doug: I don't think it would matter to him, but in our application today it's easier to implement. Executives see it as step one, step two, step three, step four. You make the system visible, identify areas of high variance and negative psychology, then you run PDSA experiments to find ways to improve the system. When we articulate it as four steps, it's easier for people to get started with applying the principles. That doesn't mean they don't think about other interactions of the four principles; it's just a start. This "packaging" makes it easier to apply. We are intent on finding ways to make it easy to apply, which as you know, Dr. Deming the professor refused to tell you how to do anything; he taught the philosophy.

Kevin: He never answered my questions; he'd always just tell me where to go look for the answer.

Doug: In *The New Economics* Dr. Deming wrote that production was 3% of the opportunity for company improvement. In a chart on page 37, he referred to the 97% as strategy and long-term planning, and all the company-wide systems, which I then write in simple terms as strategy, innovation, and how we work together. As a businessperson, and I fully respect the fact that you can't read Dr. Deming's mind, thinking about strategy, innovation, and how we work together, what do you feel is the greatest challenge with companies today?

Kevin: Well I think one of the biggest challenges is that they do not look at their organization as a system. Until they do that, they're trying, I think a lot of times, to make improvements when they don't really know what they need to improve.

I thought it was fascinating when I was in Singapore and a company had us come in and talk to them, and they were kind of swimming in ideas. They didn't know what to do with them, and we asked what was going on. They said they decided that they needed to innovate, because they realized that unless they innovated, that they could go out of business.

So they just started telling people to come up with ideas. Everyone was required to put at least one idea a week in the suggestion box. They had 300 people in the factory, so soon they had 1,500 ideas, and they had no idea what to do with them. They realized they hadn't even articulated to the people why they wanted to innovate. They hadn't articulated what they were trying to ultimately accomplish.

Doug: So what you're saying is that you can't separate strategy, innovation, and how we work together, because they are the collective system.

Kevin: Exactly.

Doug: One of the challenges with applying system thinking is the difference between a factory, which primarily is a collection of mechanical systems, and innovation and strategy, which are composed primarily of human systems.

Kevin: I think that's a really interesting observation. In the end it doesn't matter whether it's a mechanical or human system. One of the things my grandfather talked about was aim, and the importance of everyone understanding the aim of the system. Every system, mechanical, human, or combination, has to have an aim to it, and that aim needs to be clearly defined so that everybody understands whether it's strategy, innovation, or how we work together.

Doug: Without that alignment on aim, there is chaos.

Kevin: Without alignment, you can't have the Constancy of Purpose that my grandfather talked about.

Doug: When we mention Deming to executives, they often say we already did "Deming." However, when we say yes, you did mechanical systems in your factories, but we're here to talk about in the new economy, it's the human systems that are the challenges.

Kevin: That is interesting, because you know that's also one of our challenges. It's hard to get people to stop and think that Deming is not just about the factory, you know? It's not just about the shop floor. It's not just about, like you said, the mechanical things.

I think that was part of what he came to realize at the end of his life. I think he probably became a little bit frustrated that a lot of people really looked at system thinking as just for factories. In truth it can and should apply to everyone in every organization, as you've found out.

Doug: To add to that, as I mentioned, in Dr. Deming's last book he wrote that application of system thinking to the factory, was only 3% of what was to be done. This number is important, as he was a statistician who understood order of magnitude. He could have said 30%, but he didn't; he said 3%. He declared that his life work, at least from when he started in Japan, was only 3% of the opportunity. This is an example of his frustration at people not getting the fact that he wasn't talking about factories; he was talking about leadership, and how you ran the company.

Kevin: Yes. We talk about it when we do our seminars, that organizations realize impacts from 6 Sigma, Lean, or other tool-focused applications, but they tend to eventually hit a ceiling on innovation and improvement. Until you actually start to think about the other elements that you're teaching people—those company-wide systems, the interactions like he said in that diagram, the personnel, the training, detrimental systems of reward—you are not going to realize the full potential of system thinking.

Doug: When I interviewed Bill Conway [CEO of Nashua Corporation—the first leader in the USA to embrace Dr. Deming], I asked what's the one most important thing Dr. Deming taught him? He said Constancy of Purpose, Constancy of Purpose, Constancy of Purpose.

Kevin: Yes.

Doug: Then of course I went back to Dr. Deming's book and read the section on Constancy of Purpose—that is the long-term survival of the organization—and the first thing he says on how to do it is to innovate.

Kevin: Yes.

Doug: It really hit me how strongly he supported innovation. It's the first thing he tells people to do. And his primary focus is on leading customers, not just cost-cutting and optimizing the existing offering. Despite that, he's not known as being an innovation expert.

Kevin: No, it's interesting that he's not. He spends time talking about how important innovation really is. He gives that famous example that you can optimize the carburetor all you want—but fuel injection came along and replaced the carburetor. He was clear that if you're not going to innovate, you will ultimately go out of business.

Doug: I recall a quote from him: "It is not necessary to change. Survival is not mandatory."

Kevin: Yes. **Deming is all about having the proper aim.** If your aim is to build the best, lowest-cost, highest-quality carburetor, and you're working your tail off to hit that aim, you're improving quality and productivity on that aim, but that doesn't mean you're going to stay in business. I mean you've got to have an aim, and that Constancy of Purpose that gives you the guiding principles that say wait a second, I need to look outside. I think you call it LEAP innovation. I don't remember the exact words, but he suggested that ultimately the aim should have been for the carburetor company to put a mixture of air and fuel in the combustion chamber and innovate something new and more effective.

Doug: Dr. Deming's higher-order aim always was the long-term success, survival, and growth of the organization. The long-term was always key. To him, the only measure of a CEO was did they do things to maintain the long-term success. I love to add to it "no whining"—my guess is that Dr. Deming was pretty much a no-whining guy too. What do you think is the greatest barrier to leadership embracing the system thinking mindset?

Kevin: I would say, and this is my personal belief, that most of the people who are in leadership roles have been trained and taught for decades in an existing system of management. They were never taught system thinking. They've been taught in school and at work, a style of management where you're graded, you're rated, you're ranked, you improve performance by focusing on people, not the system.

Now all of a sudden they're walking into an Innovation Engineering class or a Deming seminar, and we're asking them to do a 180 in their thinking. From talking with David P. Langford, who leads our education initiative, one of the hardest things is to all of a sudden say I'm going to change my brain. I mean, **you literally have to change the way your brain works, and it's not easy to do that.**

Doug: They're used to just blaming people instead of taking responsibility for the system.

Kevin: Exactly, and the biggest thing that I see when talking to leaders, in terms of getting them to embrace a system-thinking mindset, is their existing belief that the problem isn't the system, it's the people. They believe that if they can cut off the bottom performers, and just have top performers, that they're going to be better off. So what they end up doing is working on the people, where maybe 6% of their problems are. Eventually they have to come to realize that it's the system that's the greater issue.

Doug: When working with an executive who has been in the job for a few years, you can sometimes create a "Eureka" moment for them by pointing out that they've changed their VP of sales three times in five years. And each time the person hired failed to hit their numbers. It appears that either we have a bad system for hiring or maybe the problem is the system, not the people we put in the job.

Something executives don't often realize is that if a worker is provided no system, training, or tools to do their job, which is usually the case when it comes to innovation, then it's not their fault when they don't achieve the aim of the system. Lack of training is a common cause error of the system and a classic source of high variance. Workers aren't supposed to just magically know how to innovate. The need for training, training, training is throughout Dr. Deming's writings and the Deming Video Library. If you haven't provided employees training in what to do, why to do it, and how to do it, you can't complain or blame them when things go wrong.

Kevin: Exactly. Organizations will show us their control charts, and they say they're mapping everything out. We then ask them what do you do with them? They say, if there's a point here in this chart we don't like, we take a look at it. We then point out that you're looking at a point that's within the control limits…a common cause. This tells us they don't really understand Dr. Deming's teaching on variation. If the system is stable, and you don't like the variation you are realizing in sales or in the volume of products that you're producing, then you need to work on improving the system. And that will require training, like you said, Doug, in methods for reducing that variation.

Doug: I was interested to read that when Dr. Deming was asked how he would summarize his overall message in a few words, he said, "I'm not sure, but it would have something to do with variation." Later he said, "I said earlier that my message had to do with variation. I've given it some more thought, and I would say it has to do with pride of work." Sadly, our research of over 12,000 employees found that just 5% feel high pride of work. In your opinion, what stands in the way of pride of work today?

Kevin: When I read your research, it depressed me. It's what my grandfather wrote about more than 25 years ago. It's terribly demoralizing that things have not improved.

All the same mistakes still exist, such as not understanding the system. And point 12 of my grandfather's 14 points, where he said **remove the barriers that rob employees and those in management of their right to pride of workmanship,** this means abolishing the annual rating, MBO, management by objective, MBR, and all of those MBs. As we talked about earlier, we need to enable the workers, enable the people in the organization. We need to give them a chance to advance their learning and actually contribute their talents. Everybody has some level of talent, and we never talk to any workers unless they're so beaten down that they don't want to contribute. Employees want to have their talents have impact in a positive way on the business.

Doug: The internet has accelerated the rate of change that business leaders face. How do you feel the application of system thinking can help with this?

Kevin: The internet has accelerated the rate of change, and unless you're thinking from a system standpoint, more than ever you just can't waste time. I think it was Robert Rodin who said, "Right now there is somebody looking at you who is right around the corner or around the world who wants to do what you do, better, faster, and cheaper."

To be able to compete, you've got to break down the barriers so that you can be innovative. You've got to drive out the fear that may preclude people from being innovative, or being interested in it. System thinking is what's going to enable you to innovate. Because if all you're going to do is manage by objective, or manage by results, then all you're going to do is just run harder doing the exact same thing you're doing right now, and I think ultimately you'll be out of business.

Doug: Bill Conway told me that Dr. Deming had told him it was important to work with the willing. What advice would you give to an employee who is working for a leader who is "unwilling" to learn/change?

Kevin: I agree, you've got to work with the willing, whether it's at the bottom, at the middle, or at the top.

I know my grandfather said quality starts in the boardroom, and I've heard many people say unless you're at the top, it's not worth doing. I disagree because you're not always going to get the person at the top right off the bat. **I believe that every single person, in every single organization, has some sphere of influence they can impact.** Ultimately, that's what I did. When I started out working, just out of college, I had leaders who were fantastic people, but they really didn't want to change, because what they were doing at that time was working well.

I started out as an assistant to an assistant. But I realized that I could use my grandfather's ideas and thinking to improve the areas that I had some influence over. In time, it had a real impact, and people started noticing that this guy did something really interesting and different. What it enabled me to do was to move up in the organization. Eventually those who are willing to learn the new way of thinking and applying it could end up being in charge of that leader who is unwilling to learn or to change.

Doug: I agree 100 percent; we cannot wait. We need to find the willing, get started, and let it grow from there. Based on what you've learned and read about Innovation Engineering, do you think a company on their Deming journey would find it to be a natural extension of his work?

Kevin: I believe in any process and approach that starts with—and I'll actually quote you from the book—**"innovation requires a learning mindset. You can't create a new idea without learning. It's a never-ending journey."** You combine that with a focus on education of leadership, which you do; an understanding of the system-driven innovation principles, which we call System of Profound Knowledge; getting leaders to drive out fear; and then many others you combine, all combined lead to a Constancy of Purpose, which brings about innovation.

My grandfather said it's critical to innovate; having satisfied loyal customers is great, but it's not enough. The moral is that it is critical to innovate, to predict the needs of the customer, and by customer, as you know, Doug, he meant internal and external. But having a goal to innovate is also not enough, because everyone may want to hit that goal, and most everyone does, but the key is by what method do we do it?

I believe if you learn the Deming philosophy and incorporate proven innovation systems, then you can truly be innovative. I love what you wrote: **"A system mindset, explore stimulus, leverage diversity, and drive out fear principles are simple and unquestionable in their impact. Their application is anything but. To develop them as a new mindset across a culture takes time, education, and repetition."**

Doug: It's funny, as you read that to me, I can just hear your grandfather saying similar things.

Kevin: Yes.

Doug: It's the same basic message, isn't it?

Kevin: Yes, you've got to have that system mindset.

Doug: Dr. Deming said in his experience, most troubles are 94% a result of the system, 6% special causes. In my dad's speech in 1980, after working with your grandfather, my dad declared 94% of problems were due to the system, 6% the workers, and only management can change the system. What do you think about this concept—94% system, 6% the workers?

Kevin: In my experience it is about right, from what I've seen, and what I've heard talking to a lot of different people. I've even heard people say my grandfather thought it might even be 96, or 98%.

Some of the people will say okay, 6% is the worker, but if it's special causes, those special causes are actually unwanted variation, which may be or may not be due to the worker. It's worth looking into special causes, because while it's part of the system, it needs to be identified, determined if it's a false signal, or if it can reoccur.

I think the important thing for leaders to understand is if special causes can recur, you've got to identify them and eliminate them. Because until the special causes are eliminated, the system is unstable, and thus the leader is working on trying to improve an unstable system, and if you're trying to improve an unstable system, you're trying to improve a performance that's unstable, which means it can't be predicted. You really need that process to be in control in order to improve it, so you've got to get rid of whatever those special causes are.

Doug: Let's look again at human versus mechanical systems. If I'm in a mechanical system, there are things that could happen such as an electrical surge, but in a human system, then it becomes much more about management and employees, human systems of how we work together.

Kevin: Yes, and you bring up an interesting point because if you're looking at trying to figure out what's a special cause, and what's a common cause in a human system, that's got to be really hard to make that conclusion.

Doug: That has been the greatest challenge in applying Deming outside of the factory. That's why we need to bring data and data systems to these human systems. What I am finding is that with innovation, it's at least 94%, especially when I say that the 94% includes having a method, training, and tools to innovate. Sadly, there are none of these for employees. The only "innovation system" that exists is a system of controls on what not to do. Nothing on what to do.

Kevin: So they don't know how to innovate?

Doug: No they don't. Innovation is a random "special cause" event. The innovation problem is 99.9% common cause error. **The truth is there usually is no system, no method, no instruction, no standardized work, no way to create ideas.** The problem is 99.9% system because there is NO SYSTEM. And for the change of mindset to happen across the organization requires leadership of a team, department, division, or organization to lead the new way of thinking.

Kevin: Well you hit it right on the head. It's rare that leadership steps back from reacting to the marketplace and their numbers. I mean that's what they're trained to do, and until we get them away from thinking about that, and until they gain the insight necessary to view their organization through a new system lens, they're not going to change.

Getting leaders to provide strategic leadership in a form that engages employees really boils down to getting them to say I've got to manage differently, I've got to lead differently, and the reason I do is that I was looking at things through a lens that didn't give me the insight that I needed to do these different things.

Doug: Dr. Deming felt that much of what is important was unknown and unknowable. With Innovation Engineering we have worked to make some of this known and visible. How important is it to make innovation systems visible and known?

Kevin: The loss from inhibitors to pride and workmanship is unknown and immeasurable, but with that all being said, obviously the more that you can measure, and the more that you have known, once you're measuring it, you can understand how stable it is, and then you can understand how to improve it.

Doug: Variation was a key element of Dr. Deming's teachings. How important is understanding variation today? What holds leadership back from understanding variation in their management and decision-making?

Kevin: I think they don't truly understand variation and the critical nature of what is a common and what is a special cause. I think it's incredibly important because **once you understand variation you can see your organization as a system.** Once the system is stable, it's predictable, you now know that it's going to produce within a certain range. It doesn't mean you like the output, but now you know what to work on. You are no longer going around playing Whack-A-Mole with special cause and the common cause elements.

Doug: I think one of the challenges with getting managers to look at common cause versus special cause is they are scared of doing the math. While we talk a lot about metrics, we use them to control, not to enable people to work smarter. There's some real value to doing the math.

Kevin: Absolutely. I agree, and with control chart tools today, like the one you've developed based on my grandfather's formulas, it is much easier than ever before.

Doug: Employees and managers have to get comfortable doing the math of variation. To enable this we've created a super-simple control charting application. It removes all excuses. But we're still finding that getting them to do the math is a challenge.

Kevin: I agree with you a thousand percent, that if you can get them to plug in their data and take a look at it, then all of a sudden they go, "whoa, I had no idea, it's the system I need to work on, not the people."

Doug: Enabling everyone, everywhere, every day is fundamental to Innovation Engineering. How important was enabling all members of an organization in understanding system thinking to Dr. Deming?

Kevin: Absolutely critical—that's almost a one-word answer for me—it's critical. Until they view their organization as a system, they're not going to see sustained improvement. **Otherwise they're just going off, as my grandfather put it, into the Milky Way.**

Doug: What do you mean by going into the Milky Way?

Kevin: If everybody in the organization understands system thinking, then they understand the aim of the system and how their work fits in. When they don't have a common mindset they are going off wandering around the Milky Way. Everyone is doing their best, as my grandfather would say, giving their best efforts, and working hard, all toward a different aim.

Here's a quick example from when I started my business. I sat everyone down at a table. I think we had 12 employees. We had each person write down on a piece of paper what the aim of the system was. I did this because I was struggling with everybody working really hard but we were not making the progress we needed to make. We were a startup company and everybody was going 24/7. Out of the 12 people, how many of them do you think wrote down the same aim? None of them, none of them—that was my problem. So I made the system visible and outlined the aim of the company. The improvements in our individual effectiveness and in the company's results were as my grandfather would predict.

Doug: What excites you about Innovation Engineering in the 21st century?

Kevin: What excites me is that I think, **without a doubt, innovation is the key. None of these companies, no organization, government can survive without innovation.** Innovation is really the key. Of course one requirement for innovation is faith that there's going to be a future, don't you agree?

Doug: Yes, absolutely.

Kevin: Innovation is the foundation of the future. We can't thrive unless top management has that unshakable commitment to innovation, quality, and productivity.

Doug: So now I'm going to ask for your personal help here. If you could wave a magic wand, where would you focus the Innovation Engineering movement?

Kevin: I think the Innovation Engineering movement needs to focus on large organizations. You are having an impact on big companies in a way the Deming Institute can't have today. **The way you're explaining system thinking and the way you're doing it is getting them to think about it in a way that we're not able to.**

We tend to have very good success with small and medium-size companies, but when it comes to bigger companies we're not, and you are. So in my mind, I think that Innovation Engineering needs to focus on the larger companies. I mean, they employ the greatest number of people and they have an enormous impact on our society.

I know that everybody talks about small business being the engine that drives the country, but when you've got 150,000 at whatever it is—at Toyota or Ford Motor Company—you can have that major impact there. My grandfather always tried to do that too. He went with the bigger companies for the most part because he saw that he could have the greatest impact. To me, that's where I think your focus is very well served. It doesn't mean it wouldn't be well served elsewhere, but I mean I think that's one of the hardest nuts to crack, and God bless you for taking on a nut like that.

Doug: I don't like your answer but I know you're right.

It's a ton more fun to work with small and medium-sized companies. However, if we're going to change the world we need to reignite system thinking in the large organizations, be they businesses, universities, or governments. It really is hard to change large organizations.

That said, to keep us sane we also support tens of thousands of small businesses and entrepreneurs through our scholarship programs and the Innovation Engineering Foundation.

Kevin: But if you're going to change the culture of business in America, or in the world, you've got to change the big guys. When I looked at some statistics for large companies going back 40, 50 years, you see that they hit a point, and they don't keep getting bigger. They start declining. I think a main part of that reason they start getting smaller is because they're not innovative anymore.

Doug: What advice would you offer to students studying Innovation Engineering on campus who are preparing to enter industry?

Kevin: When asked that by students, I will typically tell them that learning system thinking at a young age is a tremendous advantage for them as individuals. It gives them a valuable mindset at the start of their careers. Most of the time people learn system thinking much later in life. This makes it hard for them to accept the change because they've been practicing the prevailing style of management for so long, and now they're trying to reverse it, or change it. **I think it's amazingly cool to have people coming out of school who are thinking this way. It's so much easier than trying to get them to change once they realize that they've hit a wall, or they're frustrated.** We're finding that this message really resonates with them, because they're not big believers in the typical command and control mindset that exists in most big organizations.

Doug: What advice would you offer to the leadership of companies considering system-driven innovation as we do it with Innovation Engineering?

Kevin: The advice I would say is system-driven innovation, like the System of Profound Knowledge that my grandfather taught, is a new mindset that you have to commit to. There's always going to be pieces that aren't going to make sense at first, that are going to be challenging at first for you. As you gain new knowledge and insight and understanding, it's going to make more sense, and it's going to be easier. It's not one of these things where you do it once or twice and it's over and you're done with it. Your market's going to change, your business is going to change. It gives you such an amazing advantage, because it teaches you how to look at and deal with those changes by thinking differently.

Doug: Anything else that I didn't ask you that we should talk about? You've been very, very kind. I've learned a lot through this interview. In my view it's always a good day when you learn something.

Kevin: Well that goes both ways, Doug, because frankly I always learn as well from your questions. They get me thinking in new ways. They cause me to think about my grandfather's work from a different angle or approach. So I've got to tell you, I appreciate the opportunity to do this.

Doug Hall

Doug is an inventor, author, and whiskey maker. He's a chemical engineer who rose to the rank of Master Marketing Inventor at Procter & Gamble. At P&G, using the principles that would become Innovation Engineering, his team invented and shipped a record 9 innovations in just 12 months.

He has been named one of America's top innovation experts by A&E Top 10, *Inc.* magazine, *The Wall Street Journal, Dateline NBC,* CNBC, *CIO* magazine, and the CBC.

In 1986 he founded the Eureka! Ranch, focused on a singular mission to find, filter, and fast-track big ideas. Today, the mission is the same; however, through the application of Innovation Engineering system-thinking to innovation, Eureka! Inventing projects (by the Ranch team and Planet Eureka! Network partners) invent 10 times more "big ideas" and make them real up to 6 times faster then existing innovation systems.

In 2009 he founded the Innovation Engineering Institute, focused on changing the world through systems that enable innovation by everyone, everywhere, every day. It's a new field of academic study and leadership science that is taught as an undergraduate minor and graduate certificate on college campuses and off campus through Innovation Engineering Blue Belt and Black Belt courses, coaching, and certifications.

In 2016 he founded Brain Brew Custom Whisk(e)y on the belief that the world doesn't need another whiskey, but everyone needs their own whiskey. The Brain Brew team is powered by the Eureka! Ranch culture and the Innovation Engineering systems. They collaborate with craft whiskey companies to accelerate the development of luxury smoothness through application of Brain Brew's time-compression technology.

Doug is the best-selling author of seven books. He has starred in two network television series (ABC's *American Inventor* and *Backyard Inventors*) and a nationally syndicated radio program (*Brain Brew Radio*). Doug authored and performed a one-man play, *North Pole Tenderfoot,* on his adventure re-creating Admiral Peary's last dash to the North Pole.

For his pioneering work on system-driven innovation he was awarded an honorary doctorate in engineering from the University of Maine and a doctor of laws from the University of Prince Edward Island.

Doug is a citizen of Canada and the USA. He is married to his high school sweetheart, and they have three children. They divide their time between Cincinnati, Ohio, USA and Springbrook, Prince Edward Island, Canada. He is passionate about sailing, craft pizza, craft whisk(e)y, cross-country skiing, and bagpiping.

Index

A Rookie's Adventures & Misadventures Traveling in Admiral Peary's footsteps to the North Pole

By Doug Hall

Excerpt from Prologue

The next hour and a half could very well be the worst 90 minutes of my life. I was standing in the wings of the nearly 100-year-old Victoria Hall, home of the Victoria Playhouse in the Village of Victoria-by-the-Sea in Prince Edward Island, Canada. It's a big name for a very small Village, that not long ago was listed as one of the fastest shrinking municipalities in Canada as a result of the conversion from year-round to seasonal residents.

I was preparing to perform the play of the same name as this book. I had always dreamed of performing a play of my creation. But somehow, as I stood in the wings, I wondered if I was about to fulfill a dream or live out a nightmare.

The house was sold out, for reasons I still don't understand. In the second or third row—in the center was Charles Mandel, the theater critic from The Guardian, the largest newspaper on Prince Edward Island. It had been the summer of nightmare reviews by Charles. He even took some cheap shots at the College of Piping and Celtic Performing Arts performance of Highland Storm—performed by Island Youth.

Following this performance, he would write a review of the play that would expose me. And given that I was the playwright and the actor, I had no one to blame the bad review on.

Though I'd delivered over 1,000 talks to business groups and cohosted national radio and television shows for millions, this was different. This was 90 minutes, plus intermission, with just me and the audience—performing in my first play since my high school appearance in The Pajama Game, performing the first play I'd ever written about my rookie experience as an Arctic explorer.

On the stage was the actual dog sled we'd taken to the North Pole, plus a near-perfect replica of one of Admiral Peary's sleds we'd photographed at the Berkshire Museum in western Massachusetts.

To bring the full theater experience alive, we had Styrofoam blocks, cut to look like ice, and a team of four Inuit dogs—well actually they were children's stuffed animals. At the back of the set was a monstrous rear projection screen that would bring the images, video, and audio of my 1999 adventure to life as I told my story.

I'd chosen to create and perform this one-man play to fulfill a dream.

My literary inspirations for this adventure include George Plimpton's classic *Paper Lion* and Bill Bryson's *A Walk In the Woods*. Their adventures and misadventures inspired me to not let inexperience get in the way of participating in a great adventure.

I do not presume that this book matches their literary genius. My goal is more humble, to help you experience what it's like for an ordinary, middle-aged, overweight male to travel to the North Pole as Admiral Peary did.

On this expedition I was a TENDERFOOT, as Admiral Peary called George Borup, Donald MacMillian, and Dr. John Goodsell, the arctic rookies on his 1909 expedition. On this expedition I was a first-timer who frankly had no business going to the North Pole.

I was 40 pounds overweight and even more out of shape. If there were such a thing as an obese-o-meter, I registered somewhere beyond plump. Sure, I knew a textbook ton about exercise. But there is clearly a vast difference between KNOWING about fitness and ACTUALLY BEING fit. I was a 40-year-old man in a 50-year-old body.

•   •   •

Erskin Smith, the artistic director of the playhouse and the director of North Pole Tenderfoot, explained to the sold-out house that there would be one intermission. He explained that it was an exciting summer at Victoria Playhouse. Following my show, in a few weeks, was the world premier of Anne and Gilbert, based on the writings of islander Lucy Maude Montgomery. It would be a full musical that tells the story of Anne Shirley's life after Anne of Green Gables.

He ended with my cue: "But first we travel to the top of the earth. Ladies and gentlemen, the Victoria Playhouse is proud to present the world premier of North Pole Tenderfoot."

The prelude music was the jazz classic "I'm Looking Over a Four-Leaf Clover" as performed by my father's Dixieland band the Presumpscott River Bottom Boys. I'd selected it as it was a personal favorite and I figured four-leaf clovers were lucky.

As the song came to an end, the lights came up and I sprang onto the stage, reciting as Erskine had directed.

> *Tonight we're going on an adventure to the North Pole—to the top of the earth, to the spot around which the whole earth spins. Leading our expedition will be Paul Schurke of Ely, Minnesota— a genuine adventure hero. My name Is Doug Hall. By day I help the world's leading companies invent big and bold innovations. On this trip I'm a rookie, a raw beginner, a tenderfoot, as Admiral Peary called rookies.*
>
> *The purpose of our expedition is to recreate Admiral Peary's last dash for the pole.*
>
> *Tonight's performance is like those performed in halls like this at the beginning of the century before last. It's an adventure story told with slides and audio as Admiral Peary, Shackleton, Admundsen, and Nansen would have recited to raise funds for their next adventure.*
>
> *I'm not here to raise funds—rather I'm here to raise awareness for the need for parents and grandparents to help inspire children's aspirations. To that end, as you entered the theater you received a free audio CD with a program designed to help you inspire your children.*

> *As a special BONUS—tonight on this stage I will reveal
> the answers to the three great mysteries of Robert Peary's 1909
> North Pole Expedition. Tonight you will learn the answers to
> three questions*
>> *1. Why was Peary so silent upon his return to the ship?*
>> *2. Why did he take Henson instead of Bartlett to the pole?*
>> *3. Did he actually make it to the pole?*

And that was how the story that became this book began . . .

Excerpt From Chapter 12: Splish Splash

About 3 a.m. I woke up freezing. I couldn't understand it. I'd followed my same routine, gone for a quick run, placed a water bottle with boiling water in the bag.

What had happened?

I did a quick scan of my body and the sleeping bag. Everything seemed right. Then I rolled to the left and discovered it. In my good feelings that evening, I had overstuffed my sleeping bag with wet socks, hats, and mittens. My body didn't have enough energy to dry off all the socks and gloves I had in the bag. They were "sucking away" my heat. I tossed the wet clothing out of the bag and instantly felt warmer. I pulled my hat down and went back to sleep.

At 7 a.m. the consequences of my 3 a.m. actions became evident. Beside me lay a frozen sculpture of gloves, hats, and socks. I picked it up and knocked it against my backpack. A glove fell off. The fingers frozen in the shape of a demented monster. The balance of the mess was frozen solid.

Ugh.

I placed the entire mess inside my yellow bivy sack between my sleeping bag and sleeping pad. The space was still warm from my body heat the night before. I lay down on top of the mess to soften it.

Craig noticed and asked what I was up to.

"Just a little problem with frozen gloves," I said.

I'm like a mother bird sitting on her nest of eggs. The eggs being my complete collection of gloves and socks.

After about 5 minutes, I got up and pulled at them. They came apart. Next was the ugly part. I pulled one pair of gloves and one pair of socks inside my sleeping bag with me. Within about 5 minutes—they defrosted and I could at least put them on.

I'd learned the hard way that you have to pay attention to every detail. Lack of attention results in consequences. This morning it's my gloves. Yesterday I was sloppily drinking from my water bottle; the water got on my gloves and they froze solid.

Paul was the first into the cook tent. "How are the boys doing?" he asked.

Craig and I being among the youngest and smallest were not only rookie tenderfeet; we were also the "kids" on the trip.

Paul reported that the weather wasn't good.

Craig reported, "We have fuel for today and tomorrow."

I piped in that "we don't have a landing strip."

For some reason it all seemed funny to us all. We laughed. It was a different laugh. Not a nervous laugh. Rather it was a fun laugh, as in: *Boy, won't it be exciting to see how we get out of this one.*

I asked Craig, "We're 1,600 miles north of Alaska, traveling on a moving sheet of ice, with little fuel left, with weather that looks like it'll storm any minute. Most amazing of all, we volunteered to go on this trip. When do you think we should reevaluate our sanity?"

●　　　●　　　●